UNDERSTANDING DEPRESSION
Second Edition

UNDERSTANDING DEPRESSION

Second Edition

Paul R. Robbins

McFarland & Company, Inc., Publishers
Jefferson, North Carolina, and London

LIBRARY OF CONGRESS CATALOGUING-IN-PUBLICATION DATA

Robbins, Paul R. (Paul Richard)
    Understanding depression / Paul R. Robbins.— 2nd ed.
        p.   cm.
    Includes bibliographical references and index.

    ISBN 978-0-7864-3542-5
    softcover : 50# alkaline paper ∞

    1. Depression, Mental — Popular works.   I. Title.
    RC537.R58   2009
    616.85'27 — dc22   2008023087

British Library cataloguing data are available

Cover art by Boris Zaysev (iStockphoto). Front cover by TG Design

Manufactured in the United States of America

*McFarland & Company, Inc., Publishers
    Box 611, Jefferson, North Carolina 28640
    www.mcfarlandpub.com*

To the memories of Maurice and Edith Robbins
and Marguerite Horyna

Acknowledgments

The author would like to thank Sharon Hauge and Herschel Shosteck for their continued interest in and many contributions to the manuscript. He would also like to thank Linda Lewin for her contribution, Allison Nugent of the National Institute of Mental Health for her helpful explanations concerning the genetic research now going on at the Institute, Lynn Nelson for sharing his knowledge about medieval medicine, Donald Jewell for providing a case study of the psychotherapeutic treatment of depression, Karen Kraft for providing information about the Depression and Bipolar Support Alliance and Leroy Resnick and George Winfield for help in preparing the final version of the manuscript.

Grateful acknowledgment is made to the following for permission to reprint excerpts from their copyrighted materials: Plenum Publishing Corporation for S. D. Hollon and P. C. Kendall, "Cognitive self-statements in depression: Development of an automatic thoughts questionnaire," *Cognitive Therapy and Research,* 4 (1980): 383–95, and J. D. Safran, M. Vallis, Z. V. Segal, and B. F. Shaw, "Assessment of core cognitive processes in cognitive therapy," *Cognitive Therapy and Research* 10 (1986): 509–26; Clinical Psychology Publishing Co., Inc., Brandon, VT 05733, for P. R. Robbins, and J. F. Nugent, III, "Perceived consequences of addiction: A comparison between alcoholics and heroin-addicted patients," *Journal of Clinical Psychology* 31 (1975): 367–69; Farrar, Straus and Giroux, for J. Anouilh, *The Restless Heart,* in *Jean Anouilh Five Plays,* Volume 2, copyright 1959 by Hill and Wang.

Table of Contents

Preface to the
Second Edition

When I had nearly completed my perusal of the recent scientific literature on depression, and was about to commence writing the second edition of *Understanding Depression*, I took some time to reflect on the history of the subject. While it was clear that the disorder had been a source of distress from the early days of recorded history, our reliable knowledge about the nature of depression and how to treat it could be collapsed into our own era, into a lifetime or even half a lifetime. Given the rudimentary knowledge that existed over the centuries, the progress that has been made during recent years strikes me as rather remarkable.

In the literature of the ancient world one finds examples of the expression of a lingering sadness ritualized into lamentations. These lamentations may be found in the Bible or even earlier in the writings of the Sumerians—lamenting the fall of the ancient city of Ur. Ritualized sadness also comes down to us in the plays of the ancient Greeks, such as Aeschylus' *The Persians*. Clinical depression as we conceive of it today shares some core common elements with these ancient lamentations—particularly prolonged sadness and guilt and self-reproach.

The earliest descriptions of depression that have come down to us may be those found in ancient Egyptian writings and later in the work of the inspired Greek physician, Hippocrates. Hippocrates described a condition called *melancholia* which he believed was caused by an excess of one of four hypothesized bodily fluids called *black bile*. Melancholia was characterized by a number of depressive-like symptoms including long lasting despondency.

In the dark ages of Europe following the destruction of the Roman Empire, much of Greek teaching was lost leaving a vacuum of knowledge for most Europeans that persisted for centuries. The Greek theories about bodily humors, however, survived and found their way into medieval medicine. The idea that depression was a disease was also present in the Arab civilizations that developed in North Africa, Spain and the Middle East in the wake of the spread of Islam.

1

We know next to nothing about how ordinary men and women through the dark ages and the early medieval period conceived depressive symptoms or what anyone could do about the condition. Perhaps, some people might have believed that the malaise was the work of demons, the evil-eye, or some malevolent spirit that needed casting out. In my novel, *Medieval Summer*, one of the characters, a monk, Brother Peter, went into a prolonged depression. The Abbott of the monastery reacted by relieving him of his duties, and when the illness lingered sent him off to the mother house of the order — a kind of benign exile. The concept of exiling people with mental or emotional disorders became institutionalized centuries later in western countries. These places of exile were known as insane asylums. And unlike Brother Peter's fate, such exile was not benign; often, insane asylums were little more than the brutal warehousing of sick people. In mid–twentieth century, Albert Deutsch wrote a riveting book complete with photographs describing the overcrowded, sometimes squalid conditions of American mental hospitals where treatment was almost nonexistent. The photographs showed women strapped to beds and even more appalling scenes when viewed from our contemporary mental health perspective.

The first rays of sunlight that came into this rather bleak picture of treatment for mental disorders were the insights of Sigmund Freud. Freud treated people who were depressed using the new approach to treatment he developed for emotional and mental disorder: psychoanalysis. Based on his clinical observations, he offered theoretical contributions to the understanding of depression highlighting the role of loss and self-directed anger. While Freud was a brilliant thinker and clinician, he was not a research psychologist in any sense of the word and had no way of testing his theories in an objective and replicable way. This had to wait until both psychiatry and psychology matured which was well into the 20th century.

Psychiatry began to assume its modern form with the work of pioneers such as Emil Kraepelin who made a careful study of the symptoms of mental patients and developed a system of classification of mental disorders. One of the important disorders recognized was manic-depressive psychosis now known as bipolar disorder.

For its part, psychology evolved rather tentatively, initially focusing on problems that were easily measurable like calculating reaction times and studies of memory, and then under the influence of the behaviorists analyzing behavior of rats in mazes and later Skinner Boxes. It was well into the post–World War II years before psychologists began to apply their developing research techniques to study serious problems such as depression. With research funds coming through the National Institute of Mental Health, psychiatrists and psychologists began to study depression in earnest, slowly at first and then in a more accelerated manner. By the time I wrote the first edition of *Understanding Depression* in 1993, researchers had developed both a very respectable science base and new methods for treating the disorder.

With the continued influx of new information about depression, it seemed a propitious time to write a second edition of *Understanding Depression*. Since the publication of the first edition of the book, there have been important changes in both our understanding of the disorder and in our approach to treatment. The new edition reflects these new realities. In particular, I have given increased emphasis to recent studies highlighting the biological foundations of depression, the development of and wide use of antidepressant drugs, the shift in the means of dispensing these drugs from mental health professionals to primary care physicians, the development of alternative medicine approaches to the treatment of depression, and the critical need to find ways to prevent the recurrence of the disorder.

Introduction

Most people "get depressed" now and then. It's a sad feeling, being in the dumps. The feeling is usually transient, vanishing in hours or days, like the proverbial dark clouds that give way to sunshine. We think of such short-lived depressed states as *depressed moods,* not to be confused with the often chronic, severe problem called *clinical depression.*

Transient depressed moods may be as common as the cold. My colleague Roland Tanck and I carried out a series of studies on college students in which we asked the students to fill out a special type of diary before they went to bed for a period of ten nights. The diary included the question "Did you feel depressed today?" There were very few students who did not answer the question yes at some time during the ten-day period, and many students said yes repeatedly.

Going to college is not easy. There are major adjustments that must be made in being away from home. Problems in relationships develop with frequent disappointments. Term papers are due and examinations generate a great deal of stress. One might expect to observe depressed moods in students, and one finds them in abundance. Still, most of the students do not stay depressed. They get over romantic disappointments, pass their exams, and continue to study and go about their daily lives. Brief periods of depressed mood give way to more pleasant moods. Good times are often right around the corner.

In clinical depression there is a sharp contrast. Often, the clinically depressed person doesn't see a corner. He or she may not even see that there is a possibility of a corner. Clinical depression is something like being in a black hole. The person feels trapped and the future may appear hopeless.

This perception of hopelessness is often accompanied by deep feelings of sadness, loss of interest in what had previously made life meaningful and sometimes thoughts of suicide. The depressed person often has slowed reactions, trouble concentrating and remembering, difficulty in sleeping and sometimes a marked weight loss. When such problems persist over time, we are talking about an emotional illness that merits careful evaluation and appropriate therapy. I shall have much to say about the options for treatment that are available and I hope the discussion will prove useful if seeking professional help is under consideration.

5

Between the occasional blue moods of everyday life and a severe clinical depression, there are millions of people who experience periods of mild to moderate depressed mood. They may experience some of the same symptoms of the clinically depressed person, such as difficulties in sleeping and feelings of sadness. Such people enjoy life much less than they would like. At times, their daily routine seems like drudgery, but they continue to function, going to school, working and taking care of their children. The depressed state diminishes the quality of life, but life goes on.

There is a lot that such depressed people can do to create a happier, more rewarding life for themselves. In this book I shall present some ideas and information that I hope will assist them in moving toward this goal. However, the book is not intended as a substitute for professional treatment if that is what is needed. For many people who experience chronic low levels of depression, getting good professional help can make a world of difference in their lives. I believe that this book will also be helpful to those who know or live with people who are prone to depression. The information that shall be presented may help these people better understand what is happening to their friend or loved one.

To fulfill these objectives, I shall present in the first seven chapters of the book a wide-ranging picture of what is currently known about depressed moods and depression. We shall look at how depression is currently defined, examine its demographic, biological, and psychological aspects, consider its antecedents in childhood experiences, examine the role of stress in bringing on depression, and look at its relation to alcohol and drug abuse. Then, I shall offer some ideas about how to prevent depressed moods and how to cope with these moods when they occur. The later part of the book will be devoted to the treatment of depression, with a discussion of antidepressant medicines, psychotherapy, electroconvulsive therapy and alternative treatments for depression. We will conclude with a discussion of the very troublesome issue of the recurrence of depression, presenting some current views about how to lessen this risk.

1. Depressed Mood and Depression

A grief without a pang, void, dark, and drear
A stifled, drowsy, unimpassioned grief,
Which finds no natural outlet, no relief,
In word, or sigh, or tear...
— Samuel Taylor Coleridge, "Dejection: An Ode"

Your mood colors the way you perceive your environment, the people about you and yourself. If you are in a happy mood, you tend to look at others and yourself through rose-colored glasses. Everything seems right with the world. There is, indeed, some truth in the feeling that when you're happy, the whole world seems happy, too. People may not be happy in reality but if you're happy, it may not matter that much.

When you are feeling in a sad mood, you tend to look at things with a negative perspective. Gone are the rose-colored glasses. Now you are wearing very dark ones. And this overflow of bleak mood can affect the way you look at yourself. An interesting experiment demonstrates how mood may influence judgment. Before describing the experiment, I should state that researchers have developed techniques that can be used to alter the mood of normal subjects.

One of these mood induction techniques is hypnosis. Another comparatively simple technique that has been widely used is to ask the subject to read a set of standardized phrases that are sad in content.[1] An example would be, "The way I feel now, the future looks boring and hopeless." It has been repeatedly demonstrated that when people read these phrases and *feel the mood* as they do so — they become more depressed. In contrast, reading happy phrases tends to elevate mood. Mood can be that sensitive to change!

The experiment I am going to describe was carried out by Joseph Forgas and his colleagues.[2] For the experiment, the subjects were first interviewed for a while on a variety of topics. These interviews were videotaped with the subjects' consent. On the following day, the subjects were given a mood induction technique to make them feel either happier or sadder about themselves. The subjects were then asked to make judgments about their own videotapes. The subjects in the positive mood judged their performance as competent, confident and socially skilled. The subjects who had been put in a negative mood saw their previous performances as incompetent, clumsy and unskilled. Objective judges did not see any difference in the two sets of interviews. It was all in the minds of the subjects.

If depressed mood can make you think more negatively, it is equally true that negative thoughts can depress your mood. Drawing on this observation, Aaron T. Beck has developed one of the most influential theories about the cause of depression, as well as an effective form of therapy, called *cognitive therapy*.[3] When mood and thinking patterns are negative, you may also see changes in behavior, such as slowed reactions and a loss of interest in your usual activities. Moreover, there may be changes in the way you feel physically. A person may have a variety of physical complaints and not sleep or eat as well as before. Instead of a simple depressed mood, what we now have is a more complex situation — a mixture of symptoms. This group of symptoms is called *depression*.

The clinical description and understanding of depression has become refined in recent years, but as we indicated in the preface, the notion that people can become saddened and immobilized goes back a long way. Hippocrates and Aretaeus, physicians of ancient Greece, wrote about people who suffered from a form of depressive illness and advanced a naturalistic, biologically based theory to explain it.[4] Although the theory was inaccurate, their views of depression remain a testament to careful observation and the importance of building testable explanatory models in scientific inquiry.

The world's literature has its share of characters who appear depressed. One finds depressed people in literary works ranging from the tales of, "A Thousand and One Nights" to the writings of the German poet and dramatist Johann Wolfgang von Goethe.[5] Remember the despondent figure of King Lear in Shakespeare or the guilt-ridden Lady Macbeth?

Among historical figures, Abraham Lincoln was described as a melancholy man. He wrote to his law partner, John Stuart, "I am now the most miserable man living. If what I feel were equally distributed to the whole human family, there would not be one cheerful face on earth. Whether I shall ever be better, I cannot tell: I awfully forebode I shall not. To remain as I am is impossible. I must die or be better...."[6]

In her carefully documented book *Touched with Fire: Manic-depressive Illness and the Artistic Temperament*, Kay Redfield Jamison presents a long list of well known poets, novelists, composers, and painters who may have been afflicted with one form or another of depressive illness including bipolar disorder.[7] This list includes poets Lord Byron, Emily Dickinson, T. S. Eliot, John Keats, Edgar Allan Poe, Sara Teasdale, and Walt Whitman, novelists Charles

Dickens, Ernest Hemingway, F. Scott Fitzgerald, Herman Melville, and Leo Tolstoy, composers Hector Berlioz, George Frederick Handel, Robert Schumann, and Peter Tchaikovsky, painters Michelangelo, Vincent van Gogh, Paul Gauguin, Jackson Pollock, and Georgia O'Keeffe. Jameson's list includes some of the major artistic talents in the history of Western civilization. Is there indeed a link between depressive illness and artistic creativity? Jamison's bibliographic work suggests that this is the case.

While the concept of depression has its roots in early times, the attempt to clearly define it as a clinical-disorder had to await the development of psychiatry in the nineteenth century. The description and classification of mental and emotional disorders gained great impetus during the latter half of the nineteenth century, much of it resulting from the pioneering efforts of German psychiatrist Emil Kraepelin. In eight editions of his *Textbook of Psychiatry,* he distinguished between different types of mental illness, using such terms as manic-depressive disorder, which remain part of psychiatric language today.[8]

The attempts to describe and classify what appeared to be different types or shadings of depression have continued since Kraepelin's time. Various descriptive terms have entered the psychiatric literature, proving more-or-less useful, including *involutional melancholia, endogenous depression, reactive depression, neurotic depression,* and *dysthymic disorder.* Dysthymic disorder may be the least familiar of these names, but is a term in current favor that refers to depression which is typically not severe but is long lasting, the type of problem that may linger for years. Despite this formidable sounding list of diagnostic categories, the problem of meaningfully distinguishing between varieties of depressive problems is not fully settled. The American Psychiatric Association, through its task forces and committees, has been wrestling with the problem. The Association's current thinking is embodied in its *Diagnostic and Statistical Manual of Mental Disorders.*[9] While there is some uncertainty concerning the subtypings of depression, there is general agreement about the typical symptoms of depression. I shall now describe these symptoms.

Symptoms of Depression

As a starting point it is important to recognize that the diagnosis of depression is based almost entirely on the patient's report of symptoms. The physical exam that is often essential in making a diagnosis of a physical illness is of little help in making a diagnosis of depression nor are there yet laboratory tests which are specific to depression. The diagnosis is based on what the patient reports. In making the diagnosis, the physician or psychotherapist relies on a list of nine symptoms. The rule of thumb is that if a patient reports five of these symptoms and they have persisted for a period of time (at least two weeks) the patient is diagnosed as experiencing major depression. Among the five symptoms, the patient must report either feeling sad or having lost interest in his or her usual activities. So among the nine symptoms, these two can be viewed as being particularly diagnostic.

Here then is a short list of the nine symptoms used in diagnosing depression.

1. Depressed mood
2. Diminished interest or pleasure in usual activities
3. Weight loss or gain
4. Insomnia, or excessive sleep
5. Psychomotor agitation or retardation
6. Fatigue
7. Feelings of worthlessness, guilt
8. Diminished concentration or indecisiveness
9. Suicidal thoughts

Let's take a look at these symptoms in more detail.

One of the clearest signs of depression is mood. A sad, blue mood that persists is usually a dead giveaway that something is wrong. Sadness is sometimes visible in facial expressions. Depressed people may look glum and downcast. Using the electromyograph to measure activity of the muscles, one can study the facial muscles of depressed people. For example, electrodes can be placed near the eyes to monitor the corrugator muscles, which pull the eyebrows down. EMG readings for these muscles tend to be higher in depressed people and may be even higher when depressed people think unhappy thoughts.[10]

There are times in life when sadness is a normal, expected response to unhappy or tragic events. Bereavement is such a time and we expect a period of grief and mourning as part of a psychological healing process. But protracted sadness under any circumstances is something to be concerned about.

A second sign that a person is depressed is a loss of interest and pleasure in his or her usual activities and pursuits. The person may simply go through the motions or even stop the activities altogether. An example would be Arlene, once an enthusiastic gardener, interested in cooking and entertaining, active in her church. Her enthusiasm for all of these activities has dwindled. When her friends asked her about this, she replied, "I don't care anymore." What was important and fulfilling in her life had lost its meaning.

Changes in appetite and significant weight loss or gain can be a sign of depression. Because changes in weight can also reflect a variety of medical problems (e.g., anorexia nervosa, cancer) as well as changes in living arrangements and circumstances (e.g., leaving home for college, marriage, joining the army, going on a diet to lose excess weight), one should be circumspect in applying this criterion. If, however, you hear such statements as, "I've totally lost my appetite, I don't care about food anymore," it certainly has the ring of depression.

Trouble in sleeping is another possible indication of depression. Obviously, not everybody who has trouble sleeping is depressed, but so many people who are depressed have difficulty sleeping that this problem is often a tell-tale sign. Sometimes the problem is what is called *sleep onset insomnia*. The person goes to bed at night and can't fall asleep. Instead of lapsing into sleep, the person may begin to rethink and replay the events of the day or troubling unresolved problems. As the person lies in bed, these thoughts may repeat themselves over and over, something like a phonograph record that is stuck in a groove. When we ask a depressed patient what he or she was thinking about while struggling to sleep, we often gain a pretty good encapsulation of what some of the person's major problems are.

Overeating and oversleeping are signs of what has been called *atypical depression*. Some depressed patients appear to be restless and agitated. In contrast, others have slowed reactions. They seem both slow in sizing up a situation and in responding. While it is difficult to separate these two components of reaction in real life, efforts have been made to do so in laboratory experiments. Research has shown that compared to normal controls, depressed patients are slower in making physical reactions.[11]

The slowed reaction times which one finds in many depressed people can show themselves in a variety of everyday activities including driving. In an interesting demonstration of this tendency, Canadian researchers compared the driving behavior of 18 non-medicated patients diagnosed with major depressive disorder with a group of control subjects.[12] Using a driving simulator which took all of the subjects through a trip on a country road, the researchers reported that the depressed patients showed slower steering reaction times and were more likely to veer out of their lanes and/or collide with other vehicles. We would need a large-scale study of the driving safety records of people who are clinically depressed to see what kind of implications, if any, these findings might have in the real world.

When people are extremely depressed, their body movements may have a uniform, monotonous, limited character. Picture in your mind the graceful movements of a dancer, then imagine what the opposite of that might be like. In a metaphorical sense, it is as if the restriction in the patients' movements mirror the restriction in their current lives. When depressed patients begin to improve, constricted body motion begins to become more mobile, complex and dynamic.

Chronic fatigue is yet another sign of possible depression. While all of us get tired at times, depressed people often feel tired and lethargic. To get out of bed in the morning may seem like a tremendous task. For some depressed people, the day seems to drag like a clock going in slow motion and the person may feel about as energetic as the clock. The combination of dysphoric mood and fatigue can be immobilizing. Allison, a writer and teacher who was in the midst of a depressive episode described this lethargic state well. "I began to feel immobilized. I did not want to get out of bed. I remember needing to move my car to keep from getting a parking ticket, but it felt like a major undertaking to get up, get dressed, walk a couple of blocks and do it."

When a person reports chronic fatigue and there is no clear physiological basis for it, one must be alert to the possibility of an underlying depression.

Another sign of depression is excessive self-reproach. Therapists who have worked with depressed patients have observed that many depressed patients are overly self-critical. Freud described depressed patients in the following way: "The patient represents his ego to us as worthless, incapable of any effort, and morally despicable; he reproaches himself, vilifies himself and expects to be cast out and chastised."[13] Depressed people may feel responsible for events they really have no control over. They are often overly concerned with their own faults, shortcomings and failings. The message may boil down to "I'm no good." The flip side of this conclusion is often, "I deserve to be punished."

Many depressed people carry with them a large burden of guilt, a painful feeling that they have violated the standards of what is right and wrong, what is acceptable and unacceptable. These standards have strong emotional roots in childhood learning experiences and particularly in the moral teachings of parents. To feel you have violated these expectations can be a wrenching experience.

In addition to the substantial clinical observation that feelings of self-reproach and guilt are often part of a depressive picture, there is some experimental evidence that activating guilt may deepen the depressed mood, and that this may happen on an unconscious level.[14] The process may take place without any awareness. The experimental procedure used in these studies is interesting, though controversial, as it utilized the not-fully-understood technique of subliminal perception. Depressed subjects viewed short sentences or phrases at such rapid speeds of exposure that they were unable to make out what they were looking at. What the subjects saw was something like a flash or a blur. When researchers used phrases like, "leaving Mom is wrong" or "I have been bad," the subject's mood after the experiment became more depressed. The effect was clearest in subjects who seemed more guilt-prone on psychological testing.[15] Diminished ability to concentrate is also a possible sign of depression. Patients will often complain of this problem in their jobs or school work. A task that normally goes easily may not go along at all. Experimental studies suggest that attention and learning may be particularly compromised if the matter at hand stirs up unpleasant emotions.[16]

In the most recent edition of the *Diagnostic and Statistical Manual of Mental Disorders*, indecision has been coupled with difficulties in concentration. I have been puzzled by this coupling because focusing attention and decision-making seem like quite different phenomena. Indecision often flows from conflicts. While wrestling with choice — playing Hamlet — may be a sign of depression in some people, why it should be included in a category with troubles in focusing escapes me.

Thoughts of suicide are another sign of depression. Sometimes these thoughts are expressed in verbal statements that are direct and unmistakable. Sometimes the idea of suicide is expressed obliquely and not easily recognizable. The possibility of suicide in depression must be taken very seriously. Estimates are that the lifetime risk of suicide in persons with serious depression runs on the order of 15 percent while it is only about 1 percent for the general population.[17]

Researchers have been carrying out studies to better understand the risk factors that increase the chances of suicidal behavior in depressed patients. Recent data suggest that among the classic symptoms of depression, some of the ones to look out for are loss of appetite and weight, insomnia, and feelings of guilt and worthlessness, and as one might expect, thoughts of suicide. Personality tendencies of impulsivity and aggressiveness are other signs to watch out for. A concomitant problem of alcohol or drug abuse, and even as one study suggests, heavy smoking — any such substance abuse could be indicators of increased risk. Previous attempts at suicide are a marker for possible future acts, and lack of a partner may also contribute to the risk.[18]

In addition to these nine symptoms that currently serve as the basis for diagnosing depression, there are other characteristics which one often finds in people who are depressed. These include difficulties with memory, a tendency to ruminate about one's problems, and the development of physical complaints.

Difficulties in memory may reflect difficulties in paying attention. People who are having trouble concentrating and focusing may not absorb and remember what they are insufficiently attending to. And, indeed experimental studies of the memory of depressed people for verbal materials have found that their memory was not as good as that of control subjects. In an early review of these studies, Mark Johnson and Peter Magaro stated, "Given the frequent complaints of memory impairment reported by depressed patients, a number of investigators have attempted to verify this phenomena experimentally. The majority of these investigations have examined memory processes in depressed inpatient samples. Most have demonstrated some memory impairments when depressed patients are compared with normal nonpsychiatric control groups."[19] Generally speaking, the more severe the depression is, the greater the problems with memory. A recent study carried out in Norway suggests that the negative impact of depression on memory may not be evident with patients who are mildly to moderately depressed.[20]

One possible explanation for the difficulties in memory experienced by many people who are depressed is that they are often very preoccupied with their own problems. This self-focusing may interfere with their ability to concentrate on the external world and communications coming from others. It is hard to remember things when it is a challenge to pay attention to what is going on about you.

Many depressed people have a tendency to ruminate about their problems. Sometimes, they think about what is bothering them to the point it becomes obsessive. And what often happens is that their thoughts and conclusions are quite negative in nature which may only deepen the depression.

When a person has been feeling in a depressed mood — even in a mild one — she or he will often report more physical complaints. As an illustration of this pattern, consider some research Roland Tanck and I carried out using our student diaries. We asked the students whether they were feeling depressed during the day. We also asked them whether they had been experiencing any physical symptoms during the day. To assist the students in recording these symptoms, we provided a list of physical complaints such as headaches, nausea, dizziness, weakness and diarrhea, and asked the students to check off any of the complaints they had experienced. The students who reported feeling higher levels of depressed mood reported more physical complaints.[21]

Depressed mood has a relation with physical symptoms. It is not, however, easy to establish what is cause and what is effect. It is possible that the depressed mood may cause physical problems. However, it is also possible that a person may react to physical problems by becoming depressed.

In exploring the symptoms the patient reports in a clinical interview, the mental health professional will often gain enough information to go beyond the basic diagnosis of major depression. He or she may be able to add some "specifiers" to the diagnosis, asking such questions as is this a first-time event or as frequently happens, a recurrent problem? Is the level of depression, mild, moderate, or severe? Does the patient's depression have atypical features? For example, instead of experiencing insomnia, the patient reports sleeping too much.

While the approach we have outlined to diagnosing depression has been widely accepted for a number of years, a number of people working in the field have raised questions about it. For example, some researchers have asked, do all of these nine symptoms contribute to the diagnosis of depression? Perhaps some of them do not and may be irrelevant in making a diagnosis. Recent studies carried out by Martin Zimmerman and his colleagues suggested that leaving out weight loss or gain and indecisiveness would do little to change a diagnosis of depression.[22]

Some psychologists have gone beyond making attempts to refine the current approach to making a diagnosis of depression; they have raised fundamental questions about the the nature of depression, itself. They have asked, is depression really a diagnostic category like tuberculosis or asthma that people either have or don't have or is it more like a dimension that ranges from a little (most of us have times in which we feel depressed) to a lot. In the dimensional view, what we call depression is really being high on this depression continuum (scale), somewhere beyond an arbitrary cutoff point. These differing views of depression — categorical verses dimensional are clearly quite different and these differences have implications for the way we think about depression, treat depression, and the way we carry out research on depression. If we were inclined to follow the dimensional model we would be more attuned to study levels of depression rather than simply compare two groups of people, one of which is categorized as depressed and the other as not depressed. While the views of the mental health profession seem currently firmly rooted in the categorical camp, there has been some research which seems to support the dimensional view.[23] As it is a hallmark of science to change its models and theories when data contradicts currently held views, it seems important to keep an open mind about this question. It is possible that further research may cause us to revise our thinking about the nature of depression.

Measuring Depression

These, then, are some of the typical symptoms of depression. How do we measure depression as a practical matter? How do we say that this person has a mild depression or that person has a more serious problem? The best method we have to date for diagnosing a person as depressed is a clinical interview conducted by trained psychiatrists or psychologists using a set of benchmark criteria similar to the symptoms we have described. The most widely used guide for such clinical interviews—considered the gold standard for diagnosing depression is the *Hamilton Depression Rating Scale*.[24]

A good deal of research has demonstrated that one can get a reasonably good estimate of what the clinicians would find in their interviews by using questionnaires in which people report their own symptoms. One of the most widely used of these self-report measures is a 21-item inventory developed by Aaron Beck and his colleagues.[25] Another inventory used in community studies on depression was developed by the National Institutes of Health's Center for Epidemiological Studies.[26]

The scale developed by Beck and his colleagues generally referred to as the Beck Depression Inventory (BDI) has been revised twice since its original development in the early 1960s. The BDI uses a dimensional approach with scores ranging from zero (no indication of depression) to a theoretical maximum score of 63. Beck and his colleagues have suggested cutoff points for the scores indicating various levels of depression such as mild, moderate, and severe. Because the BDI is self-administered and in my experience easily understood by those using it, it has been a workhorse for psychological research on depression over the years. I have used it myself in a number of studies, exploring problems such as the relation of depression level and recall for very early memories.[27] The BDI has been translated into a number of languages ranging from Japanese to Arabic and has proven useful to researchers abroad as it has in the United States. While I will not reproduce any of the items from published inventories such as the BDI, I would like to give you an idea of the types of questions that are used in self report measures of depression. The following are some questions that are similar to those used in depression inventories:

1. Have you experienced extended periods of sadness during the past few ,weeks?
2. Have you been having problems sleeping?
3. Has your appetite been poor lately?
4. Have you been more withdrawn from people in recent weeks?
5. Have you felt tired a lot of the time?
6. Have you noticed that you have little enthusiasm about doing things?
7. Have you been down on yourself lately?
8. Do you find that you are getting much less satisfaction from your usual activities than you used to?
9. Have you recently been troubled by feelings of guilt?
10. Do you often feel like crying?
11. Have you been experiencing feelings of deep pessimism?
12. Have you recently been troubled by physical symptoms such as headaches, nausea, or dizziness?
13. Have you noticed a decline in your desire for having a sexual experience?
14. Have you been feeling that you are very much alone in life?
15. Have you noticed you have had difficulty lately in concentrating on your work?
16. Do you find yourself sluggish in your reactions?
17. Do you have feelings that nothing in life seems worthwhile?
18. Have you been feeling overwhelmed by the problems you have been facing in life?
19. Have you been thinking that you are a failure in life?
20. Have people been telling you that you seem depressed?

The sample of preceding questions is a collection of items, *not a psychological test*. We would have to show by research that a score based on the responses to such items is a reliable and valid measure before we could interpret the results with any precision. Having said this, if you answered the questions and found that you had only a few "yes" answers, it seems unlikely that you would have a serious depressive problem. On the other hand, if you answered most of the questions yes, you might want to consider consulting a mental health professional to discuss the things that are bothering you.

As we have indicated, most of us experience times in which our mood is sad or blue and we may experience some of the symptoms of depression. What makes these symptoms more serious or less serious is how *intense* they are and how *long* they persist. Take mood for example. You can feel a little blue or you can feel just terrible. It is the latter condition you worry about. There is no absolute rule of thumb for how long depressed feelings persist before you should begin to feel concerned, but certainly a couple of weeks of intense symptoms is more than enough time to recognize that you ought to do something about it. The American Psychiatric Association's *Diagnostic and Statistical Manual* suggests that two weeks of intense symptoms is enough to classify what is happening as a major depressive episode.

While we are discussing measurement, let's consider the measurement of mood. In contrast to the measurement of depressed states which may require use of a variety of questions to explore a number of different symptoms such as sleep and appetite disturbances—the measurement of mood seems straightforward. We are able to assess a person's mood in surprisingly easy ways. One such technique is to use the Adjective Check List.

Let's say a researcher is trying to find out what your mood is like at this moment. To do this, he or she might ask you to respond to a list of words that describe various moods. The list will have been refined with the aid of statistical procedures so that the researcher can derive scores to represent the intensity of different moods, such as anger, anxiety or depression. To give you an idea how these techniques work, we have drawn up a list of words that are similar to those used in standardized adjective check lists. As was true for our questions about depression, this is not a psychological test, simply a way of showing how researchers study mood.

If you are interested, try responding to the list of words using the following procedure. Look at each word in the list in turn. If you don't feel in the mood described at all, check the box on the left. If you feel a little bit in the mood described, check the box in the center. If you definitely feel that way, check the box on the right.

	Not at All	*A Little Bit*	*Definitely*
Affectionate	0	0	0
Alert	0	0	0
Angry	0	0	0
Anxious	0	0	0
Blue	0	0	0
Cheerful	0	0	0
Dejected	0	0	0
Distraught	0	0	0
Downhearted	0	0	0
Energetic	0	0	0
Fearful	0	0	0
Friendly	0	0	0
Glad	0	0	0
Gloomy	0	0	0
Happy	0	0	0
Irritable	0	0	0
Jittery	0	0	0
Joyful	0	0	0

Kindly	0	0	0
Lethargic	0	0	0
Merry	0	0	0
Optimistic	0	0	0
Pessimistic	0	0	0
Pleasant	0	0	0
Relaxed	0	0	0
Restful	0	0	0
Sad	0	0	0
Sociable	0	0	0
Suspicious	0	0	0
Thoughtful	0	0	0
Tired	0	0	0
Worried	0	0	0

Look at the words for which you checked "Definitely." What kinds of moods do these words suggest? Look at the words you checked "Not at All." What kinds of moods do these words suggest? Do you see any patterns? Now, take a closer look at the words Blue, Dejected, Distraught, Downhearted, Gloomy, Pessimistic and Sad. If you checked "Definitely" for several of these words, chances are that your mood at the moment is depressed. Mood changes: If you check this list again tomorrow, you might find a different pattern. When depressed mood persists, however, there is a problem.

Mood Swings

It would be a very rare person indeed whose moods are constant. Some of us have moods like shifting winds. We react to changes in body chemistry, to events in our environment and to our thought processes consciously, and in the psychoanalytic view, unconsciously as well. As we have indicated, it is possible to induce a depressed mood by simply reading and trying "to feel" a list of depressive phrases.

If you think about it, you can probably recall books that you have read or movies you have seen that left you feeling depressed. Try listening to the last movement of Tchaikovsky's *Pathétique* Symphony (No. 6). It can be a real downer.

The other side of this process is mood elevation. Try thinking of people, parties, music, vacations, books, sporting events— good times that have elevated your mood, producing a sense of well being.

We mentioned that body chemistry can influence mood. A good example of this is the premenstrual syndrome (PMS) experienced by many women. These women may feel depressed, anxious and irritable during the premenstrual phase of the menstrual cycle. It is a little difficult to estimate how many women experience *premenstrual depression* because many women who have this problem also experience intermittent depression at other times during the month. However, there are studies which suggest that about 40 percent of the women who report PMS depression experience an increase in depressed mood *only* in the premenstrual period and return to a normal mood after menstruation ceases.[28]

What kind of variation in mood do you experience during a day? Are you more likely to be bursting with enthusiasm during the day and dropping off as the day ends? Or are you a grumbler in the morning and a free spirit in the evening? Are you a night person?

Roland Tanck and I were interested in the problem of mood swings within the day and used our diaries to obtain some information from college students.[29] The results might surprise you. If you feel brighter during the day and your mood deteriorates somewhat as evening falls, you are not alone.

In reflecting upon their day's experiences, most of the students reported that typically the downside of mood was in the evening. The students felt best during various times of the day, but by evening, the day's activities seem to have taken a toll on them and their mood deteriorated. A night's sleep seemed to clear things up and they were ready to go in the morning.

We found fewer instances of the reverse pattern, of "night people" students who felt more depressed in the morning and peaked in the evening.

Some students in our sample reported having periods of depressed mood that persisted right through the day with little evidence of mood swing. It was these students with stretches of rather constant depressed mood who were more likely to report the typical symptoms of depression such as a plethora of physical complaints.

Mood Swings in Clinical Depression

SEASONAL AFFECTIVE DISORDER

Over 100 years ago during an early exploration into Antarctica, the expedition physician, Frederick Cook noted that during the darkness of winter, members of the expedition became markedly depressed. He wrote that, "The curtain of blackness which has fallen over the outer world of icy desolation has descended upon the inner world of our souls. Around the tables, in the laboratory, and in the forecastle, men are sitting about sad and dejected, lost in dreams of melancholy from which, now and then, one arouses with an empty attempt at enthusiasm."[30] Writing in *the American Psychologist*, Lawrence Palinkas noted that Cook endeavored to treat the symptoms by having, "Crew members sit in front of large blazing fires" and this may have been the "First recorded attempt to use light therapy to treat symptoms of winter depression, or seasonal affective disorder."[31]

In recent years scientific studies carefully carried out in laboratories in both the Arctic and Antarctica have confirmed the general thrust of Cook's observations. Prolonged exposure to a dark environment has a deleterious effect on mood and behavior. In reviewing these studies, Palinkas concluded that, "When viewed collectively, therefore, these results suggest that behavior in Antarctica is influenced by patterns of exposure to daylight associated with time of year and latitude."[32]

Cook's observations were telling and his choice of therapy astute. But, I would imagine that long before his time the depressing impact on humans of the darkened days of winter could not help be noticed. Shakespeare employed the idea metaphorically in one of his plays chronicling the War of the Roses in England, the struggle of the houses of Lancaster and York to control the English throne. In the opening of the play Richard the Third, Shakespeare penned the lines, "Now is the winter of our discontent made glorious summer by this sun of York."[33]

My first exposure to Seasonal Affective Disorder occurred during my early years of private practice before the disorder had found its way into the established listing of mental disorders, the Diagnostic and Statistical Manual of Mental disorders. The patient, a man in his late 20s came to see me reporting some of the usual symptoms of depression such as a sad mood, loss of energy, and a loss of interest in his usual activities. Interestingly, he told me that his life seemed so "draggy" in the winter, but how he felt so much better in the summer when he played tennis and softball. I thought part of the problem might be the recent holiday season and we talked about the feelings he experienced in being alone and away from home during Christmas. Still, this did not seem to be the crux of the problem. During therapy he alluded several times to the feeling that everything seemed so dark and dreary in the winter. I suggested that he try lighting up his apartment with bright lights and see if that might help. I don't know whether he thought going to a therapist who offered such simple-minded advice was a poor investment, but he ceased coming soon afterwards.

Some years later, I began to read of a new concept called *seasonal affective disorder*. Patients report they feel OK in the sunlit days of summer but feel terrible during the dark days of winter. Norman Rosenthal and his colleagues have been largely responsible for developing the idea.[34] Among the therapies that seem effective in treating this mid-winter case of the blahs are very bright lights. Interestingly, artificial light therapy seems to work best when it is carried out in the morning. Perhaps it mimics the pleasant sensation of awakening on a bright summer day. In any event, I was delighted to learn that my off-the-cuff suggestion to a patient was not idiotic after all. To feel less cheerful, less happy and energetic in the dark days of winter is a common experience. A telephone survey carried out in Montgomery County, Maryland, a state in which the winters are not especially severe, almost everyone surveyed (92 percent) noticed seasonal changes in their moods. About a quarter of those surveyed reported that these seasonal changes presented a problem and for about four to 10 percent of the sample, the problem was severe enough to suggest Seasonal Affective Disorder (SAD).[35]

Between the nuisance level of mild winter blahs and the frank depression of SAD, there is a category which has the imposing name of Subsyndromal Seasonal Affective Disorder. One might think of this category as "almost, but not quite" SAD. It is difficult to estimate the prevalence of SAD and its subclinical variety because if we are correct in our thinking, the prevalence of these problems should vary with latitude and climate. And indeed a study carried out in the mid 1984 found this to be true. The title of the study could not be more explicit in this regard, "Seasonal Affective Disorder: prevalence varies with latitude and climate."[36] Go to northern lands and you would expect to encounter more SAD.

There have been reports that seasonal depression may work the other way as well-feeling OK in the winter and depressed in the summer. This seems somewhat harder to explain than its counterpart. A case of this atypical pattern of seasonal depression was described by Thomas Wehr and his colleagues:

Ms. A, a 66-year-old married retired secretary, had had recurrent summer depressions, beginning in March-April and ending in August–October, for at least 15 years. When depressed, she was indecisive, had negative thoughts, and scarcely spoke. She had frequent crying spells and suicidal thoughts. Because of lethargy, lack of motivation, and difficulty concentrating, she engaged in no activity voluntarily and tried to sleep as much as possible. In the fall and winter she was energetic and outgoing. She required less sleep, was talkative and had racing thoughts. Her clinical state appeared to be influenced by changes in climate and weather. Her depressions began earlier than usual during spring vacations in Florida, and remissions occurred during midsummer vacations in New England.... We observed a temporary remission when an unusual cold front reduced the temperature to 39°F in June. Furthermore, she appeared to improve after an experimental cold treatment, as just described.[37]

Researchers have been studying people reporting seasonal depression, comparing them with people whose depression is not seasonal. One interesting observation is that the seasonal depressives do not have difficulties in getting enough sleep. They often sleep too much. In addition, they may have very good appetites—and often have a tendency to crave carbohydrates. This pattern is very reminiscent of what has been called atypical depression.

Since the behavior of animals as well as humans is affected by seasonal changes—one thinks of the hibernation of bears, it is no great leap to look for the causes of SAD in our biology. Among the prime suspects are our circadian rhythms (our biological internal clocks) which seem to shift with the seasons and the action of melatonin, a hormone secreted by the pineal gland in the brain. Melatonin influences the sleep-wake cycle and when administered as a drug can alter the sleep-wake cycle. The neurotransmitter, serotonin, of which we will have much to say about in later chapters is an almost automatic suspect in any depressive illness and has been linked to the craving of carbohydrates which is a characteristic of SAD. Psychological vulnerabilities to depression can also play a role in transforming normal unenthusiastic reactions to long dark days into SAD. We shall consider these causes in later chapters.

Bipolar Disorder

The clinical disorder of *bipolar disorder* is characterized by pronounced shifts in mood. The disorder was recognized in the mid nineteenth century by a physician named J. P. Falret, who published descriptions of manic excitement and depression and used the term *circular insanity* to describe the phenomenon.[38] This legalistic and pejorative term never received much currency and was replaced by the diagnostic labels of *manic depressive disorder* and *bipolar disorder,* which have essentially the same meanings. The key elements in bipolar disorder are dramatic swings in mood. At times the patient may be very depressed, reporting many of the symptoms in our earlier description of clinical depression. However, at other times, the patient will be in a hyperelated state, which has been termed *mania* or *hypomania,* depending on severity. The patient may engage in a whirlwind of activities, thoughts firing rapidly from one idea to the next and speech difficult to interpret. The need for sleep seems to vanish. Self-esteem becomes inflated. Prudence may disappear and the patient may do some very rash things.

In a manic state the patient may make all kinds of plans, look up old friends — sometimes calling them in the middle of the night — go on buying sprees, even drive recklessly. This state of euphoric mood and hyperexcitement seems like it is 180 degrees away from the patient's depressed state. Hence the term bipolar disorder.

In their booklet, *A Story of Bipolar Disorder,* the National Institute of Mental Health included a very useful checklist of signs of mania presented in the form of first person statements.[39] The statements provide a good sense of what mania is like.

I feel like I'm on top of the world
I feel powerful. I can do anything I want, nothing can stop me.
I have lots of energy.
I don't seem to need much sleep.
I feel restless all the time.
I feel really mad.
I have a lot of sexual energy.

I can't focus on anything for very long.

I sometimes can't stop talking and I talk really fast.

I'm spending lots of money on things I don't need and can't afford.

Friends tell me that I've been acting differently. They tell me that I'm starting fights, talking louder, and getting more angry.

These signs are indicative of bipolar disorder. If the symptoms are clear enough to call it a manic episode, then the condition is classified as *bipolar disorder Type I*. If the symptoms of manic behavior are less severe — what we call *hypomanic*, the condition is called *bipolar disorder Type II*. People who are hypomanic might exhibit some of the same behaviors as people who are manic; they may appear to be very energetic, even euphoric, but their thoughts and behavior are not as erratic and disorganized as people who are clearly manic.

People who have bipolar disorder typically go through cycles with manic episodes, depressive episodes and normal periods. A revealing study carried out by Richard Depue and his colleagues tells us a good deal about the behavior of people with bipolar depressive problems.[40] The subjects in the study had bipolar problems but were not at that time impaired enough to require hospitalization. They reported increased and decreased energy patterns, uneven patterns of productivity, mental confusion, high and low sociability patterns, high and low interest patterns, increased and decreased sleep patterns, and highs and lows in sexual interest.

Depue reported that typically depressed episodes lasted from three to six days. The duration of manic episodes was about the same — two to six days. About two-thirds of his subjects had between two and six depressed episodes per year with about the same numbers holding for manic episodes. The impression one gets from these statistics is that the outbreaks of bipolar symptoms were fairly frequent, but time limited. For Depue's sample of people whose problems were not serious enough to require hospitalization, the episodes seemed to run their course.

The researchers described a case that illuminates some of the clinical features of bipolar disorder. The subject, Ms. S, was an 18-year-old college student. The researchers first described some of the behaviors of her hypomanic phase. The following are some excerpts:

> *Mood.* Feeling clearly higher or happier than is usually the case, "as if I have a different personality, I feel hyper, and I fool around a great deal, laughing and joking all the time." Other people notice the change in mood and comment to her about it.
>
> *Energy and need for excitement.* She has greatly increased energy that "goes with the high feelings." People comment on this, usually saying that she "ought to slow down" or that she is "wearing them out." She participates in many more sports activities, goes more places than usual ("to see people, stores, bars, anywhere"),

and does other activities that she might not ordinarily do. During these active times she can get so excited that she is unable to sit still, and she jumps from one activity to another.

She reports an intense need for excitement, and begins new activities with lots of enthusiasm and then quickly loses interest in them. For instance, in one recent phase, she started skiing lessons, two new embroidery works, needlepoint lessons, learning a new complicated card game, and she joined a women's group, but dropped all of them at the end of her 2-week hypomanic period....

Thoughts, speech and distractibility. During these phases her thoughts race so fast that she "can say about one half of a thought and then it is gone." Also, her attention jumps rapidly from one thought to another so that she loses her "train of thought totally" At these times, she talks very fast, and stumbles over words, and others complain that they cannot hold a conversation with her....

Irresponsible behavior. She spends money she cannot afford or other people's money.... [S]he is sexually active with new male friends, which leads to trouble with her steady boyfriend; she gets into a lot of verbal, and sometimes physical, fights; she frequents bars and drinks more when she goes to bars; she drives recklessly (goes through red lights and stop signs) and faster than usual (more than 10 miles over the speed limit, whereas this is not usual for her).

The authors then describe the behaviors of her depressive phases.

Mood. Both depression and irritability, but mainly the former. Others always tell her she looks sad or depressed during "lows," and the feeling is described as "painful." Nonverbal cues of depression are apparently evident in facial expression, since others always comment on her depression, and she has frequent crying spells, without understanding why, and has an almost constant urge to cry....

Energy and motor activity. During "lows" she feels very tired and worn out. She does not do school work ("couldn't if I tried"). She could manage to go out, but she "wouldn't go out on my own initiative." She reports that she is "slowed down" and that "moving is more difficult."

Concentration. Her concentration is poor; it is "difficult or impossible to read."

Somatic complaints. Her somatic complaints are frequent during "lows" (headaches, blurred vision, constipation; vacillates between feeling too hot and too cold)....

Cognitions. She reports a range of negative cognitions, including indecision over small matters, pessimism about present and future, being a burden to her family, that she would be better off dead....

Ms. S had been experiencing hypomanic and depressive periods since her first year of junior high school. It was reported that she might experience four phases in a year, each of which would last for at least two continuous weeks.

With four manic and depressive episodes a year, Ms. S would meet the minimal criteria for what is called "rapid cycling." Four or more manic or depressive episodes in a year is a benchmark for rapid cycling and it is not at all uncommon for bipolar patients to reach this benchmark. In a recent study carried out in the Netherlands, nearly 40 percent of a large group of bipolar patients studied were classified as rapid cyclers. In the study, it was found the rapid cyclers were more likely to be diagnosed as bipolar type I than bipolar type II, were likely to have experienced abuse as a child, and to have abused drugs.[41] A long-term follow-up study carried out in Italy suggests that for many patients, rapid cycling can become a way of life — a pattern that continues over the years.[42]

There are some patients who experience very rapid cycling — a complete turn around in only 48 hours, and some patients who cycle even more rapidly than that. One can imagine how bewildering that must be, not only to the patient but to his or her friends and family.[43]

What are bipolar patients like when they are in a non episodic, normal state? Do they have characteristic features of personality, and if so, how would they differ from unipolar patients? A large-scale study using a variety of personality tests found some interesting differences between bipolar type I, bipolar type II, and unipolar depression patients when they were in a recovered state. The unipolar patients tended to be insecure and introverted. The bipolar type I patients were surprisingly most nearly normal on the tests while bipolar type II patients were very conscious of experiencing dramatic, uncomfortable changes in mood. They were the ones who saw themselves as emotionally unstable. It may be that the Type I bipolar patients in the study (who actually experienced more pronounced manic episodes) were going through a process of denial when it came to viewing themselves and their symptoms during recovery.[44]

As is true for their counterparts with unipolar depression, people who have bipolar disorder tend to perform less well than control subjects on tests of attention and memory. Recent studies have reported contradictory results as to whether bipolar type I or bipolar type II patients experience these deficits more severely, but it seems clear that such deficits are a part of the picture of both types of bipolar disorder.[45]

Thoughts of suicide and attempted suicide are characteristic of patients with bipolar disorder. Studies carried out in Finland indicated that about half of the bipolar patients studied had at some time in their lives made a suicide attempt.[46] Bipolar patients are a relatively high risk group for suicidal behavior. During depressive episodes, if the patient reports feeling *hopeless*, this should be taken very seriously.

2. Depression in the United States

We shall now turn to the questions of how prevalent depression is in the United States and who appears most vulnerable. In pursuing our inquiries, we are going to put on the hat of an epidemiologist–the statistically trained scientist who collects and analyzes data on diseases. In this role, we will ask such questions as: How many people in this country suffer from depression and which groups in the population seem to be at higher risk of becoming depressed? Are men or women more likely to become depressed? Does being in a minority group increase one's vulnerability? Does it make a difference whether one lives in an urban area or in the countryside? And what relation does the onset of depression bear to one's age? The answers to such questions will help us better understand the scope of the problem of depression in this country and identify groups of people at greater risk.

How does one estimate the number of people who suffer from depression? The problem is more difficult than it may seem. One possible approach would be to survey the nation's mental health centers, psychotherapists in private practice and family physicians, asking how many people are being treated for depression and who these people are. The problem with this approach is that a very large number of people who are depressed do not seek professional treatment. Moreover, the people who do seek treatment are not likely to be representative of the entire population of depressed people; they are likely to be more affluent and better educated. Minority groups will be underrepresented.

Probably the only way to estimate how many people are depressed in the United States is to go knocking on doors in our cities, towns and farms, to survey representative samples of our population and to ask questions that will accurately tell whether a person is depressed. And you have to do this in a way so that people will not slam the door in your face. After all, information about emotional health is sensitive.

In the 1980s The National Institute of Mental Health (NIMH) made the first concerted effort to address the problem. Researchers working under the auspices of NIMH developed an interview guide — a series of questions that enables one to identify with reasonable accuracy people with different mental and emotional disorders. The technique was validated by comparing the results obtained using the interview guide with the results from clinical evaluations. The interview guide was found to be acceptable for community surveys. Having said this, the technique should be viewed as a screening instrument and not as an ideal measure of depression. Like any other self-report measure of depression, it will classify some people who are actually clinically depressed as not depressed and some people who are not depressed as depressed. There is an error rate.[1]

In large scale studies, researchers used the interview guide in selected communities in Connecticut, North Carolina, California, Maryland and Missouri. Thousands of people were interviewed in their homes. The results from these surveys indicated that about 5 percent of the adult population have suffered at one time or another from a major depression and 3 percent have experienced a protracted period of moderate depression (dysthymic disorder).[2] Translating these percentages into raw numbers, something like 9 million adult Americans were thought to have experienced a major depression and 5 million dysthymic disorder. At any given point in time, the number of persons experiencing depression would be less, though still numbering well into the millions.

A large majority of the cases of depression uncovered in the 1980 surveys were cases of unipolar depression. While the rates for experiencing a major depression were about five in one hundred, only one out of one hundred people interviewed reported ever experiencing a manic episode. Bipolar disorder was clearly less prevalent than unipolar depression.

Studies carried out using the NIMH interviewing technique suggested that the chances of a person becoming depressed in the 1980s were higher than they were in past generations. This conclusion is based on the findings that people who were in their twenties were much more likely to report having experienced a depressive illness in their relatively short lives than people who were senior citizens. If this was indeed the case, it was a provocative observation.

There are, of course, problems in making comparisons between people at very different age ranges with different memories. One may raise questions about how reliable the memories of older people are about emotional troubles experienced many years earlier. Still, the apparently large increase in the rate of depression cannot be easily dismissed.

Other more recent straws in the wind buttress the possibility that the prevalence of depression in the population has been on the rise. Two recent large scale surveys of the prevalence of depression in the American population indicate that the figure now is substantially higher than was estimated from the studies carried out during the 1980s. In one of these studies, "The National Comorbidity Survey Replication," carried out between 2001 and 2003, a nationally representative sample of American households was surveyed using professional interviewers of the University of Michigan School of Social Research. In this study over 9000 people were interviewed. It was found that the lifetime prevalence of major depressive disorder — the percent of people who have experienced such depression at some time in their lives was not of the order of 5 percent as was reported in the 1980s, but more than three times as large — nearly 17 percent.[3] In an even larger study, "The National Epidemiologic Survey on Alcoholism and Related Conditions," over 43,000 people were interviewed. The prevalence of depression in this study was 13 percent.[4] In discussing their results, the researchers noted that their data suggested a higher prevalence of depression than was noted in earlier studies. In both of the recent studies the highest lifetime prevalence of depression had shifted from younger people to middle-aged people.

As was true for the previous analysis, one cannot rule out the possibility that the differences between the findings of the 1980s and the more recent findings may be the result of artifacts rather than represent real differences. For example, there were differences in the samples used; the more recent studies used nationally representative samples while the earlier studies sampled selected geographical areas. However, it seems unlikely that these different sampling procedures would have produced such dramatic differences in the findings. Another line of explanation involves possible changes in public attitudes about depression. With the extensive flow of public information about depression in recent years and the heavy advertising of the pharmaceutical industry promoting antidepressant medicines, it seems likely that people today are both more knowledgeable about depression and more open about revealing the problem than they might have been 20 years earlier. Perhaps, the earlier estimates for major depressive disorder were on the low side because the people interviewed may have been more reluctant to admit having the problem.

Given these cautionary notes, we still cannot dismiss the possibility that the data means exactly what it says, that there has been a substantial increase in the prevalence of major depressive disorder in the United States over the last several decades. If this is indeed the case, it is an intriguing question as to why this would be so.

Why should people today be more prone to being depressed than people of past generations? While this is a tantalizing question, there are so many differences between the lifestyles of today and earlier generations, that it is difficult to ascribe the apparent increase in depression to any one reason. One would be comparing an era of smaller communities to sprawling cities and suburbs, to jobs using manual typewriters and card filing systems to those using high speed computers and ever more sophisticated information technology. If I were forced to pick one reason to explain the apparent increase in depression, my candidate would be the breakdown of social support systems and most importantly, the family. The family has traditionally provided the individual with meaning and security. However, there has been a large increase in the number of families experiencing divorce and separation. Moreover, one is less likely to have one's extended family — aunts, uncles, cousins and grandparents — within hailing distance as might have been the case in the past. Today's lifestyle tends to scatter families. An individual may feel isolated, even rootless. In times of trouble and emotional stress, there may be no one close to turn to.

The idea that family ties, or to use a broader sociological term, *social integration*, has a relation to depressive behavior, is not a new one. One of the founding fathers of sociology, Emile Durkheim, reported in nineteenth-century France that persons who were more integrated into the society (e.g., married persons, persons coming from larger families) had lower suicide rates than those who were less integrated.[5] I shall return to this theme — that social support has protective value against depression in later chapters.

Sex Differences in Depression

When we compare groups of men and women we usually find that women are more likely to be depressed. It should be stated that this is not always the case. For example, I once studied a sample of over 200 college students using the well-respected Beck Depression Inventory to assess depression and found no difference between the male and female students. However, when we examine the case records in treatment centers such as mental hospitals and outpatient clinics, we typically find that more of the cases diagnosed as depressed are women. Moreover, in all of the major household surveys undertaken, we find that more women than men report being depressed. This is a very robust finding.

A number of explanations have been offered to account for the higher rates of depression found in women. One theory is that women may be more biologically vulnerable to depression. It has been suggested that this vulnerability may relate in part to the reproductive system in women. Many women experience depressed reactions during the premenstrual phase of the menstrual cycle. When such distress is pronounced, it may be given the name of *premenstrual dysphoric disorder*. Moreover, many women experience depressed reactions following the birth of a child. This *postpartum depression* is a widespread phenomenon, with a mix of biological and social elements. In Western societies estimates are that about one in 10 new mothers will experience this problem.[6] A recent study of over 4000 American women reported a figure of nearly 18 percent with depressive symptoms.[7] Postpartum depression has been reported in such widely differing societies as Hong Kong, Dubai of the United Arab Emirates, Turkey, and India.[8]

Researchers have carried out studies trying to ascertain what factors tend to be associated with postpartum depression. It was thought that the method of childbirth — vaginal verses cesarean might make a difference in this regard — that cesarean delivery might be associated with postpartum depression but a recent meta analysis of existing research casts doubt on such a linkage.[9] Having a history of depression is a risk factor for postpartum depression as is smoking.[10] Poor relationships with partners and negative feelings about pregnancy are probably not helpful.

Postpartum depression has implications for child care. Research suggests that women who develop postpartum depression are less likely to play with and talk to their infant children and more likely to use harsh punishment.[11]

The influence of biology in promoting depression may be most evident when a girl enters puberty. Prior to that time, research shows that boys and girls do not differ in the likelihood of their being depressed. When girls reach the age of about 13, all that changes. The frequency of depression increases markedly for girls. Not so for boys, at least not yet. But, for girls, mid-puberty is the time in which depressive symptoms tend to increase, and the difference between males and females in the report of depression begins to emerge.[12]

Studies attempting to tie ovarian hormone levels directly to the experience of depression in both adolescent and adult females have produced some positive and quite a few negative results. For example, a study reported by Brooks-Gunn and Warren found no relation between levels of depressive symptoms and any of five hormones tested.[13] If, as this study suggests, it is not the hormonal changes themselves that are directly associated with depression, then it seems plausible that it is the way girls deal with these changes in their everyday lives that may influence vulnerability to depression. The onset of puberty may place a girl into a new status within her family and among her friends, with new expectations and challenges. Going into the teen years is a major adjustment which for many girls can be difficult and threaten their self-esteem. Because many girls tend to internalize problems, they may react by feeling low and dispirited.

A second type of explanation for the gender differences in the report of depression emphasizes such psychological vulnerabilities. Studies show the girls tend to experience more negative events during childhood and adolescence than boys.[14] Such negative events, by themselves, can promote depressed feelings. Negative mindsets can exacerbate the meaning of these events, making them seem worse than they actually are and there is some evidence that girls may be more likely than boys to have such mindsets.[15] Girls tend to place more emphasis on social relationships than boys and may be more likely to experience personal rejection in the insensitivities that often characterize these relationships. Finally, girls tend to place a great deal of importance on their personal attractiveness and studies show that a large majority of young adolescent girls are dissatisfied with their body image.[16]

A third, more sociological type of explanation is that the role of women in our society often places them at a disadvantage, both economically and psychologically, leaving them in situations that increase their vulnerability to depressive reactions. Let's illustrate this idea with two case examples.

Tracy tells a story of being in an unhappy marriage. She was married shortly after high school graduation and had three children over the next six years. In the last two years her relationship with her husband has deteriorated, and he has been physically abusive. Tracy would like to leave him, but feels she can't. She has small children to support and sees no way of doing it. She feels dependent and powerless.

Denise is a single mother. She has near total responsibility for bringing in money from a job, keeping up the house and raising two children. This triple responsibility puts her in a perpetual time squeeze that creates high levels of stress, particularly when something goes wrong, like sickness in the children or herself. While both Tracy and Denise are vulnerable to depression, because of their circumstances, I suspect that it is Tracy who may be the most vulnerable of the two for Denise can make adjustments to reduce the stress load in her life; while Tracy faces a very difficult road.

A fourth type of explanation is that the cultural definition of being female permits women to more easily admit having emotional problems. From early on, males in our society are raised to be self-reliant and not to appear weak. The need to project a strong image may deter some men from admitting that they have a depressive problem and from seeking the help they need. According to this theory, men may have a higher rate of depression than is believed, but it is simply not reported.

Many men feel that if they express the fact that they are depressed to others, they may not only feel a loss of self-esteem, they may experience rejection. Constance Hammen and Stefanie Peters ran an experiment that suggests such fears are not groundless.[17] Try the experiment on yourself. Read the following description of a young woman:

> Susan is 18 years old and a freshman in college. She was a good student in high school, well-adjusted, and got along well with her schoolmates. However, a couple of problems have developed since she started college. She is finding the course work quite a bit more difficult than she had expected, and lately it seems like her boyfriend from high school is losing interest in her.
>
> For the past few weeks, Susan has been feeling pretty down. She's feeling really miserable about what's been happening in her life and can't imagine that things will ever get any better. When she goes out with her friends or her boyfriend, she can't seem to shake her gloomy feelings and enjoy herself. Susan's been trying to keep up with her schoolwork, but she's falling farther and farther behind because most of the time she gets so discouraged and pessimistic that she gives up. The other day one of Susan's friends asked her if she wanted to get together for lunch, but Susan said "no" because she hasn't really felt like eating lately and found that she had no appetite at all. Often she feels like there's no point in even getting up in the morning, and, in fact, Susan has been staying in bed longer and longer every morning. It seems like she just doesn't have any energy left for anything.

Now ask yourself the following questions: How much would you like to have this person as an acquaintance? How much would you like her as a co-worker on a task? How much would you like her as a close friend?

Now go back and read the description of the person again, only this time, substitute a name like Bill or Jack for Susan, and girlfriend for boyfriend. When you finish, ask yourself the same three questions.

The subjects in the study carried out by Hammen and Peters were more likely to reject the person described when identified as a male than when identified as a female.

Urban and Rural Comparisons

One can make a case that the atmosphere of many cities is more turbulent than that of small towns and rural areas. Many big cities have serious problems with crime and drugs. They are congested, noisy and seem impersonal. In these respects, the stress-arousing potential of the city seems higher than that of rural areas. At the same time, the stress buffering potential of family and close friends often found in integrated small communities may be diminished in the city. One might expect that these conditions could lead to higher rates of depression in urban areas.

The idea that one might find less depression in low-stress environments receives some support from research conducted in close-knit, less technologically advanced communities. For example, researchers studying a preliterate society in New Guinea in 1984 found little evidence of depression or suicide. A study of the Amish people in Lancaster County, Pennsylvania, also found low rates of unipolar depression.[18] In a systematic study, researchers compared rates of depression in several urban and rural American communities. The research team surveyed five counties in North Carolina. One of the counties (Durham County) was part of a major urban center containing several well-known universities and an industrial park. The four rural counties contained no major industries and were described as representative of the rural South.

Carefully chosen samples of people in these communities were interviewed using the NIMH interview guide. The results? Reports of current major depressive episodes were *three times* as frequent in the urban county. When the researchers controlled statistically for a number of important social and demographic factors, such as sex, education, race and selective migration, they continued to find a substantial difference in the rates of depression between the urban and rural areas. The results indicated that urban life is associated with a higher risk of depression.[19]

The tendency observed in the North Carolina study for residents of urban areas to more frequently report being depressed than residents of rural areas has been observed in other countries. Several studies carried out in the United

Kingdom as well as studies carried out in Canada have reported this tendency and there is some suggestive data along these lines that was collected in Nigeria. There appears to be elements in urban living which increase vulnerability to depressive reactions.[20]

There is another interesting pattern which may tie in here, if only loosely. Studies have found that some groupings of people who immigrate to the United States are less depressed than their counterparts who were born in this country and reside here. This is particularly true for white immigrants, presumably coming in the main from Europe and English-speaking countries and is also the case for Mexican immigrants.[21] If a person moves here from such countries, the data suggest that he or she is not as likely to be depressed as their counterparts who have become acculturated to our society.

One possible explanation for this difference is that the lifestyle of the country of orgin and particularly the routines of the workplace may be more relaxed than what we find here in America. Lower levels of stress tend to be reflected in lower levels of depression. The individual choosing to immigrate to America may come here to take advantage of the economic opportunities that this country offers. However, as the immigrant becomes acclimated to America, he or she may find that the workplace is very competitive, and as studies have shown generates high level of stress.[22]Living with such increased levels of stress, we might hypothesize that, in time, the immigrant's level of depression would increase and eventually match that of his or her native born counterparts. And, as we have noted, there may be a link, here, to the observation that people living in urban areas tend to have higher rates of depression than people living in rural areas.

Depression in Members of Minority Groups

Let's turn our attention to the question of whether depression is more likely to occur among members of minority groups. Our focus will be on three of America's largest minority groups: Asian, Hispanic and African Americans.

In considering the potential risk for depression among these minority groups, we might start with the observation that African Americans and Hispanics are likely to be economically poorer than non–Hispanic whites. These groups have a higher chance of living in poorer, more crime-ridden neighborhoods. They may also be subjected to prejudice based on racial and ethnic bias. In addition, African Americans have a higher rate of single parent families than other groups, which brings additional burdens. All of these factors might lead one to speculate that at least some minority groups are exposed to relatively high levels of environmental stressors, which might be reflected in higher rates of depression.

Is this deduction correct? Let's look at the research, beginning with studies of depression among African Americans. In the large National Comorbidity Survey Replication we cited earlier, comparisons were made between Non-Hispanic whites and African Americans in terms of whether they had ever experienced a major depressive disorder. The data revealed that lifetime prevalence rates for African Americans were not higher than for whites; rather, they were far lower (African Americans 11 percent, non–Hispanic whites 18 percent). The figures for dysthymic disorder were about the same for African Americans and whites, while the figures for bipolar disorder were higher for African Americans (5 percent versus 3 percent). In regard to the other psychiatric categories used in the survey, lifetime prevalence rates for anxiety disorders were lower for African Americans. African Americans and whites were generally similar in the report of impulse control disorders while African Americans had lower figures for alcohol abuse and dependency.[23] It seems fair to conclude from this study that the added stresses that were traditionally experienced by African Americans in this country do not show themselves in increased rates of unipolar depression or most other major psychiatric categories. This is an interesting, in some ways counterintuitive finding and raises the intriguing question as to what it is in the African American experience that protects against the development of such emotional disorders. The important role of the church in the African-American community has been suggested as a factor. It would be interesting to see studies looking at the possible influence of the patterns of social relationships in the African-American community as well as studies of attitudes and beliefs that might be protective against the onset of depression.

Hispanic Americans have a diverse history in this country. Mexicans resided in California and the Southwest long before people from the eastern United States settled there in large numbers. Puerto Ricans have been living in such cities as New York for generations. Recall the wonderful Leonard Bernstein-Stephen Sondheim musical West Side Story. Many Cubans immigrated to Florida following the establishment of Fidel Castro's regime. And more recently immigrants have come from Central America and the Caribbean islands. While Hispanic Americans share a common language and for the most part a common religion, household surveys which place all Hispanics under the same rubric may obscure important differences between groups of Hispanics.

The National Comorbidity Survey Replication provides us with an overview comparison of non–Hispanic whites and Hispanics for the lifetime prevalence of depression. Because the survey used only English speaking people, it probably excluded many Hispanics whose command of English would not permit them to participate in the survey. The sample would be non-representative in this respect. With this caveat, the bottom line is that the survey found that for both major depressive disorder and dysthymic disorder, Hispanics have lower lifetime prevalence figures. For major depressive disorder the figures are 14 percent for Hispanics versus 18 percent for non–Hispanic whites.

For Dysthymic disorder the figures are 2 percent versus 4 percent. There were no differences for bipolar disorder. Interestingly, the difference in lifetime prevalence for depression applies only to the younger people sampled (age 43 or younger). For the older people sampled, Hispanics and non–Hispanic whites did not differ.[24]

In regard to specific groups of Hispanic Americans, probably the best available data is on Mexican Americans. The National Epidemiological Survey on Alcoholism and Related Conditions found that the risk of psychiatric problems among Mexican-Americans was lower than among non–Hispanic whites. This was also reported in an earlier version of the National Comorbidity Survey.[25]

A particularly revealing study on depression was carried out on Mexican Americans living in two Los Angeles communities. As was true for the national household surveys, the lifetime prevalence of major depressive episodes was lower for Mexican Americans than for non–Hispanic whites. There were some very interesting findings reported for Hispanic women. In the younger age range Hispanic women were *much less* likely to be depressed than young non–Hispanic white women. However, when the researchers looked at Hispanic women over 40, they found a relatively large number of women who reported long-lasting, moderate levels of depression.[26] This finding seems to jibe with the findings from the more recent national survey which found that the lower rates of depression (dysthmic disorder) for Hispanics was limited to the younger people sampled.

One wonders what it was about growing up in these Mexican American families that offered young women protection against depressive reactions? Was it the protection of a close-knit, extended family, where one has many links to other people? Was it the immersion in religion that often assumes a predominant place in Hispanic culture? Was there more certainty in the future roles of young women, with less pressure toward career achievement? One also wonders what happens in later life that breaks down this early protection leaving these Mexican American women more vulnerable toward a protracted malaise.

For purposes of statistical analysis, "Asian Americans" are often grouped together, but Chinese Americans, Japanese Americans, Vietnamese Americans and Americans whose origins are in the Indian subcontinent have diverse languages and cultures. A recent study carried out in California showed that the use of mental-health services by people categorized as Asian Americans varied considerably, with people whose origin was in East Asia more likely to use the services than people coming from South East Asia, the Philippines or other areas.[27]

There are some difficulties in obtaining a clear answer to the question of the prevalence of depression in Asian Americans. For many Asian Americans and in particular recent immigrants there may be a language problem in answering questions phrased in English. The use of interpreters can lead to misleading conclusions because of the subtlety of the language used in the description of psychological states. An example of the error resulting from the use of a translator is provided in an article by Luis Marcos.

A clinician wanted information from a Chinese-speaking patient. He asked, "What kinds of moods have you been in recently?" The interpreter turned to the patient and asked, "How have you been feeling?" The patient replied to the interpreter, "No, I don't have any more pain, my stomach is now fine, and I can eat much better since I take the medication." The interpreter said to the clinician, "He says that he feels fine, no problems."[28]

A second problem that may affect the validity of the data obtained is a feeling held by many Asian Americans that being treated for a mental illness such as depression carries with it a stigma. People who feel this way may be unwilling to reveal having the disorder. In writing about mental illness in Asian Americans, David and Stanley Sue observed that the, "amount of stigma or shame associated with emotional difficulties is probably much greater among Asian American groups. Mental illness in a family member is considered a failure of the family system itself. For Eastern more than for Western families, the failure or weakness of an individual is considered a disgrace to the family unit.... [Researchers] reported that the stigma of mental illness in Asian Americans remains so great that, even among individuals of the third and fourth generation, there is hesitation to admit to psychological problems."[29] A recent study of a sample of depressed Asian Americans drawn from Internet users suggests the observation voiced by David and Stanley Sue continues to hold true. Compared to whites, Asian Americans more strongly felt that being treated for depression carried a stigma.[30]

Researchers have reported that Asian Americans seem willing to describe their problems in terms of bodily complaints— headaches, fatigue, insomnia, dizziness and heart palpitations, but are reluctant to admit to demoralized psychological states. This denial of an emotional problem may even persist into treatment. Given this cultural tradition, which would lead to underreporting of the problem, there is a need for caution in interpreting the findings from household surveys which assess the prevalence of depressive problems among Asian Americans.

Here are some findings from two large-scale studies. The first study reported in 1999 surveyed over 18,000 people from a number of selected sites. It was found that Asian-Americans had lower rates of bipolar disorder than whites.[31] The second study called the Chinese American Psychiatric Epidemiological Study was carried out in Los Angeles and reported in 1998. The sample consisted of over 1700 Chinese-Americans who spoke either English, Mandarin, or Cantonese. The variety of languages used in the study was at remedy for the problems caused by an unfamiliar language and helped keep the sample of Chinese Americans representative. Lifetime prevalence estimates for both major depressive disorder and dysthymic disorder were considerably lower than the figures for whites reported in the two recent national surveys.[32]

Age at Onset of Depression

At what age do people become depressed? Is it likely to begin in early childhood? Adolescence? Young adulthood? Some preliminary answers to this question were suggested by a study carried out in Oregon. Over 2,000 people who had shown some evidence of depression on psychological screening tests were interviewed in detail about current and past episodes of depression.[33] About 1,000 of the people were diagnosed as having at least one current or past episode of unipolar depression. During the interviews, the researchers tried to ascertain the time at which the first episode of depression occurred. They found that the risk of developing depression in childhood was *very low*. Before we accept this conclusion as gospel, however, we must point out that there have been real difficulties in diagnosing depression in children. As we shall see, we really can't estimate these numbers very well.

As an anchoring point in what has been an area of controversy, we should note that children are being treated today in psychiatric hospitals for depression. Using the benchmarks described in the American Psychiatric Association's *Diagnostic and Statistical Manual*, children have been diagnosed as having major depressions and are being treated using psychotherapy and antidepressant drugs.

What is a young child who is diagnosed as having a major depression like? Here are some excerpts from a case study presented by Javad Kashani and his colleagues.[34]

The depressed child, a five-year-old boy named Mike, became a matter of considerable concern to his teacher, "when he told her that he wanted to 'kill himself and die.' The teacher found him to be sad, worried, overactive, restless and irritable. He had feelings of self-reproach, self-blame, and hopelessness about the future and had difficulty in concentrating and following rules." Mike had physical complaints such as stomach aches and pains in his legs and arms. He was also fatigued. His mother reported that he had crying spells, was irritable and had a poor appetite.

When Mike was interviewed by the researcher, he did not smile, but appeared solemn. He said he didn't like himself and that nobody liked him. When he was asked what was going to happen to him when he became a big man, he replied, "I'll be dead."

Mike is a depressed child, not difficult to recognize as such. So, too, are other children in psychiatric hospitals being treated with drugs and psychotherapy. When we move away from such severe cases, however, the problem becomes murkier. It is hard to say how many children in this country should be considered depressed.

One of the reasons for this uncertainty is that the clinicians and researchers who have studied depression in children have disagreed about the very nature of childhood depression. In describing the disorder, some writers have included symptoms that go well beyond those listed in the *Diagnostic and Statistical Manual* for adults. They have interpreted a number of troublesome behaviors in children as "masking depression," behaviors that disguise an underlying depression. Behaviors as wide-ranging as hyperactivity, aggressiveness, delinquency, temper tantrums, boredom and restlessness have been cited as evidence of depression. In a paper on childhood depression, Monroe Lefkowitz and Edward Tesiny observed that such a "catalogue of symptoms must, at one time or another, encompass all children."[35]

At the other extreme, it has been argued that much of what has been called depression in childhood is really transitory problems in development–problems that often disappear as children grow up. An example would be poor appetite, a symptom of depression in adults. One study identified a number of children at age six with poor appetites. By age nine the problem in most of the children had disappeared.[36] It would be stretching things to infer that these children had been depressed.

How do we identify children who are depressed? Parents and teachers are usually in the most strategic positions to recognize that something is troubling the young child and that he or she appears to be depressed. Research suggests that by around the age of nine, the children themselves can be good reporters of their own moods.[37] Child behavioral checklists are available for researchers and clinicians to help in evaluating depression. And there are self-report measures for children which measure depression. These self report measures of depression for children, somewhat similar to those used to assess depression in adults, probably increase in usefulness and accuracy as the child grows older.

The Children Depression Inventory (CDI), developed in 1981 and commercially published in 1992 has been the principal self report measure used for assessing depression in children.[38] The inventory consists of 27 items that sample various aspects of depression in children such as self-blame, suicidal thoughts, feelings of sadness, and feelings of loneliness. The scale is internally consistent and has shown a moderate correspondence with the ratings of clinicians. The scale has been translated into foreign languages and used both in this country and abroad.

While the Children's Depression Inventory has shown itself useful in a variety of research studies, its value as a reliable instrument in diagnosing depression in children has been questioned. A recent study carried out in Belgium concluded that the test was a useful diagnostic instrument, but earlier studies have not always found this to be the case.[39] In one study, for example, researchers used the measure to try to distinguish between children in a clinic diagnosed as depressed and children diagnosed as having "conduct" disorders such as truancy or over aggressiveness. The test misclassified about two-thirds of the children. The researchers concluded, "The level of discrimination achieved from the CDI factor scores falls far short of the necessary level of differentiation required of a diagnostic tool. Thus, the use of the CDI as the sole criterion for the selection of depressed youths for treatment or research purposes is not recommended."[40]

In another example, researchers administered the test to children in the schools of four rural communities. To estimate the prevalence of depression, the researchers used "cutoff" scores suggested by the developers of the instrument. A score above a certain number was thought to indicate the likelihood of depression. Using these recommended cutoff scores for identifying depression, the researchers would have come up with the astonishing figure that 46 percent of the children in the community were depressed.[41] This figure, of course, is ludicrous and just emphasizes the fact that we do not yet have accurate ways of identifying depression in young children that can be applied to large, heterogeneous samples with confidence.

The difficulty of identifying children with subclinical (less than full-blown) levels of depression was highlighted in a study carried out by Reed Larson and his co-workers. They monitored the moods and behavior of 483 fifth-and ninth-graders for a week, comparing the behavior of children who scored high on a measure of childhood depression with those who did not. They reported, "In general, we were struck by how few associations there were between depression and how children and young adolescents experienced the different contexts of their lives. Outwardly, the daily patterns of depressed children and adolescents are quite like those of nondepressed peers."[42]

In reviewing the state of the art, Mary Kerr and her colleagues likened attempts to conceptualize and measure depression in children to the story of the blind man examining the elephant.[43] Because of these troublesome problems in definition and measurement, I think it is fair to say that we do not as yet have a trustworthy estimate of the number of children who are depressed in this country. While it seems likely that the prevalence of depression in young children is a good deal less than what we find in adolescence, to provide precise estimates of the prevalence of depression in children, and particularly younger children would be a very difficult undertaking. As we have suggested, depression in children is not always easy to recognize. It is not difficult to spot a "problem child" who bullies his playmates, has recurrent nightmares or sets fires at home, but a child who seems lonely or sad may not be viewed as being all that unusual. The child may be described as "quiet" or "shy," rather than depressed. The parents or teacher may not identify a depressive problem for what it is, and young children should not be expected to diagnose themselves.

While we may not often recognize depression in young children either because it occurs infrequently, as suggested by the Oregon study, or because we are not sophisticated enough to identify it when it does occur — the situation is quite different for adolescents. Depression in adolescence is a widespread problem. Suicide among teenagers, for example, has received a great deal of publicity and for good reason. Suicide is the second leading cause of death among people in the 15 to 24 age range. Surveys carried out on teenagers reveal that large numbers of them have thought about committing suicide at some time during their lives. Many of these teenagers feel that they would find it difficult to tell their parents or teachers about these thoughts.[44]

How extensive is depression among adolescents? In an early study William Reynolds surveyed high schools using a battery of self-report measures of depression and reported that he found levels of moderate to severe depression running in about 11 to 17 percent of the students.[45] A more recent self report survey carried out on a large number of French high school students reported figures in the 10 percent range for boys and more than twice as high for girls.[46] Correcting for the possibility that self-report inventories may overestimate the extent of depression when compared to interviews conducted by trained clinicians, it still looks as if depression in adolescents is a widespread problem.

As is true for unipolar depression, the prevalence of bipolar depression tends to increase sharply during adolescence. If you examine graphs showing the age of onset of bipolar disorder, you will see a pronounced spike in the late teens extending into the early twenties. While bipolar disorder can occur at almost anytime, this is the time of life that bipolar disorder very frequently begins.[47]

Psychologists studying "loneliness" have found that these very unpleasant feelings, which often coincide with depression, frequently are at high levels during the teenage years. Adolescents are noted for their gregariousness but frequently feel lonely and sometimes alienated. The experience of loss such as the divorce of one's parents sometimes precedes the onset of a major depressive disorder in adolescence. Tensions within the family have been linked to the longer lasting dysthymic disorder.

Studies carried out in Finland where SAD might be expected to be a particular problem indicates that the disorder is especially prevalent in young women.[48]

Turning to college students, Roland Tanck and I included in our diary the questions, "Did you feel depressed today? And if *yes*, what do you think was causing these depressed feelings?" In perusing the students' responses, we noticed that while on occasion the students were at a loss to identify the cause of their depressed moods, they usually offered a reason, and often a specific event. Frequently, the students attributed their depressed feelings to problems relating to school work. A few examples of such responses were, "I feel very behind in my school work as though I will never catch up," "Without a doubt-the chemistry exam," and "Big test that I did poorly on."

The students pointed to relationships as another source of depressed feelings. Sometimes, the depressed feelings were caused by problems in a romantic relationship. For example, "He is interested in someone else more than me," or "A problem with a boyfriend." Sometimes there was friction in a relationship. Some examples are, "A fight with a friend," or "An unpleasant conversation with the girl upstairs." And sometimes there was the possibility of a breakup of relationships: "I thought too much about two good friends who are transferring next semester."

At times, the students identified the source of their depressed feelings not as events, but as their own thought processes. Sometimes the students spent time looking within themselves, questioning their own performance. "My lack of motivation to do things," or "I'm wasting too much time." Sometimes they thought about the future and felt uncertain about where they were going: "I was wondering where my life is leading." And occasionally, there was a vague feeling of concern, such as, "I was worrying about life in general."

Reading through our collection of student diaries leaves one with the impression that a great many college students experience periods of mild to moderate depression. Using the Beck Depression Inventory, we estimated that about 14 percent of the students in our research project were moderately depressed.

The data, then, suggests that the risk of becoming depressed increases sharply in the late adolescent and young adult years. A case example would be Allison who I briefly mentioned in the proceeding chapter. Allison has suffered from recurrent depression for many years. She experienced her first episode as a young adult and interestingly had no clear understanding of what was happening to her during this first episode. She related, "As far as the history of my depression, it began at age 20, when I was between my junior and senior years of college. I began feeling strange and did not know why. I did not know it was depression. Then I decided to try committing suicide. I told my brother and he drove me to the doctor who put me in the hospital overnight until they arranged for me to go to a clinic for treatment. While I was at the clinic I had no inkling of what was bothering me and I did not know what to talk about with the psychiatrist. I was cut off from my feelings...."

Even with the wide dissemination of information about depression in recent years, I can still see how the first episode of depression may not only be very unsettling, but confusing and in many cases bewildering both to the patient and the family.

The recent National Epidemiological Survey on Alcoholism and Related Conditions indicates that the highest lifetime risk of becoming depressed occurs in middle age.[49] Interestingly, the Oregon study suggests that period of high risk may occur somewhat earlier for males than for females. For males, the risk is significant by the early twenties and remains so until it begins to decline in the later years of life. The years of higher education, of starting a career, of developing relationships, of marriage, and starting and raising a family — these years of ever increasing responsibility are the years when depression is most likely to occur in men.

Kevin, a young musician whose career ambitions had been sidetracked by the pressures of an early marriage, is an example of this age related risk in men. From an early age, Kevin had hoped to become a pianist. In his second year of college, he met Julie, an art student, fell in love, married and within a year became a father. His musical studies slipped into the background as he took jobs that were unrelated to music in order to support his family. He waited on tables, tried selling real estate, then took a job as a bank teller. The birth of his second child made it still harder to seriously resume his studies. The press of responsibilities and the fading of his dreams posed an emotional strain to both Kevin and his wife. Kevin became irritable and difficult to talk to. He became morose and withdrawn. Eventually, he entered therapy for depression.

The Oregon researchers reported that the risk of becoming depressed for women did not reach its highest point until well into middle age. This difference in peak age of onset of depression indicated in the study may reflect traditional differences in sex roles. For example, society has placed a higher premium on physical attractiveness in women than in men and the fading of physical beauty may have more of an emotional impact on women. In addition, the responsibilities and satisfactions that come with childrearing traditionally provide a great deal of meaning in the lives of women, and when these diminish as children leave home, many women experience an emotional letdown and a sense of emptiness in their lives.

Women differ greatly in the way they adapt to these role transitions. Many women find that diminished family responsibilities and increased time for themselves provide an opportunity to fulfill longstanding ambitions. Janice, for example, always wanted to write children's books and now has the time to do so. Ellen always wanted to travel and decided to take a tour of Europe with her husband. In contrast, Rose, who was a housewife for many years, found herself with few meaningful things to do after the children were gone. She did not want to incur the risks involved with reentering the job market and was at loose ends. She was caught in what has been called the "empty nest syndrome" and would appear to be the most vulnerable of the three women.

As is true for men, there is a decline in the onset of depression in women during the later years of life. In reflecting on these trends, it appears that the most likely times for the onset of a depressive illness are the prime years of life. What may be some of one's best years in terms of drive, earning capability and fulfilled relationships may also be one's most vulnerable years for becoming depressed.

Depression Among the Elderly

Some years ago I was a member of an organization of volunteers, physicians, nurses, psychologists and social workers, which provided free health services to people who did not have easy access to medical services. My assignment along with another psychologist was to offer therapy to the residents of a large public housing project for the elderly. Many of the residents came to our weekly evening clinic, but only a few people ever asked for an appointment with a therapist.

At the time I was surprised by the apparently low prevalence of emotional problems among the residents. In reading articles on aging, I was struck by all of the things that can go wrong: chronic illness, slowdown in mental acuity, financial deprivation, widowhood, loss of friends, and so on. Given these conditions, I expected to encounter a lot of emotional problems, particularly depression. However, in the senior citizens' apartment complex, that did not seem to be the case.

The senior citizens' housing complex offered a wide range of social and recreational activities. The complex was not just a roof over one's head; it was a place to live and socialize. Perhaps it was these opportunities for an active lifestyle that helped keep psychological distress to a minimum.

Consider a contrasting situation. I once acted as a consultant to another senior citizens' facility, a very large metropolitan nursing home. The residents were not as well off physically as the residents in the housing complex, nor did they enjoy the same quality of life in terms of housing, social life and recreational activities. With the aid of the institution's nursing staff, we carried out a study of psychological problems among the residents of the nursing home and found evidence that about 15 percent of the residents experienced at least one depressive episode during a six-week observational period.

These two isolated observations point to a conclusion that is buttressed by considerable research. The physical health and social environment of senior citizens can make a difference in whether they are likely to experience depression. A study carried out in Canada indicated that the factors promoting depression in the elderly might vary somewhat depending on whether the people lived in rural or urban areas, but in general living alone or lacking companionship, inadequate financial resources, poor physical health, and declining mental functioning tended to relate to depression in the elderly.[50]

The impact of these factors in promoting depression in the elderly is illustrated by Kathy Biggs, an elderly, retired librarian. Kathy led a quiet, fairly solitary life in a suburban community. She read a great deal, worked in her garden and spent a lot of time with a lifelong friend, Joan. Joan died suddenly and unexpectedly. It was a terrible blow to Kathy. The loss, coupled with increasing physical disabilities of her own, left Kathy alone and isolated. Her quiet, comfortable world had been turned upside down and she had no one to turn to. She began to experience many of the symptoms of depression.

When we pose the question "What is the prevalence of depression in the elderly?" we encounter some difficulties. A significant number of elderly people suffer from brain disorders such as Alzheimer's disease and unless some care in diagnosis is made, it is possible to confuse some symptoms of depression with brain dysfunction. Another problem is that elderly people all too often learn of the death of family members and close friends and experience the grief that comes with such loss. Grief and depression are not the same, but may appear similar and can easily be confused. It is quite possible that when the researcher looks for the symptoms of depression, he or she may find them, even though the person is not clinically depressed. All of these considerations then lead to some caution in making hard and fast estimates of the prevalence of depression in the elderly. The Oregon study suggested that depression is relatively infrequent in older people. Findings from the National Comorbidity Survey Replication indicated that the percentage of cases of major depressive disorder that have their onset after the age of 56 or so is not that large, less than 10 percent.[51]

A long term study of elderly depressed people carried out in Amsterdam in the Netherlands indicated that the depression was more likely to persist than to clear up. In about 40 percent of the people studied, the depression had an unfavorable although fluctuating course while in another 32 percent the depression had a severe chronic course. Remission occurred in only 23 percent of the people studied.[52]

When an older person becomes depressed, it can foreshadow poorer health and overall functioning in the future. Researchers at the National Institutes of Health assessed older persons on a measure of depression and tested them on a variety of physical performance measures such as a timed walk and a timed test of five repetitions of rising from a chair. Four years later the older people were retested on the performance measures. The elderly subjects who were assessed as more depressed at the original assessment had a higher risk of experiencing physical decline.[53]

Because of the risks presaged by depression in the elderly for an overall decline in health, it is important to treat depression in the elderly when it occurs. Too often, however, depression in older people is ignored. Both the individual who is depressed and his or her family may not recognize depression for what it is, believing that what they see is only a normal part of aging. In the limited time that physicians have to spend with individual patients, the physician may not recognize the depression, either. The problem may remain untreated. A research study reported in the late 1980s suggested that there may be a need for more emphasis in medical education in identifying depression in the elderly. In the study of a sample of elderly patients at a Veterans Administration Hospital, only 2 of 23 depressed elderly patients were correctly identified by the house staff as depressed.[54]

Some studies, though not all, indicate that the risk of depression is higher among seniors in the less affluent stratas of society. Being caught in a daily economic squeeze and not being able to do much about it can create constant psychological pressures, which may lead to depressed reactions.

In this chapter I have presented some statistics about the prevalence of depression in the United States. The figures presented depend on the methods used to obtain the information, and these methods are far from perfect. Still, it is very clear that the problem of depression is widespread and probably increasing in scope. We are talking about many millions of adults who have experienced moderate to severe levels of depression and a problem that happens to all of the groups that make up our society. And we are talking about a problem that is likely to arise in the best years of our lives.

3. The Biological Bases
of Depression

I remember looking through a textbook on abnormal psychology written for undergraduate students in the 1950s and being struck by the effort to explain the causes of mental illness in purely psychological terms. Manic depressive disorder and schizophrenia were viewed as exaggerations of normal psychological tendencies. Little attention was given to biological bases for these emotional and mental disturbances. One of the reasons for this approach was that scientists looking for biological links to these disorders had not yet been able to find much. The paucity of biological findings reflected the lack of sophisticated technologies to adequately research the problem.

In recent years, the situation has changed drastically. There have been dramatic improvements in technology that allow researchers to both obtain images of the different regions in the brain and using positron emission tomography (PET) and functional magnetic resonance imaging (fMRI) to measure activity levels within these regions.[1] The discovery that many clinically depressed people have imbalances in the neurotransmitters in the brain has spurred intensive interest in the biological bases of depression. The pendulum has swung so far that people talk about depression as a biological illness.

With the perspective that increasingly sophisticated research provides, it now seems likely that both biological and psychological factors play major roles in depressive disorders. The task that lies ahead for scientists will be to integrate the findings from both disciplines to provide a comprehensive model that will best explain depression.

What I will attempt to do in this chapter is to present thumbnail sketches of some of the important findings showing biological bases for depression. We will look first at the influence of heredity on depression. Then we will consider structural differences in the brains of depressed patients, the role of the neurotransmitters in depression, the possibilities for a laboratory test for depression, the links between depression and physiological measures of sleep, and the impact of depression on the immune system. We shall conclude with a discussion of the search for genes that may underlie depression.

46

Many diseases "run in families." Some examples that come to mind are allergies, hypertension, Alzheimer's disease and schizophrenia. When we say that an illness "runs in families" we simply mean that someone in a family in which one person has been afflicted is more likely to develop the problem than someone in a family where there is no history of the disease. It does not mean that everyone in the family will develop the problem or that the onset of the disorder is inevitable. We are saying that the risk is higher.

When we observe such family patterns, we often suspect that there is some genetic basis for what we see. This may not always be the case, for environmental conditions can trigger both physical and emotional problems and members of a family are usually exposed to a similar environment. A high level of stress, a pattern of poverty, or destructive parenting practices can affect all exposed persons. Still, the possibility of a hereditary basis for an illness is an obvious place to start looking when we observe familial patterns of illness.

Depression has some tendency to run in families. If someone in a family is clinically depressed, a very close relative — such as a sister or brother has about twice the risk of developing the problem then someone in the general population. For children of parents with major depressive disorder — the risks of developing depression are even higher — perhaps over a threefold increase. For close relatives of depressed people the onset of such a depression is likely to be relatively early. Some research suggests that the problem might initially present itself as an anxiety disorder.[2]

When we move away from very close relatives to more distant relatives such as aunts, uncles, cousins and grandparents, the risk of depression decreases appreciably.[3]

The fact that depression does run in families suggests the possibility of a genetic basis for the disorder. Is this the case? One of the best ways to establish that heredity plays a role in a disorder is to carry out studies that use the twin study method. In such studies, one compares the concordance of depression in identical twins (monozygotic twins) and fraternal twins (dizygotic twins). The reasoning behind such studies goes something like this: Monozygotic twins have exactly the same heredity, coming from the same fertilized ovum. Dizygotic twins happen to be born at the same time and share a common environment, but come from different fertilized ovums. Such twins have the same hereditary makeup as any other pair of siblings. If heredity plays a role in depression, we would expect to find more cases among monozygotic twins than dizygotic twins in which when one of the twins becomes depressed, the other also becomes depressed. And this is just what we find in research.

An example of this type of study was carried out by a research team in Australia. The team, led by Kenneth Kendler, mailed questionnaires to people listed on the Australian Twin Register. They received about 4,000 replies from both members of twin sets. The questionnaire included items that asked about depressive symptoms. The researchers found much more similarity in the responses of the monozygotic twins to these items than in the responses of the dizygotic twins.[4]

Kendler as well as other researchers have carried out additional twin studies to estimate the extent to which depression is genetically based. Two large-scale twin studies reported in 1999 estimated that major depressive disorder is about 40 percent "heritable."[5] So, while the studies indicate that genes play a major role in the development of depression, one's environment and unique experiences also play a significant role, probably larger than heredity. While twin studies clearly support the important role of heredity in unipolar depression, it is equally clear that heredity is not totally determinative. If it were, both members of identical twins would invariably come down with depression if one were afflicted and this is simply not the case.

These two major twin studies yielded conflicting results as to whether heredity plays a more significant role for males or females in the development of depression. One study found that heredity played a less important role for males, the other did not. This question needs further study.

What we have in some people is a genetic vulnerability that increases the risk of becoming depressed should environmental conditions develop that promote depression. The interplay of genetic and environmental factors needs to be clarified by further research.

While heredity appears to play a significant, but probably not dominating role in the development of unipolar depression, the influence of heredity on bipolar depression appears to be very considerable. Two recent twin studies in which a twin had bipolar illness yielded very high heritability estimates, in the 80 to 90 percent range.[6] Bipolar illness would seem to be an attractive target to search for implicated genes.

Magnetic Resonance Imaging (MRI) provides a powerful tool for measuring the size of various regions in the brain. Using this technique researchers have been able to compare regions in the brains of people who are clinically depressed with those of people who are not. Much of the attention of researchers has been focused on two structures in the brain which are known to be involved in emotions. These structures are the hippocampus and the amygadala.

The hippocampus, named for its shape which resembles a sea-horse lies in the medial temporal lobe of the brain. Researchers believe that the hippocampus plays an essential role in the development of new memories. Damage to the hippocampus can produce amnesia.

A number of studies have been carried out which compare the size of the hippocampus in depressed subjects with that of control subjects. A meta-analysis examining the overall trend of these studies indicated that in patients with long standing depressive illness, the hippocampus appears reduced in size. This brain structure has appeared to atrophy.[7]

It is believed that the diminished size of the hippocampus in depressed patients may reflect a decline in the number of neurons (nerve cells). One of the reasons for this decline may be the high level of stress many depressed people have experienced. Studies using animals have demonstrated that stress has a negative effect on the production of new nerve cells. As the duration of the illness appears to be a factor in the reduced size of the hippocampus, it may be that the depressive process, itself, contributes to this decline in the genesis of new nerve cells. Interestingly, there is research on animals which suggests that the action of antidepressant treatments may reverse this tendency towards decline.[8]

The amygadala is an almond shape mass located in the anterior portion of the temporal lobe of the brain. Many studies have shown that it plays a significant role in emotion, particularly in the genesis of fear reactions. Some studies have found that the amygadala in depressed subjects are enlarged when compared with control subjects. However, other studies have not reported this finding. While the question of amygadala enlargement in depressed patients remains unsettled, there is some suggestion that patients with a short-term illness are more likely to show this enlargement than patients who have been depressed for a long time.[9]

In an interesting study carried out in Germany, patients with major depressive disorder who have an enlarged amygadala tended to have difficulties in processing emotional materials (photographs of fearful, surprised, and disgusted faces) into memory. Their ability for dealing with these materials appears to have been compromised.[10]

Some MRI studies of the brain have been carried out on patients with bipolar disorder. A review of the studies concluded that for adult bipolar disorder patients, the brain regions studied appeared heterogeneous in volume; there were no clear indications that the regions studied were either larger or smaller than those of controls. In contrast, in the fairly rare form of bipolar disorder called *early onset bipolar* disorder in which the disorder strikes children and adolescents, there appeared to be volumetric differences between patients and controls. Several studies have reported that the amygadala and probably the hippocampus as well were reduced in size and the total cerebral volume seemed also smaller in patients with early onset bipolar disorder. To fully understand the meaning of these findings, we need to follow early onset bipolar disorder over time to see whether these differences persist or tend to normalize as the child matures into an adult.[11]

The Neurotransmitters

The search for biological bases for depression has opened up another rich vein of ore in the study of the action of the neurotransmitters. To appreciate the important role neurotransmitters play in our functioning, keep in mind that there are billions of nerve cells (neurons) in the brain. These nerve cells are separated by small gaps called *synapses*. Electrical messages transmitting signals within the brain and relaying instructions to various parts of the body cross these gaps through the action of certain chemicals. When nerve cells release these chemicals, they seep across the gaps to a receptor in an adjacent nerve cell, transmitting the message to "fire" or "not fire." These chemicals are called *neurotransmitters*.

Now, an interesting thing happens to some of the neurotransmitters as they are discharged from the terminal of a neuron to stimulate the adjacent neuron. Some of these neurotransmitters do not complete their appointed rounds; instead, they are reabsorbed back into the transmitting neuron. In this reabsorption process called *reuptake*, there is less availability of the chemical to do what it is doing. Reuptake reduces the active levels of the neurotransmitter which as we shall see has important implications for the pharmacological treatment of depression.

Researchers have identified a sizable number of neurotransmitters. Two of these neurotransmitters, serotonin (5HT and norepinephrine (NE) have especially interested researchers for the role they play in depression. To date, serotonin has attracted the most attention. Serotonin, an organic compound synthesized from the amino acid tryptophan was discovered about 60 years ago and was initially recognized as a vasoconstrictor in blood serum. Subsequently, serotonin was found to be involved in emotions, sleep, and memory, all of which can be part of the depressive picture. The recognition that serotonin might be involved in depression led to considerable research that has substantiated the hypothesis. In addition, the development of drugs that acted to inhibit the reuptake of this neurotransmitter, thereby increasing the availability of active serotonin have proven effective in ameliorating symptoms in many depressed people.

If, as we believe, serotonin levels influence the development of depression, a classic approach to demonstrate this would be (1) to increase serotonin levels in depressed people to see if the depressive symptoms are ameliorated and (2) decrease serotonin levels in normal people to see if depressive symptoms develop. There are obvious ethical concerns that have to be addressed in carrying out the latter procedure.

Now serotonin cannot be used directly in such experiments because serotonin cannot cross the blood-brain barrier. However the precursor of serotonin, the amino acid tryptophon can be used in such research. Richard Wurtman and his collaborators found that tryptophan controls the amount of serotonin the brain produces. They found that injecting tryptophan solution into laboratory animals increased the level of brain serotonin.[12] Tryptophan is sold as a food supplement and its effects have been studied on depressed people. There is some evidence that increasing the amount of tryptophan in the diet can have an antidepressant effect. Indeed, in some countries, tryptophan has been marketed as an anti-depressant.

What happens when tryptophan is depleted in people who are not depressed? Does this bring on depressive symptoms? The answer appears to be *no*. The procedure that has been used is to give the subjects capsules containing all the essential amino acids the body requires with the exception of tryptophan. This procedure depletes the amino acid to a fraction of its usual concentration in plasma. Several studies including a recent investigation at the National Institute of Mental Health showed that tryptophan depletion did not induce depressive symptoms in normal people.[13] Nor did brain imaging (PET) show increased brain activity in suspected areas of the brain. However, if you try this experiment with people who have suffered major depression disorder and are now in remission, you are likely to find that some of these patients will experience transient returns of depressive symptoms. Moreover, they may show increased activity in a number of areas of the brain including the orbitofrontal cortex, the medial thalamus, and the anterior and posterior cingulate cortices.

The findings that tryptophan depletion has depressive effects on people who have been clinically depressed but not on controls points to the conclusion that while serotonin is clearly involved in depression, there is much more to the story. Clearly individual differences in vulnerability to depression are very important and that is likely to reflect both genetic and experiential factors.

One of the interesting findings concerning serotonin is a link to suicide. Autopsies of suicide victims have revealed low levels of serotonin activity, particularly when the victim's suicide was a violent act.[14]

Norepinephrine, also known as *noradrenaline,* may be more familiar in its role as a stress hormone that when released into the blood helps prepares the body to react to emergencies. You know the feeling, the "fight or flight" reaction. Your heart races, you feel alert, primed, and sometimes acutely anxious. Norepinephrine is also synthesized within the brain and is used in the transmission of signals within the brain. So, norepinephrine has a dual capacity, as a stress hormone and as a neurotransmitter.

As is the case for serotonin, norepinephrine, as a neurotransmitter is subject to the reuptake process. Researchers have developed norepinephrine reuptake inhibitors in a manner analogous to the serotonin reuptake inhibitors. These drugs have been used alone or combined with serotonin reuptake inhibitors. Both types of drugs have been shown to be effective in the treatment of depression. It seems possible that the unique profiles of the two types of neurotransmitters might lead to drugs with somewhat different types of effects on depression. J. M. Gorman and his colleagues at Columbia University suggested that influencing norepinephrine might be useful in relieving energy and interest deficits in depressed patients.[15]

It now seems clear that in many depressed people there are problems in the way these neurotransmitters are working. At this point, the dynamics of these abnormalities in the neurotransmitters in depressed people are not fully understood. Some researchers have questioned whether the abnormalities are simply a matter of too low an activity level. They have raised the question of whether these neurotransmitters are regulated correctly, suggesting that these systems may be out of kilter. It would be something like the thermostat in your house or automobile was malfunctioning.

Researchers have used the term *dysregulation* to describe some of the abnormalities observed in these biological systems. In elucidating the concept of dysregulation, Larry Siever and Kenneth Davis discussed such ideas as impaired mechanisms, erratic output, disruption in normal periodicities, less selective response to environmental stimuli, and slower return to basal levels. These ideas conjure up an image of an engine that is out of sync.[16]

A Possible Biological Test for Depression

When a person is confronted with stress-provoking situations (stressors), the body reacts in a number of ways. We have already mentioned the role of norepinephrine in activating the sympathetic nervous system. Another hormone that is released into the bloodstream as a response to stressors is cortisol. Cortisol has a multiplicity of effects. It helps regulate blood pressure and the way the body uses its sources of energy; the brain receives more glucose and fat cells are released into the muscles.

The release of cortisol in the body involves the action of the HPA axis which includes the hypothalamus, the pituitary gland, and the adrenal glands. Briefly, the hypothalamus, based deeply within the brain releases a hormone called CRH that stimulates the pituitary gland located in the base of the skull, which, in turn secretes a hormone, ACTH, which regulates the actions of the adrenal cortex, located in the chest cavity next to the kidneys. The adrenal cortex then secretes a hormone, cortisol into the bloodstream. Cortisol secretion as a response to stress seems to be greater when people are in situations in which they feel they are being evaluated and when the stress-provoking situation appears to be uncontrollable.[17]

Now what does this mean for depression? HPA system dysfunction is frequently found in depressed patients. In a large number of depressed patients, perhaps as many as 60 percent, one finds evidence of hypersecretion of cortisol. Researchers have attempted to capitalize on this observation to develop a test that would be a biological marker for depression. A procedure that has generated a lot of interest is called the *Dexamethasone Suppression Test (DST)*.[18]

For most people, the chemical dexamethasone suppresses the secretion of cortisol for a period of at least 24 hours. Under the influence of this agent, plasma levels of cortisol measured by standardized laboratory procedures are low. While this suppressive effect is found in most normal people, it is not found in many people who are depressed. In many depressed patients, cortisol levels continue to remain high even after taking dexamethasone. The failure to suppress cortisol, then, could be an indication for depression.

The procedure for the DST may go something like this: dexamethasone is administered at 11:00 P.M. During the following morning, afternoon and evening, blood samples are taken from the patient to check the level of plasma cortisol concentration. An elevation of cortisol in any of the blood samples indicates a failure of the expected suppression activity of the drug, and is considered a positive test result.

How accurately will positive results on the DST identify persons with diagnoses of major depression? After several thousand people had been tested, the provisional answer to this question is that the test picks out about half (45 percent) of individuals with major depression. About one out of ten normal subjects also test positively on the DST.[19]

You can see from these figures that the DST is not as accurate as one would like as a technique for identifying persons with major depression. It would be something like a lie detector test that could pick out people who actually lied about half of the time, although it was reasonably good at clearing people who were telling the truth.

With the evidence mounting that the DST was not a definitive biological marker for depression, researchers have looked for other possibilities. The abnormalities in the HPA axis observed in many depressed patients still seemed like a good bet for further study and there are alternative ways of looking at these abnormalities. In pursuing this objective, researchers devised a new test to assess HPA system functioning.

The test which combines the usual DST procedure with a second procedure, that of corticotropin releasing hormone stimulation, is called the DEX/CRH test. In this combined procedure, the usual procedure for the DST is followed and then on the following day corticotropin releasing hormone is administered to the subject. Blood samples to determine plasma cortisol are taken at intervals over the next few hours. This new test appears to be more sensitive in identifying people with depressive disorders than the DST procedure when used alone. Interestingly, research studies have found that the test is more likely to show abnormalities in patients with major depressive disorder when the patients are in the acute state of the disorder then when depression becomes chronic.[20]

A study carried out in Japan found that the DEX/CRH test results appear more normalized after treatment for depression.[21] In contrast, in bipolar disorder patients, research indicates that the test results are abnormal both when the patients are symptomatic and when the dis-order appears to be in remission.[22] The combined DEX/CRH test shows promise as a neuroendrocinological tool in the assessment of depression.

Depression and Sleep Patterns

We know that difficulty in sleeping is one of the more common symptoms of depression. Apart from the fact that people who are depressed have trouble falling asleep and may wake up frequently, there are physiological differences in the sleep patterns that distinguish depressed and nondepressed individuals. These differences have been identified in sleep laboratories.

Sleep laboratories were developed as controlled scientific settings to monitor sleep and dream activity. While subjects sleep, their breathing and heart rates are monitored, their brain waves are recorded by an electroencephalograph (EEG), and the movements of their eyes that take place during sleep are recorded with the aid of electrodes pasted on the scalp.

Using this equipment, researchers are able to monitor the various phases of sleep, including the periods of jerky rapid eye movements (REM) during which dreams are most likely to occur.

When persons diagnosed as having a major depression are compared with nondepressed controls in terms of these instrument recordings, a number of differences emerge. For example, there are periods in the sleep cycle in which the EEG pens mark out a pattern of slow, high amplitude waves. This slow wave sleep, called delta sleep, is usually characterized by deep sleep. When people are experiencing depression, they tend to get less delta sleep than nondepressed controls. There is also a tendency for delta sleep to be shifted back further into the night's sleep.

Differences have also been observed for REM sleep. One of the findings that has been reported is that depressed patients tend to have shorter REM sleep latencies (the interval of time between the beginning of sleep and the first period of REM activity). There is also increased eye movement density (number of eye movements per period of REM sleep).[23]

In a paper reviewing these and other findings on sleep research, Cindy Ehlers, Ellen Frank and David Kupfer pointed out that about 90 percent of patients with major depression have at least one indicator of sleep abnormality. Subsequent studies put this figure a bit lower, but still quite sizeable. Ehlers and her colleagues suggested that these disruptions in sleep rhythms could be an important clue in the understanding of depression.[24]

These researchers also looked at depression as a state in which there is a dysregulation or disruption of certain biological processes. These processes include both the neuroendocrine system, which we have already discussed, and the sleep-wake cycle. In the latter instance, it is as if one's biological clock is out of kilter, something like a case of perpetual jet lag. There is a possible tie-in of this view to one particular type of depression — seasonal affective disorder, the depressed state that typically sets in during winter and abates in spring. This tie-in is based on circadian rhythms.

All of us—for that matter — all animals— have circadian rhythms (approximately 24 hours cycles) wired into our biology. These rhythms inform us when to sleep and when to wake. The master biological clock in mammals is located in a specialized group of cells in the hypothalamus. Destruction of these cells results in destruction of the sleep-wake cycle.

Now the rhythms controlled by this pacemaker may fall out of sync with the sleep wake cycle. In winter, for example, daybreak occurs later in the morning; it is dark outside, and awakening may be delayed while the clock ticks on the bedside table well past the usual time of opening one's eyes and letting out that morning yawn. Research suggests that when the circadian rhythms are not synchronized with respect to the clock and the sleep-wake cycle — this may be a factor in promoting the symptoms characteristic of seasonal affective disorder. Bright light therapy immediately upon awakening is effective for many people with SAD in ameliorating symptoms. This therapy may be effective, in part, because it can correct the disconnect between the circadian rhythms and the sleep-wake cycle.[25]

Extending the theory of dysregulation into the realm of social interaction, Ehlers and her colleagues note that environmental events can affect biological rhythms. They point to the commonplace observation of how one's sleeping and eating habits are affected by living with others. Think of life before and after marriage.

The biological desynchronization that takes place in depression and the influence of social and environmental causes in producing this condition are important ideas to keep in mind as we pursue our inquiries in subsequent chapters, particularly when we consider the effects of stress in triggering depressive reactions.

The effects of antidepressant medicines upon sleep are interesting. Sleep disturbances such as insomnia, poor quality of sleep and over sleeping are common symptoms of depression. One would expect that anti-depressant medicines would be effective in diminishing these symptoms, but paradoxically they sometimes make the problem worse, at least in the initial phase of treatment. The drugs may cause daytime sleepiness and promote night time insomnia.[26]

Antidepressant drugs have noticeable effects on REM parameters, increasing REM latencies and reducing the amount of REM sleep. These drugs tend to reverse the abnormalities observed in untreated depressed patients and can even swing the pendulum in the other direction. One class of anti-depressant drugs, MAO inhibitors wipes out our REM sleep altogether for an extended period of time. An antidepressant drug which appears to be particularly promising in the treatment of depressive-related sleep problems is agomelatine. This drug demonstrates electroencephalograph changes which seem consistent with patterns of more normal sleep. Patients with depressive related sleep problems have responded favorably to this antidepressant drug.[27]

We know from much research that REM sleep is associated with dreaming, and we also know that the REM patterns of persons with major depression are atypical. These observations raise questions about the dreams of people who are depressed — what are they like?

My own research carried out on normal subjects indicated that when people are in a depressed mood, they tend to have better dream recall than when their mood is more positive. This better recall may simply reflect a tendency for people not to sleep as well when they are troubled; nocturnal awakenings help one remember one's dreams. In contrast to normal subjects, people who are very depressed tend to have rather poor dream recall. Their dreams are usually short and banal. During the height of depression, recall for dreams, many of which can arouse uncomfortable feelings, seems to be at a low point. There may be some kind of psychological or biological mechanism operating to reduce stress.[28]

Researchers working out of the University of Alberta have carried out some intriguing studies on the dreams of bipolar disorder patients. They found that the latency of REM tended to increase in bipolar patients as their moods improved. The researchers did not find this to be true for their unipolar patients. Generally, the dream reports of the patients collected in the morning tended to reflect their moods. The researchers noted that bipolar patients frequently reported dreams about death, and most interestingly, these death dreams presaged an upward shift in mood. In ancient times, dreams were widely thought to predict the future. A dream of death might have been viewed as an omen of catastrophe. For the moods of bipolar disorder patients, however, the opposite might sometimes be true.[29]

A final note about sleep. Depressed mood is sometimes associated with sleep-related respiratory disturbance, a condition characterized by loud and disruptive snoring. In the sleep laboratory, researchers have reported that in elderly males, this sleep respiratory problem was associated with depressed mood.[30]

Depression and the Immune System

We have noted that when people feel depressed, they are more likely to experience stress-related physical complaints such as headaches, dizziness, nausea and diarrhea. Moreover, there are reports that when people are clinically depressed, they have higher rates of infections,.[31] These observations have led researchers to ask the question: Does depression lower the body's resistance to fighting off disease? And more specifically, is there a relation between depression and the functioning of the body's immune system?

Because of inconsistencies in research findings, one must be cautious about drawing conclusions about these questions. These inconsistencies were highlighted in a 1992 review carried out by Carol Weisse of 23 studies looking at the relation of depression to immune system function.[32] Weisse cited over a half dozen studies which found that depressed patients had lowered immune responses using in vitro response to mitogins as a measure. Included in these depressed counts were lower numbers of T-cells and T-helper cells. A number of other studies reported that depressed patients had lower numbers and percentages of leucocytes. If we were to judge solely from these studies, we would have the proverbial slam dunk: depression is associated with lowered immune function. The problem, however, is that a fair number of other studies found nothing — no evidence of lowered immune function.

What do we make of it all? It seems to me that there is clear evidence of some relation between depression and immune function. Too many studies have found positive results. But the conditions under which this effect is likely to happen needs to be further specified. We know, for example, that stress is associated with lowered immune function so it seems likely that depressed patients with a high stress component in their clinical picture might be particularly vulnerable to immune system decrements. In her review, Weisse noted that hospitalized unipolar depressed patients may be particularly vulnerable to immune system alterations.

If we successfully treat depressed patients with lowered immune system function, we should expect to see an improvement in immune system functioning. Some studies have reported this to be the case, although there is a need for additional research to be more certain of this.[33]

The Search for Genes That Underlie Depressive Disorders

The family and twin studies on major depressive disorder and bipolar disorder pointed to a substantial basis in heredity for the former and an even more substantial basis for the latter. These findings raise the question: Can we identify the genes that underpin these disorders? To date, this has proven to be a challenging undertaking. For one thing as we currently understand it, depression is a complex entity, a constellation of a variety of disparate symptoms ranging from fatigue to suicide. One would not expect to find a single gene underlying such a disorder. In addition, there are a very large number of genes in the human genome. Given the complexity of the disorder and the number of genes to choose from, the task of linking specific genes to the development of depression is inherently difficult.

One of the approaches that researchers are currently using to better target their search for genes is to break down depression into its psychological and biological components and then try to link these components to genes. For example, a researcher might be interested in looking at the psychological aspects of depression which relate clearly to brain function such as memory and attention deficits or the biological aspects of brain function such as dysfunctions in the neurotransmitter systems. The researcher might use measures of these deficits as intervening variables and try to link these to genotypes. The hope is that these intervening measures which are termed *endophenotypes* may provide simpler clues to the underpinning genes. The best bets for fruitful endophenotypes are thought to be those which are associated with candidate genes or gene regions and have shown significant heritability in family and twin studies.[34]

Within this targeted approach, researchers have been examining the potential role of a number of genes. Here is an example. We know from a variety of studies that serotonin is involved in depression. We, also, know that the reuptake process that diminishes the concentration of serotonin in the synapse plays an important role in whether a person vulnerable to depression experiences depressive symptoms. Inhibiting reuptake of serotonin often ameliorates symptoms. Researchers are learning a great deal about the reuptake process. As a neurotransmitter, serotonin's action is regulated by a *transporter* (5HTT), a molecule located in the plasma membrane of the presynaptic (firing) neuron. This serotonin transporter returns serotonin to the presynaptic cell where it may be recycled or degraded. Now, here is where the genes come into the story. This serotonin transporter is under the regulation of a gene, and in the regulator promoter area of the gene (designated 5-HTTLPR) two distinct forms are encoded — a short variant (S) and a long variant (L).[35] Researchers have uncovered a number of differences in the action of these two variants which, though not fully understood lead to the conclusion that the short variant is associated with a relative loss of transporter function. Current thinking is that the short variant may not regulate serotonin activity in a way that is as optimal for the person as the longer variant and under certain circumstances such as exposure to stressors, this can lead to differences in the processing of emotion, particularly anxiety and depression.[36]

As part of the effort to link these genotypes to anxiety, researchers have been studying the possibility that people who carry the short variant of the transporter gene will score higher on personality measures of anxiety and related states. The findings, so far, appear unclear with both positive and negative results.[37] While the data seems equivocal as to whether people carrying the short variant have a trait-like propensity to experience anxiety in many life situations, there is accumulating evidence from brain imaging studies that they may have a tendency to react strongly to potentially threatening situations. Consider a study carried out by using reactivity of the amygdala as a bench mark. Recall that the amygdala plays a major role in fear reactions. The study carried out by Ahmad Hariri and his colleagues compared people carrying the short variant with those carrying the long variant on a perceptual task of matching anxious and angry faces while the subjects were being monitored by brain imaging for amygdala activity. The people carrying the short variant showed much greater reactivity. It was reported that the difference in amygdala activity between the two groups was nearly fivefold.[38] The suggestion from these and other findings is that people carrying the short variant might experience hyperactivity of the amygadala when confronted with unsettling situations. People who are prone to phobias or suffer from panic reactions might have particularly strong reactions.

Let's consider depression. A very intriguing study carried out in England found that people carrying the short variant showed more depressive symptoms in response to stressful life events than people carrying the long variant.[39] Studies have also linked the short variant along with another recently recognized variant called L(G) to severity of depression in a clinical sample.[40] However, the role these variants play in depression is still far from understood. Recall the study carried out at the National Institute of Mental Health in which remitted depressed patients were given the tryptophan depletion procedure. While tryptophan depletion increased depressive symptoms in all genotypes, the largest increase in depressive symptoms occurred in the patients carrying the long variant.[41] This surprising result tells us that much remains to be learned about the complex links between genes, neurotransmitter activity and depression.

One of the areas of research that could have important implications for patient care will be comparisons between patients carrying the long variant and the short variant in terms of response to various antidepressant drugs. One can envision the use of genetic typing as a factor in choosing drugs for patients.

The studies combining genetic assessment, neuroimaging and exposure to stress are exciting, groundbreaking research, often calling for a team of researchers coming from several disciplines. Because of the complexity of the procedures required, the sample sizes used are sometimes small. This underscores the importance of replication of findings.

It is clear from these thumbnail sketches that our biology plays a very important role in depression. One can envision a time in which people who are clinically depressed will be asked to take a variety of laboratory tests which may help in both diagnosis and the formulation of a treatment plan. However, it is also clear that biological factors are only a part of the picture. We can already see that stress plays a large role in depression and we shall see that the way people interpret the situations in life that cause stress and react to these situations can make an important difference in whether the person becomes depressed. This brings us to the consideration of psychological factors in depression and an array of ideas that underpin the psychotherapeutic treatment of depression.

4. A Psychological Perspective on Depression

People who feel depressed tend to have different views of themselves and the world about them than people who are not depressed. These differences have been identified by clinical observation of depressed patients and confirmed by subsequent research. Some theorists like Aaron Beck have proposed that these beliefs or thought patterns play a large role in bringing on depressed mood, assuming that these thought patterns give rise to the sadness experienced in depression.[1]

This theory is an interesting one because it leads to the idea that if you can change thinking patterns, you may be able to alter depressed states. This is the basis for *cognitive therapy* for depression (the word *cognitive* coming from cognitions or ideas). In cognitive therapy, the therapist tries to help the patient change his or her depressive beliefs. The good news is that many studies have found this approach is helpful.

How do the world and the self look to the person who has become depressed? Let's consider two people whose moods have recently become depressed. Debbie is a housewife. She stays at home and looks after two school-aged children. Her husband, Tom, works long hours at his job and is usually tired when he comes home. Tom is a good provider, nice with the children when he has the time, quiet spoken, never abusive — but he doesn't give Debbie the attention she feels she needs. She feels the spark has gone out of their marriage. The romance of courtship and the early days of marriage seem like a distant memory. Now her life seems like an endless series of chores — shopping, cooking, cleaning, and chauffeuring. She feels people expect things from her all the time and she feels little sense of accomplishment or fulfillment. Lately she feels trapped. She's taken to watching soap operas and fantasizing about having affairs. But the idea leaves her very uncomfortable and it remains only a fantasy. She has been drinking a lot and sleeping badly. Occasionally she "blows up," giving some hint of the resentment that has been building. Most of the time, however, she just goes through the motions. When her best friend asked her what was wrong, she only replied, "What's the use?"

Alan is a 20-year-old sophomore student at a suburban community college. His mood plummeted after his first day of class in economics. During the class, the professor had outlined what she was planning to cover in the course. When the class was over, Alan sat down on a bench on the campus and pictured in his mind what lay ahead. The course outline sounded difficult. He didn't understand some of the things the professor had said. The student in the class who asked questions seemed very sharp. Alan wondered whether he could compete. During the previous semester he had had a bad experience in a math class, and didn't economics involve math? Maybe the best thing was not to take the risk. Better to drop the course than fail again. Alan felt a sense of defeat, a sense of giving up that he had experienced before, both in school and out of school.

There is a pattern running through these cases. In both instances, the individual looks at her or his situation in life in a negative way and feels pessimistic about the possibility of change. The outlook boils down to this: "My situation is bad and I cannot do anything to make things better." A tendency to view one's situation in a negative way and a feeling of powerlessness to do anything about it are important cornerstones of a depression related mind-set.

The Negative Perspective

In a bit of whimsy, or perhaps in a flight of cynicism, someone once suggested that the only things that are certain in life are death and taxes. I would expand on this short list with the notion that there are a lot of other negative events, which while not as certain to occur as these two, are nonetheless very likely to happen. Such negative events may begin in early childhood with a spanking, sitting in the corner, or some other form of disciplinary measure, and continue right on through the school years with getting a bad grade on a test, or not being chosen for the team, through adolescence and young adulthood with rejection by a sought-for romantic interest, not getting accepted into the college of one's choice, not getting the job you interviewed for, and so forth and so on. Sporadic losses, disappointments, and failures are part of almost everybody's life experiences. The question is not so much will you experience such negative events; rather it is, when you do, what will you make of them. How do you evaluate them, how do you interpret them, where do you see the fault lies, and what kind of context do you place them in? People who become depressed tend to take a more profoundly negative view of such events when they occur. Moreover, this mind-set often generalizes to interpret events which are not particularly negative as more negative than they are, and to downplay or even dismiss positive events as not being all that meaningful and significant. Whether this negative perspective rises to the level of a cause of depression is not entirely clear, but it is certainly closely linked to depression and in any event is not helpful and can well exacerbate the problem. Researchers have shown that negative mind-sets are predictive of depression, the severity of its course and the probability of recurrent episodes.[2]

When we talk about having a negative perspective, we are talking about a tendency to view events in a negative rather than positive light. It is a mind-set in which you evaluate yourself and the world you live in unfavorably. Consider the proverbial glass that may be seen as half full or half empty; the negative perspective views it as half empty.

This negative perspective shows itself not only in the evaluation of events, but can even influence what would seem to be straightforward perceptions. Almost everyone can recognize a happy face. This is a near universal experience that transcends cultures. But as research suggests, if you show a picture of a happy face to a person who is depressed, they may not see it as such. The facial expression may have to look really happy before they recognize it as such. However, when researchers showed depressed people pictures of sad faces, they more readily identified them correctly as sad than they were able to do for other emotions such as anger.[3]

Aaron Beck, who has been one of the principal architects of the negative thinking pattern approach to depression, sees this negative perspective applying to one's view of oneself, the world about one and the future. It's a "triple whammy." In therapy, we often listen to patients describe their lives as unpleasant. They may relate grim details about their job and find little appealing in their home lives. Their worlds appear unpromising and unrewarding.

Now, there may be a good deal of truth in what the depressed person points out. In therapy, the patient may complain, "I'm not getting anywhere in life," and this may be true. The job situation and home life may present real problems. However, depressed people, like everyone else, have a tendency towards *selective perception*. To varying degrees, people see what they want to see and hear what they want to hear. It is something like what happens during a political campaign. You may listen to a candidate on a television program who says things you agree with, but turn off one who says things you disagree with. The depressed person may present a reasonably accurate picture as far as it goes, but it is likely to be selective. He or she may be ignoring things that could make the overall picture seem a good deal brighter than it appears.

While some persons with tendencies toward depression engage in bouts of self-analysis and reason themselves into negative conclusions, negative thinking processes often have an almost automatic character. Such thoughts seem to chase across the depressed person's stream of consciousness something like the spots or floaters that chase across people's eyes when a section of vitreous in the eye becomes detached. At times, these depressive thought patterns have an almost obsessive quality.

In his book *Cognitive Therapy and the Emotional Disorders,* Aaron Beck related how he first became sensitized to these automatic thoughts while he was doing psychoanalytic therapy. When he became convinced of the importance of these automatic thoughts, he began to ask his patients to pay particular attention to them and to report them to him. He told his patients that when they experienced unpleasant feelings, to try to recall the thoughts they had prior to the feelings.[4]

Beck observed that automatic thoughts were typically discrete and specific, resembling a kind of shorthand. The patients did not try to initiate the thoughts; they simply occurred. Once the thought appeared in the patient's consciousness, it was hard for the patient to get rid of it. These thoughts could not be easily turned off like water from a faucet.

Beck reported that while outside observers might consider the negative ideas of depressed patients to be farfetched, the patients felt they were reasonable and true. In talking with a patient, one might be able to persuade her or him that these thoughts didn't make a lot of sense, but in a short period of time, the patient might soon revert to believing the ideas as strongly as ever. The negative thoughts that may preoccupy the mind of a depression-prone person can be resilient.

The tendency for depressed people to view their own performance negatively has been demonstrated in experiments. Here is an example. Depressed and nondepressed subjects took part in an individualized learning experiment. The subjects had to learn to associate particular numbers with particular words. Each time the subject responded, the experimenter would say whether she or he was right or wrong. At a point in the learning experiment, the researchers asked the subjects to estimate what percentage of their prior responses were correct. The depressed subjects were more likely to *underestimate* how often they had been told they were correct than the nondepressed subjects.[5]

There is an increasing body of research that suggests that the negative evaluations of depressed people are only part of the equation. People who are not depressed may have a tendency to *inflate* how well they have performed in experimental studies.[6] People who are not depressed may have some degree of illusion about their performance. As we shall speculate later, this positive, optimistic perspective may act as a kind of protective shield against depressive reactions.

Powerlessness

Powerlessness is a belief that you are at the mercy of external events and there is little or nothing you can do to change things. Like negative thought patterns, feeling powerless is associated with depression.

Researchers have studied one aspect of the relation of powerlessness and depression at length, and that is the extent to which people view the sources of gratification in their life as being under the control of external forces or under their own control. The hypothesis is that the former (external) view would be associated with depression. In testing this idea, researchers have used psychological tests to measure a person's perception of internal vs. external control. How might such a test look? Suppose someone presented you with pairs of items like "getting somewhere in life is a matter of hard work," and "the most important thing about achieving success is being lucky," and asked you to check the item that is closer to your way of thinking. If you checked many items like the second, you would receive a high external score.[7]

After examining studies exploring the relation between perceived locus of control and measures of depression, Victor Benassi and his colleagues concluded, "We found strong support for the hypothesis that greater externality is associated with greater depression."[8]

One facet of powerlessness is a belief that the world you live in is composed of immovable obstacles that will prove resistant to anything you try to do. No matter what you try to do, the result will be something like running into a stone wall. The outcome of such a view is likely to be, "I won't be able to do anything, so what's the use of trying." Martin Seligman has referred to reactions like this as *learned helplessness.* The idea is that your experiences have led you to conclude that your own efforts have no clear effect on outcomes and events. Life appears something like a slot machine — a one-armed bandit that doesn't payoff.[9]

The belief that what you do is not going to make any difference is something that may be learned from repeated frustrations. Imagine an experiment in which the subject is exposed to an unpleasant condition like loud noise. The subject presses a button in an attempt to turn the noise off, but finds that pushing the button doesn't stop the noise. The subject gives up. When put into a similar situation where pushing a new device (a knob) would actually turn off the noise, the subject is less likely to even try it. He or she may sit passively and remain uncomfortable while the noise blasts away.[10]

Perhaps an even more debilitating form of powerlessness than believing that the environment is stacked against you is the feeling that you are incompetent and can't do anything. This was the feeling Alan had in response to his poor grades in school. Believing the environment is the problem at least offers some protection for your self-esteem. Believing that you are incompetent doesn't leave you many "outs" psychologically.

Feelings of inadequacy — the idea that "I can't do it" or "I won't measure up" — may be viewed as another form of learned helplessness. This belief typically has its roots in childhood, in frustrating, unsuccessful experiences, and in disparaging messages communicated from parents, peers and teachers. Repeated experiences of nonrewarded performance and derision erode self-confidence and lead to the conclusion, "I'm not capable."

Janet Altman and J. R. Wittenborn gave out questionnaires to a group of women who had once experienced a serious depression and to a group of non depressed controls. There were consistent differences between the groups in reported confidence, perceived competence and self-esteem. The women who had been depressed were more likely to respond that it was hard to credit themselves with good, doubted that they deserved praise, were uncomfortable with responsibility, often failed unnecessarily, and were not good enough to try for the top.[11]

The consequence of learned helplessness and feelings of powerlessness are likely to include a passive lifestyle. A person is less likely to take risks when the thought of failure looms large and is more willing to tolerate an unpleasant state of affairs— a cramped and limited lifestyle — if it seems secure. The chances are higher that he or she may fall into a dependency relationship with someone perceived as more competent.

The tendency to view oneself and one's environment in a negative way, in conjunction with a perception that one is powerless to change things, may ultimately lead to a feeling of hopelessness, that one is boxed into a miserable life. Things haven't worked out well to date, and there's no prospect that they ever will. When problems seem insolvable and when a feeling of hopelessness becomes lodged in one's consciousness, suicidal thoughts may develop. The playwright Jean Anouilh described the feeling aptly in his play *Restless Heart* when he spoke of "the farthest limits of his pain" and "the far end of despair."[12]

The feeling of hopelessness casts a bleak shadow over one's daily experience. The depressed person often feels that time lingers, that the day is interminable. If put to a test of estimating how much time has actually elapsed between two settings on the clock, people who are in a depressed mood are likely to do as well as anyone else — it is the subjective evaluation of experience that is different.[13] Life seems to have little movement and vitality. In some ways, it is as if the depressed person is cast in a mental prison.

A person looking from the outside with a more objective perspective can see that the depressed person's view of his or her own situation is often not a true assessment of the way things are or could be. Except for a terminal illness for which all remedies have been exhausted, there are very few things in life that are hopeless. Separation or divorce is an antidote to a very bad marriage. One can change jobs. Joining a club is a step toward ending loneliness. Few bad situations are unalterable. But the depressed person has to alter his view to see that this mental prison is more apparent than real and that some things can be done.

Some Depressive Thought Patterns

Let's turn our attention to some of the thought patterns often found in depressed people that contribute to the feeling of hopelessness. One of these patterns is a tendency to overgeneralize. It is the classic case of 2 + 2 = 5, or perhaps even 50. Take Liz, who works in a large office in an insurance company. Every week Liz has contacts with about 20 other employees. One of these employees, Barbara, had a nasty argument with Liz and now walks right past Liz without speaking to her. Another woman, Judy, is also unfriendly to Liz, but Judy is unfriendly to just about everyone in the office. What has Liz concluded? That no one likes her at the office, and worse, that she is unlikable. One could point out to Liz that if she listed all of the people in the office, and went through the names one by one, she would find there were many people in her office who are in fact friendly to her. But Liz, like many people who become depressed, has overgeneralized from a few incidents and drawn a sweeping conclusion.

Overgeneralization may take the form that if some things are wrong in life, then everything is wrong. And if things are bad in the foreseeable future, they will always be bad. The tendency for depressed people to overgeneralize has been demonstrated in psychological experiments. For example, in an experiment in which the subjects had been told they had done poorly in a "social perceptiveness test," the subjects who were more depressed tended to magnify and overgeneralize their failure. As the authors Richard Wenzlaff and Sherilyn Grozier described their results, "the failure feedback had more far-reaching effects on depressed subjects' self-perceptions than on those of nondepressed subjects. After learning they had done poorly on a test of social perceptiveness, depressed subjects not only lowered their estimates of their social perceptiveness, but also believed they were generally less proficient."[14] The subjects also tended to magnify the importance of what they had been tested on.

Charles Carver and Ronald Ganellen developed a questionnaire measure of the tendency to overgeneralize, using such items as, "When even one thing goes wrong I begin to feel bad and wonder if I can do well at anything at all," and "How I feel about myself overall is easily influenced by a single mistake."[15] The researchers found that people who scored high on this measure were more likely to score high on a measure of depression.

Perfectionism and black and white categorization are other forms of thinking that may contribute to depression. When one hears the phrase, "he's a perfectionist," one thinks of a person who has a very high level of aspiration. His goals are not only high, they may be out of sight. He may pay inordinate attention to details, imposing exacting standards that everything must be "just so." If it isn't right, you do it again. There is an obsessive striving to attain a standard that may not be reachable. What might be seen as reasonable progress by another person may be seen only as failure.

An example of problems that come with perfectionist thinking is the student who is hung up on grades. If only an A grade will do and she doesn't get an A, where is she? Disappointed, maybe depressed.

In therapy, I have often heard statements like "My father said, if you can't do it right, don't do it at all." This overly demanding standard didn't help the people who consulted me and I wonder how much good it did for their fathers and mothers. If the only standard one can accept is perfection, then who can possibly meet it? The consequence of perfectionist thinking is often not being happy with what you do or not being willing to try anything because of the belief it may not turn out good enough. Both of these tendencies can contribute to a depressed mood.

Psychologists interested in the measurement of perfectionism have identified a number of aspects of this tendency. Of these, socially prescribed perfectionism, concern over mistakes, and self criticism seem to be particularly correlated with depressive symptoms.[16] Very high standards foisted on others accompanied by criticism for not meeting them can make the recipients feel miserable. Excessively high standards accompanied by self-criticism can do a number on oneself. Interestingly, in a study of people who suffer from chronic insomnia, it was found that these people were very concerned about mistakes. In addition, they were the recipients of frequent parental criticism.[17]

Longitudinal studies on patients being treated for depression have found that perfectionism is a predictor of how well these people respond to therapy. Depressed patients with perfectionist dependencies don't seem to do as well. Part of the problem may be difficulties in establishing a working relationship with the therapist.[18]

Trying to do as well as one can is an admirable characteristic. But self-acceptance is also important. Being a perfectionist in life almost inevitably generates frustration and discontent and can set one up for a depressive reaction.

Black and white categorization is a tendency to evaluate things in an extreme way — as being either "super" or "lousy" — and to not see what is in between. One often finds some intolerance with this perspective, a predilection to classify people as wonderful or terrible and not as the mix of strengths and frailties that they really are. With this outlook, one can come down very hard on people — and pretty soon one may find oneself with few friends. Being without friends often translates into feeling lonely, which in turn may translate into depressed mood.

Albert Ellis, writing from the perspective of rational-emotive therapy, developed a list of "irrational beliefs" that are related to depression. Ellis included such beliefs as a need to excel in everything one does to feel worthwhile as a person, the idea that it is *terrible* when things are not going the way one would like them to go, and that one cannot overcome the effects of past history. [19] Aaron Beck developed a similar sounding list of attitudes that he believed predisposes people to sadness or depression. These attitudes contain elements of perfectionist and absolutist thinking, as well as a tendency to view events in one's life as being under external control.[20]

As these researchers suggest, many depression-prone people apply excessively demanding standards to themselves. Freud would have talked about a demanding superego. Imagine that your life is being run by a permanent drill sergeant who tolerates no excuses, sees no extenuating circumstances and sees no shades of gray in life. With this mental makeup, it's not a big step to arrive at a conclusion that one has fallen short of almost everything and to find one's self-esteem deflated.

People can further tear down their self-esteem and drive themselves deeper into the mental prison of depression by frequently comparing themselves with others who seem to be doing better. Comparing oneself with others on occasion is not unusual, but many depressed people have a habit of doing this, and they do so in a way that deepens their feelings of inadequacy. The comparisons emphasize their shortcomings, not their strong points. If you think about it, you can always find someone who seems smarter or better looking, or makes more money or has nicer furniture, or is a better athlete, or whatever else is important to you. Measuring oneself by the accomplishments (or perceived accomplishments) of others can leave one chronically frustrated and discontented.

Many people who become depressed spend a lot of time thinking about themselves. Attention is focused inwardly rather than on things to do in the external world. While occasional self-monitoring can be a good thing, it is not usually helpful to make a career out of it. Moreover, the problem is compounded by the tendency of depressed people to have a negative bias in their thinking. Excessive inward attention may simply be *multiplying negatives*. Constantly turning over the question of, "What's wrong with me?" is unlikely to make a person feel positive about anything.[21]

Resentment and Anger

When we accumulate these psychological patterns—a focus on the negative, a feeling of powerlessness, overgeneralization, perfectionist thinking, and the tendency to come down hard on oneself—one can see why self-esteem takes a beating and mood is likely to plummet. The person may become paralyzed in this mental prison and rendered inactive and ineffectual. He or she may also become angry.

Anger sometimes takes the form of a deep sense of resentment. We are talking about people who may become frustrated by what is happening in their lives. They may be frustrated by not being able to do what they want, or their view of reality may be so negatively skewed that they are not able to enjoy what they are accomplishing. When this happens, the person may feel like a "victim," looking at the world about her or him as unfair. Developing resentment may be directed against one's family and friends, or turned inwardly against oneself.

In psychoanalytic theory, the concept of anger turned inward occupies a central place in the causation of depression. The idea has its roots in a seminal essay of Sigmund Freud's entitled *Mourning and Melancholia.*[22] Freud was struck by some of the similarities between mourning following the death of a loved one and depression. He believed that depression, too, was based upon the experience of loss, but that the dynamics of what happened were more complex. Freud wrote that in depression the relationship between the person who becomes depressed and the lost loved one is not a straightforward positive one; rather, the depressed persons' feelings are characterized by marked ambivalence, that is, the presence of both positive and negative feelings. The negative feelings often arise from incidents in the relationship in which the person was disappointed, hurt and neglected. Freud wrote of an ensuing struggle in the person's unconscious in which feelings of love and hostility wrestle with each other. The struggle resolves itself not by the anger being overtly expressed towards the person who "provoked" it, or by the person giving up his or her love; rather, the anger is displaced, turned inwardly against the self. The person describes himself or herself as worthless, rather than describing the lost loved one, the one who rejected him or her, as such. In this process, a degree of revenge is often exacted as the depressive illness provides a means of tormenting the person who injured the depressed person's feelings.

It is an intriguing scenario, a testament to Freud's ingenuity and remarkable powers of clinical observation. And, indeed, one often sees elements of the scenario in depressed patients, the experience of loss, anger and remorse. The patient's resentment toward others, however, may be anything but buried in the unconscious. Resentment may be simmering on the surface, if not boiling. My distinct impression is that anger toward others may coexist with anger toward the self.

Roland Tanck and I were interested in the formulation that anger directed against oneself is associated with increased feelings of depression. In one of our studies, we asked university students to fill out diaries for a period of 10 nights. During each night they responded to the questions, "Did you feel angry or annoyed today?" "And, if yes, what was it that made you feel angry?" The students who reported instances in which their angry feelings resulted from their own missteps, failures and shortcomings scored higher on several measures of depression than the students who attributed their angry feelings to other sources.[23]

When we work with depressed patients, we often see self-reproach as part of the clinical picture. In interpreting this, one must keep in mind the psychoanalytic view that some of these negative feelings toward the self have as their true target someone else. A man might feel very angry toward his wife or boss, but may be unable to express these feelings, and eventually this resentment comes home to roost. It is not clear, however, that self-reproach is always an unconscious process of displaced anger. An individual may begin to recognize his own shortcomings and failures in dealing with his problems and react in self-disgust. One can picture a sequence of thoughts, "I can't do it ... I'm no good ... Damn it!" Perhaps both conscious and unconscious processes are at work in directing anger inwardly.

If self-directed anger plays a role in the depressive process, we should expect to see less of this as the patient improves in therapy. There is some research that indicates that this is the case.

The Measurement of Mind-Sets

We have discussed a number of mind-sets, attitudes and personality tendencies that seem to promote depressive reactions. Psychologists have been developing instruments to measure the various mind-sets. We have already mentioned questionnaires that assess perceived external vs. internal control of reinforcement and a tendency to overgeneralize. Other self-report measures that have been developed are questionnaires that assess the frequency of automatic thoughts, typical styles for interpreting negative experiences and the tendency to hold irrational beliefs. All of these techniques have been used by researchers in trying to more clearly understand the role of psychological factors in depression.

Let's look at a few of these techniques, beginning with a measure to assess automatic thoughts, appropriately called the Automatic Thoughts Questionnaire. Imagine a list of very short statements in front of you, such as "My future is bleak," "Something has to change," "I'm a failure," "I wish I were somewhere else," "No one understands me," "I'm so disappointed in myself," and "I feel so helpless." Your instructions are to indicate, on a five-point scale ranging from "not at all" to "all the time," how frequently these thoughts occurred to you over the last week.[24] You can readily see that if you often had such thoughts, you would qualify for a depressive mind-set.

A second measure called the Dysfunctional Attitudes Scale developed by Myrna Weisman and Aaron Beck is based on Beck's thinking about mindsets associated with depression.[25] The scale, which includes items sampling such concepts as perfectionistic standards, concern about the judgments of others, and imperatives that one must follow, is presented on a seven point scale, ranging from totally agree to totally disagree. The Dysfunctional Attitude Scale yields a total score which has been used by researchers as a measure of belief patterns that are linked to depression. In a recent study, for example, researchers use the measure to explore how such belief patterns might play a role in postpartum depression.[26]

A third approach to measuring cognitions that relate to depression is the Attribution Style Questionnaire that followed from the thinking of Martin Seligman, Lyn Abramson and their colleagues who were interested in the attributions people made about the events that occurred in their lives.[27] People are asked to look for causes of these events: Were they something attributable to one's own actions (internal) or caused by external forces. Would they view them as stable or transitory? Global in scope or narrowly confined? Researchers drew up a list of commonly experienced events, some negative, some positive, and asked the subject to imagine them and to make ratings about them on the dimensions of internal-external, global-specific, and stable-unstable. While, the resulting measure, the Attribution Style Questionnaire has been modified over the years in various ways, such as substituting real events for hypothetical events, the basic format has remained the same with the overall score representing an attributional style of viewing events as internally caused, stable, and global. When such an attributional style is applied to negative events, the assumption that is usually made, either explicitly or implicitly, is that this is a factor in increasing vulnerability to depression. And, indeed, meta-analyses looking at the relation of attribution style and measures of depression have found positive associations for both children and adults.[28]

Here is an informal exercise you might want to try. Think back to some of the more stressful or disappointing experiences of recent months and consider the way you interpreted them. For example, think about a disappointment in a romantic relationship or a stressful problem that happened on your job or at school. Take a moment and go over the situation in your mind.

What was your reaction like?

How did you evaluate the situation?

Did you tend to put the worst light on the situation by thinking, "My whole life is in shambles" or "Things will never get any better"?

Did you go through a period of time in which you blamed yourself for what happened?

Did you conclude you were not a worthwhile person?

Now go back a little further in time to another incident in which you experienced stress or disappointment. Once again take some time and think about how you felt and what was going through your mind. Ask yourself the same set of questions.

If you answered yes to most of the questions for both incidents, think back to other episodes and again ask yourself the questions. Is this typical for you? Is this your characteristic way of reacting to stressful and disappointing situations? If it is, then you could well have the type of mind-set that makes you vulnerable to depression, a concern you may want to address.

The psychological factors we have profiled for depression probably don't work in isolation from one another; most likely they augment one another producing a cumulative effect. Perfectionist tendencies, for example, are likely to increase the chances of self-reproach. A description of this interaction, offered in a theoretical paper by H. A. Meyersburg and his colleagues noted that guilt is often tied to failures in perfectionistic expectations. When perfectionism becomes an absolute, all-or-nothing issue, even, falling slightly short of the mark may be interpreted as total failure. The tighter the perfectionistic system, the more one feels a sense of inadequacy when things don't go well and the greater the chance of triggering a depressogenic process."[29]

Meyersburg and his colleagues believed that in the face of severe stress coming with loss and disappointment, a constellation of psychological factors — impulsivity, perfectionism, guilt and self-punitiveness interact with one another as a kind of reverberating mechanism, escalating anxiety to the point where it becomes overwhelming. The reverberating mechanism can turn a difficult situation into a psychological debacle.

Mind-sets, attitudes and personality tendencies act as a kind of filtering system between the stressors of the world — the things that can go wrong and often do — and our reactions as human beings. These psychological factors play an important role in determining whether a person becomes seriously depressed. While persons with depressive mind-sets have heightened vulnerability, it is important to recognize that attitudes and mind-sets can be *changed* and, as we shall see, this often takes place in therapy.

The Protective Shield

Frustration and disappointments are near universals in life. Even the best job and the most wonderful family will have their share of unpleasant times. And the less than super job that many of us have and the more typical family will engender problems aplenty. The person who is relatively free from depression seems to have a kind of protective shield against these daily stresses. He or she is able to tolerate frustrations and disappointments without experiencing sustained periods of depressed mood.

While part of what we call a protective shield is clearly biological and genetically based, there are important psychological components as well.

The idea of a protective shield was suggested in part from unexpected findings in psychological experiments carried out with depressed and nondepressed subjects. The following is an example of one of these experiments: Imagine you have been recruited to take part in the study. You were told that, "The investigators were interested in learning more about how people who are strangers relate to one another.[30] You find yourself in a room with four or five other people. You don't know that some of the people are being treated for depression at the university psychology clinic.

All of the people in the group are asked to give three-minute introductory statements about themselves. Then everybody makes conversation for another twenty minutes. At the end of the session, you fill out a rating form asking about your perceptions of the behavior of the other people and yourself during the session. The rating form includes a number of positive descriptions, such as friendly, warm, communicates clearly, interested in other people, socially skillful, and so on. While you take part in this conversational exercise, observers watch you and the other participants through one-way vision screens. They can see you; you can't see them. These observers make the same ratings that you do. Three additional sessions are held at later times.

As the researchers expected, the participants who were clinically depressed evaluated their own performance more negatively than the other subjects. What was not expected, however, was that the nondepressed subjects had a *more favorable view* of their own performance than was given them by the outside observers.

When the depressed patients improved during treatment, they began to rate themselves more favorably than the outside observers did, just like the nondepressed subjects were doing. In speculating about their findings, the researchers, Peter Lewinsohn and his colleagues, stated, "It is tempting to conjecture that a key to avoiding depression is to see oneself less stringently and more favorably than others see one."[31] The authors use such terms as an "illusory glow in their self-perceptions" to describe the nondepressed subjects.[32]

This study, as well as a number of other studies with similar results, suggests that one of the ways of resisting the stressors that promote depression is to have an optimistic, positive attitude, a tendency to put the best face on circumstances and to believe that one can bring events under control.

As an example, consider possible reactions to an unsuccessful undertaking, such as doing badly on a test at school. One could look at one's performance in a very negative way or one could frame the event in such a way as to protect one's self-esteem. These "reframing maneuvers," as C. R. Snyder called them, make things seem not as bad. As Snyder put it, they soften, bleach and repackage the act that may generate self-blame and diminish self-esteem.[33]

One may soften the poor mark on the test with explanations such as, "Most people would not have done any better," "The test was extremely difficult," "I was preoccupied with others things that were bothering me and couldn't concentrate," "The test really wasn't that important, anyway," or "I wasn't at my best — I'm not a machine." While one can't make a living by perpetually rationalizing away disappointments, protecting one's ego from a debacle when one experiences failure has the decided advantage of allowing one to pick oneself up and regroup, and to try again without going through a protracted malaise.

The concept of a psychological shield protecting a person against the storms of reality is reminiscent of Charles Dickens' character Mr. McCawber, who was able to cope with the most miserable circumstances with an outlook that, "something is bound to turn up!" The outlook is something like seeing that half full glass, three-quarters full. Or to use the cliché — to look at life through rose-colored glasses.

Such an attitude may be clearly unrealistic at times, but a strong dose of optimism may act as a deflector, bouncing off stressors like force fields repelling attackers in a science fiction story.

This notion of a psychological protective shield bears a resemblance to the concept of the defense mechanisms postulated by psychoanalytic theories. Defense mechanisms act to protect the ego from being overwhelmed.

We are not suggesting that we should all become Pollyannas or dismiss reality. Perhaps you remember the character Ilya in the classic movie *Never on Sunday*? When she related the grim story of Medea, she concluded not with the story's horrible blood bath, but with everyone going for an outing to the beach. We are not suggesting that people follow her example. We are, however, suggesting that optimistic thinking has value in warding off depression.

5. The Roots of Depression: A Look at Childhood Experiences

It is axiomatic that one's past experiences influence what one is today. The influence of childhood experiences seems particularly important, for that is where formative personality patterns are laid down. It seems reasonable to search for long-range causes of adult depression in child development and especially in the pattern of parent-child relationships.

Some patients enter therapy with this idea in mind; they assume that there are deep underlying causes for their depressed feelings and anticipate that the therapist will spend considerable time delving into their childhood recollections trying to unearth these causes. The thinking may be that when these causes are uncovered, the depressive symptoms will disappear. This can be a somewhat romanticized view of therapy, for there are usually pressing problems that confront patients in their daily lives that demand attention in therapy, problems that are currently having an impact on the patient's well being. Nonetheless, these patients do have a point. Understanding one's past often puts the depressive problem into a much clearer perspective.

As an illustration of this, a young woman, Alexandra, entered therapy. She was experiencing considerable anxiety and depression, and had serious problems relating to self-confidence. A failure in her most recent job had plunged her self-esteem to a low level. Alexandra's therapist explored her past history. She learned that Alexandra had previous experiences of failure and when new opportunities presented themselves, she had an expectation of failure. Alexandra and her therapist traced the idea that she couldn't succeed back through her school years to her early relationships with her parents and to her Aunt Josie, with whom she used to spend her summers in the country. Her mother — who had been widowed when her husband died in an automobile crash — was overprotective, not letting Alexandra play in the street with other children. She was careful to see that Alexandra "wouldn't get hurt." Her mother was always saying "Don't do this" and "Don't do that." For her part, Josie was usually critical of the things Alexandra did and left her with the feeling that she couldn't do anything right. When Alexandra tried to help Josie in the kitchen or with her garden, she was left with the feeling that she was a klutz. During the course of therapy, Alexandra began to understand that these early experiences had thwarted the building of self-confidence. She realized that her current depression had a long history underlying it and was better able to understand her problem.

Theories of child development often make the assumption, implicitly if not explicitly, that successful experiences in an earlier phase of human development will increase the chances of successful experiences in later phases of development. Think of making a structure out of building blocks; if the lower blocks are placed correctly, the growing structure will be well supported. If the supporting blocks are badly placed, the structure may crumble. If the child fails to adapt well in early phases of development, there is an increased likelihood of trouble down the line. Obviously, there are many things that can happen in later experiences to mitigate the effects of early problems; there is no inevitability that developmental difficulties will lead to depression or other psychological problems. Nonetheless, a bad start is just that and could leave the child with handicaps in the race of life that lies ahead.

When we observe emotional difficulties in children, we consider a variety of possible causes. Among the chief suspects are parent-child relationships, for these relationships are of prime importance in providing the skills and understanding the child needs to negotiate the world about her or him. When there are failures in these all-important relationships, one may anticipate a greater chance for future problems.

The Concept of Attachment

In discussing parent-child relationships, let's begin with the very early days, the first year of life. One of the fundamental processes that occurs at this time is *attachment.* Attachment has been defined by such theorists as John Bowlby as any type of behavior in which an individual maintains closeness (usually physical nearness) with another individual who is perceived as more capable of dealing with the world.[1] One can see immediately that for the infant, attachment is all important as the infant is helpless, totally dependent on others for survival. Attachment in the infant is more than being fed, cleaned or clothed; it includes the physical comfort of being held and cuddled and the sense of security that comes with this contact.

The importance of cuddly contact was underscored by Harry Harlow's ingenious experiments with infant chimps. In these experiments, Harlow used different types of mechanical "surrogate mothers." One of the mothers was soft and cloth covered, but provided no nursing; the other was simple wire mesh with a bottle. Given a choice, the infant chimps preferred the cloth mother without feeding to the wire mesh mother with feeding.[2]

Observations by Rene Spitz, John Bowlby and others in England during and following the Second World War also pointed to the importance of attachment and the hazards of prolonged separation from the mother for the normal emotional development of the child. Children who experienced prolonged separation from their mothers went through a sequence of distress reactions. The infants began by protesting; they were angry. Later, they began to show despair. Finally, they became detached and did not seek the comfort of adults. The normal attachment bonds, which offer a secure base for dealing with the world, had been severely damaged.

The writings of Bowlby were very influential in stimulating interest in attachment. Researchers have confirmed Bowlby's observations that separation from parents has a negative effect on attachment bonds. For example, a recent study compared children from divorced families with those from intact families and found that the children from divorced families had less secure attachments.[3]

Following in Bowlby's footsteps, researchers have delineated several phases in the process of attachment. In the beginning there is a *preattachment phase,* which lasts for the first eight to twelve weeks of life. By the age of two or three months, the infant begins groping for attachments, usually developing a preference for being close to the mother. Around the age of six months, a primary pattern of attachment is well established; the young child uses this relationship as a base from which to explore and test his or her environs. It is something like a safe port in uncharted seas. Eventually, as the child develops more understanding and capabilities, the child becomes less dependent.[4]

Mary Ainsworth, who has made singular contributions to the study of attachment, provided us with a descriptive analysis of this early attachment process.

"At birth, the infant is equipped with a repertoire of species-characteristic behaviors that promote proximity to a caregiver. Most conspicuous among these are signaling behaviors, such as crying, that operate to activate caregiving behavior, attracting the caregiver to come near. At first, these attachment behaviors are simply emitted, rather than being directed toward any specific person, but gradually the baby begins to discriminate one person from another and to direct attachment behavior differentially.

At about the middle of the infant's first year, a new phase of development may be identified. A number of important changes occur more or less simultaneously. These include the emergence of locomotion and directed reaching and grasping, which enable proximity-keeping behavior to become more active, effective, and "goal-oriented." Furthermore, the baby forms his or her first inner representation of the principal caregiver, having attained some capacity for believing that the caregiver exists even when not present to perception, and with this achievement comes the onset of separation distress when the caregiver leaves the infant. At this point, the baby is capable of attachment and is very likely to have become attached not only to his or her mother figure, but to one or a few other familiar persons as well."[5]

The implications of attachment and separation for the child's emotional health have been systematically studied in the psychological laboratory using a procedure developed by Ainsworth and her colleagues, called the *strange situation*. The procedure consists of a number of episodes that last about three minutes each. In the beginning segments, the mother and her infant child go into an unfamiliar room. There, they are joined by a woman who is a stranger to them. The mother leaves the infant with the woman. After a few minutes the mother returns and the stranger leaves. Then the mother departs also, leaving the infant alone. While these sequences take place, the infant's reactions are monitored. Researchers note how the infant reacts both to the separation from the mother and to the reunion with her. The researchers note whether the infant seeks contact with the mother and the stranger, whether there is avoidance and whether the infant engages in searching behavior while separated. The observers evaluate the attachment relationship as to whether it is "secure" or "insecure" in various ways. For the great majority of children, the relationship is evaluated as secure.

Attachment theorists believe that the way a mother behaves toward her child affects the security of the child's attachment. In observing the mother's behavior, they ask such questions as, How responsive is she to the child's crying? Does she spend time being close to the child? Does she hold the child when the child expresses this desire? Is she affectionate? Does she appear positive when she talks to the child? Using the child's behavior in the strange situation as a basis for measurement, researchers have found that as the theorists anticipated, the attachment relationships of infants of responsive, sensitive mothers tend to be more secure. While the mother's caretaking behavior is not the only factor that makes a difference in the security of the child, it is significant. The early research carried out on childhood attachment was very intriguing and raised a number of questions. Do children with insecure attachments as infants have more difficulties in interpersonal relationships as they grow up? Do they tend to show less self-confidence and self-reliance? Do attachments styles persist over the years? And, do insecure attachment styles make individuals more vulnerable to experience emotional difficulties and particularly depression?

Researchers have carried out studies which shed some light on these questions. To offer a broad generalization about the results of these studies, insecure attachments in early childhood are simply not helpful. It is something like beginning the adventure of life with a called "strike one." Some of the effects of insecure attachment can be seen rather early. Eighteen to 24 month old toddlers were observed in playgrounds. Children judged in the strange situation to form insecure attachments received more negative reactions to even their positive behaviors from other children. At this tender age, there was already the suggestion of interpersonal difficulties, if not rejection.[6]

One may wonder what the long-range significance of mother-infant behavior monitored in the strange situation is. Can one make predictions about what the child will be like a number of years later when she or he is well along in school? A longitudinal study carried out over many years on children born into economically, disadvantaged families suggests that early attachment ratings can be harbingers of future behavior.[7] In this study, researchers observed over 200 mothers and their infant children in the strange situation developed by Ainsworth, making assessments at both 12 and 18 months. Then, they followed these children through childhood, adolescence, and into adulthood. During childhood, they observed the behavior of the children in the nursery school and later in summer camps. Children evaluated as secure in their early attachments in the strange situation were judged to be far more self-reliant; they seemed much less dependent on their teachers. The children with secure attachment histories were consistently judged to show more self-confidence and more self-esteem and were thought to be better able to bounce back after dealing with stressors. They were more curious and exploring in their behavior. Both in the preschool classroom and on the playground, they were judged to be more successful in their interpersonal relationships; they were likely to be actively involved in the peer group and less frequently isolated. When followed into adolescence and beyond, those who had been evaluated in infancy as having secure attachment experienced fewer emotional problems. The researchers made the important point that while attachment was critically important in that it was the process that initiated many of the events that followed, childhood development is a very complex process and that attachment was only one of the factors involved. While parent-child attachments do not relate inexorably to any particular outcome, the suggestion from this study is that a secure early attachment between mother and child promotes positive emotional development in the child.

The mother-child attachment remains important with both continuities and changes as the child grows and develops. This ongoing, powerful dynamic continues to influence the child in many ways. For example, a recent study of 9 to 11 year old children which utilized children's current views of their attachments with their mothers found that children who felt insecurely attached reported less positive moods and were judged by their teachers to have less ability to tolerate frustration; they seemed to have less emotional control.[8]

Attachment continues to be an important part of the human experience as the child matures into an adolescent and then into an adult. The focus of attachment, of course, begins to shift from the initial bonds with parents, first to friends and later to romantic partners. The ability to bond without undue strain to another person can be a critical part of our emotional development, enabling us to fulfill our needs, adding gratification and security to our existence. Researchers have found that adults with insecure patterns of attachments are more likely to experience depression.[9] Fear of rejection can be an important component of an insecure attachment style and this can be a particularly difficult issue for many women. Researchers have linked this fear of rejection to both the severity of depression in a clinically depressed sample of women and to depressive tendencies in a normal sample of women.[10]

Troublesome Patterns in Parent-Child Relationships

An influential view in the child development literature was articulated in the 1970s by Sidney Blatt who observed that two patterns of parent-child relations seem particularly related to the development of depressive tendencies. The first pattern followed from the research on attachment and separation. In this scenario, the child develops a fear of abandonment by the mother and of not being loved by her. Such fears may lead to exaggerated dependency on others for support and satisfaction in life, to feelings of helplessness and fears of being on one's own. Depression with these characteristics has been termed *anaclitic depression.*[11]

Following through on this idea, we might deduce that if separation from parents in childhood increases vulnerability to later depression, the death of a parent would be particularly linked to subsequent depression in the child and perhaps in the adult as well. Researchers examining biographical information and depression inventory scores of adults have found an association between the death of a parent during the patient's childhood and current levels of depression.[12] The chances of the loss of a parent being followed by depression in the children seems to be higher if the loss occurred relatively early in the child's life rather than in later childhood or when the child is in adolescence. Interestingly, depression may happen more frequently when children experience the loss of a parent through the separation of divorce than through the parent's death.[13]

The second pattern of parent-child relationships that seems to foster depression is one in which the relationship is characterized by excessive negative parental control. In this pattern, parents are often hostile and deprecatory and inconsistent in offering affection. Under these conditions, the child learns to feel unworthy and unlovable and may develop a strong sense of guilt and a pattern of self-criticism. The child may feel that she or he has not lived up to expectations and may develop a need for super-striving in order to prove herself or himself. In a recent study the recollections of parents as rejecting and overprotective were related to feelings of self-hating self-criticism. If you tie this in with my own research which found that anger directed against the self was related to scores on the Beck Depression Inventory, you can see how this pattern of parent-child relationships could become depressogenic.[14] Depression that emphasizes these problems has been called *introjective depression.*

In the late 1970's, researchers combined the ideas of a lack of warmth and caring from parents with over-control (for example, criticism, intrusiveness) and termed the concept "affectionless control." To measure this construct, a team of Australian researchers led by G. Parker devised a self report instrument called the Parental Bonding Instrument in which people assessed these characteristics of their parents.[15] The availability of the instrument has led to a spate of interesting research. For example, affectionless control by parents in child rearing has been linked to both dysfunctional attitudes and low self-esteem in the children — both of which can promote subsequent depression.[16]

Researchers have also studied the relation of affectionless control in parenting with measures of depression in their children. In an early study Parker administered the Parental Bonding Instrument to a group of people diagnosed with neurotic depression and to a group of control subjects. He found that when analyzed separately, the parental care component of the scale fared better than the excessive control component in picking out the depressed people from the control subjects. Using both components of the instrument together to provide an index of affectionless control, Parker reported that 67 percent of the depressed people characterized one or both of their parents' behaviors this way as against 37 percent of the controls.[17] A recent review of studies conducted on the relation of affectionless control and depression reported by Lauren Alloy and her colleagues confirmed these early results. Their review concluded that depressive symptoms were associated both with a lack of care and too much control. Lack of warmth and caring appeared to be the more important of the two components.[18]

When adult depressed patients are asked about their memories of the way their parents reared them, their reports often include both elements of affectionless control — lack of warmth and over-control. In reflecting on the studies of parenting and depression, Edward McCranie and Judith Bass wrote, "Considered together, these studies suggest that depression proneness in general is influenced by parental child-rearing practices that combine elements of rejection, inconsistent expressions of affection, and strict control. Such parental behaviors could be expected to hinder the development of normal self-esteem in the child, resulting in an increased vulnerability to generalized feelings of helplessness and failure."[19]

To cite an illustrative study, women who had experienced depression and women who had not were asked to agree or disagree with a number of statements describing their mothers. The women who had experienced depressive problems more often endorsed statements that portrayed their mothers as critical and demanding, such as, "Mother wanted me to be different," "Mother felt many things about my performance should be corrected," "I couldn't live up to Mother's expectations," "Mother honored my brothers' and sisters' requests more than mine."[20]

We must introduce a note of caution here because these studies use retrospective accounts, memories of what things were like in childhood. Like perception, memory is selective; we remember some things and not others. And there are many studies that show that depressed emotion can influence what one recalls. People who are depressed often show a bias toward recalling what is unpleasant. This bias poses an obvious problem in interpreting retrospective accounts.

There is yet another problem with retrospective studies, particularly concerning early childhood. Many people have difficulty remembering very much about this period. In conducting research on this problem, Roland Tanck and I found that recall is often very poor. For the first three years of life, about half of our college student subjects couldn't remember *anything*. About one in ten subjects couldn't recall anything through age six.[21] To appreciate the difficulties that might be involved in retrospective accounts, think back to your very early memories. How much do you recall?

With this limitation in mind, researchers set about the more difficult, time-consuming task of carrying out prospective studies. In these studies, measures of parenting style were obtained, sometimes by observing parents and their children together in an interaction task, sometimes by conducting interviews with mothers and their children, and sometimes using the Parental Bonding Instrument. Then, the children were followed for a number of years to see if depressive symptoms developed. In their review, Alloy and her colleagues cited four prospective studies. Each provided some evidence that parenting styles characterized by a lack of warmth and excessive control were followed by an increase in the likelihood of depressive symptoms.[22]

So, it looks very much as if both lack of affection and over control can be risk factors for depression and the combination of the two may be particularly injurious. However, there is an important caveat here. While sub-optimal parenting can promote depression, it can also promote the development of other types of emotional problems. In one of the prospective studies on parenting, it was reported that the odds that affectionless control by the parents would be followed by substance-abuse in the children were even higher than they were for depression.[23] Sub-optimal parenting is not specific to depression; it is a risk factor for a number of unhappy developments in the children, one of which is depression.

Going beyond these two patterns, we know that parents who are angry, or worse, cruel and abusive, can leave emotional scars on children. The effects of physical abuse of children are found in poor performance in school, conduct problems, anxiety and social withdrawal, as well as depressed reactions.

In discussing their study of children who were inpatients in a psychiatric facility, Alan Kazdin and his colleagues reported that children who had been physically abused, "Evince higher levels of depression and hopelessness and lower self-esteem than do nonabused patients ... and viewed themselves and their futures more negatively than did children without physical abuse."[24] A retrospective study using a nationally representative sample found that people reporting sexual abuse as children also showed an increased risk of depression as well as other emotional problems.[25]

In reviewing the studies carried out over the years linking abuse of children with subsequent depression, Alloy and her colleagues concluded that emotional abuse by the parents—even more than physical or sexual abuse was a precursor of depression in the children. Humiliating and belittling statements that tear down the child's self esteem can have destructive effects on the child, leading to depression and other emotional problems.[26]

Other sources of potential problems are homes in which there are high levels of parental discord. Such homes are a fertile environment for children to germinate the seeds of emotional difficulties. It can be a severe strain on children to witness a declared or undeclared war between their parents. Children who go through the divorce of their parents not only experience this tension, but they experience the subsequent loss of separation. It is no wonder that anger, depressed reactions and withdrawal are among the common reactions observed in children to the divorce of their parents.[27] There are parallels here with the reactions described by Bowlby when attachments were severed in very young children.

The Importance of Confidence-Building Activities

One of the important aspects of early attachment relationships is that they give the child a secure base with which to explore his or her world and begin to develop competence in mastering the environment. This builds feelings of confidence. Competence and confidence are very important in becoming a fully effective individual. The home atmosphere that promotes these tendencies will help the child develop a sense of self-esteem. The home atmosphere that does not may promote learned helplessness, which increases the risk of a depressive reaction.

To grow in competence and gain the confidence that comes with it, children need the opportunity to explore, to try and to succeed. Parents like Alexandra's mother and Aunt Josie, whose repetitive messages to the child are "no," "don't," and "you can't," are not providing her this opportunity. The parent who is impatient with the child, who takes over and says, "Here, I'll do it," when the task is within the child's capabilities, prevents the child from developing a sense of mastery in dealing with her or his environment.

Confidence-building activities are vital in the formative years. In addition to the early home environment, school is an important setting for this kind of learning. Some children prosper in school, but not all do. Think back to your classrooms in elementary and junior high school. Do you remember some of the very bright kids in the class? It seems like their hands were always flying high to answer the teacher's questions and the teacher called on them time and again. The children were praised; their marks were glowing. Whatever else was happening in their lives, these children knew they were good students. But what about the children who were not as quick? Who praised them? Chances are many such students faded into the woodwork and were ignored. And what about the children who really had to struggle in school? Some of these children took a psychological beating.

The message of years of being ignored or worse, put down, is cumulative and clear: "You're not competent — you don't measure up." If the child has compensating talents like athletic ability or artistic or mechanical skills, these can go a long way as a self-confidence booster. The important thing is that children need to experience success as they grow up.

Self-confidence comes not only from academic success but from interpersonal success as well. Children who do not develop social skills tend to experience rejection and loneliness. Poorly developed social skills in children can be a harbinger of possible future psychological and social difficulties. Researchers have found that children who experience a "double whammy," having both poorer academic and social skills, are more likely to be depressed.[28]

We are sketching a picture of what is often a subclinical depression in children. Picture a child who is neglected or rejected by his peers and not doing well academically. Such a child is unlikely to feel very good about himself. Teachers can often spot such a lonely, unhappy child. The child's classmates may be even better at it. The consensual opinion of children about their classmates is often revealing.

It is possible to obtain such opinions in research. To cite an example, using a "peer nomination" technique, Monroe Lefkowitz and Edward Tesiny gathered groups of children into a schoolroom and read aloud a series of descriptive statements that included such items as, "Who often plays alone?" "Who thinks they are bad?" "Who says they can't do things?" "Who doesn't have much fun?" "Who thinks others don't like them?" "Who often looks lonely?"[29] The children's tasks were to think about their classmates and check all the names on their class roster that best fit the description.

What happened in Lefkowitz's and Tesiny's study was that most of the children in the class received *no votes* at all. Most of the children were not viewed by their peers as depressed. However, there were some children who were clearly picked out by their peers as depressed.

When the researchers compared these "nominated" children with their classmates, they uncovered some interesting findings. First, the nominated children were rated by themselves as depressed. They recognized that they had a problem. These children also had lower self-esteem on psychological testing.

Like adults who are depressed, they more often saw the sources of gratification in life as under external control. They were more often absent from school and performed less well on reading and math achievement tests.

Depressive symptoms in children are not only correlated with lowered estimates of self-esteem and diminished perceptions of one's competence, they are correlated with the child's perceptions of how other children view them and like them. Depressive feelings in children can deflate their views of how well other children accept them and as research has shown, this can be a good deal worse than the reality. Researchers have found that children with depressed tendencies are often both more competent and accepted than they believe.[30]

Notwithstanding this, children with depressive tendencies often have difficulties relating to other children. Part of the problem may be a self-fulfilling prophecy, in which low self-esteem and questions about one's acceptability usher in a demeanor and behaviors that may be unattractive to others and lead to rejection.

These tendencies may even influence the way the depressed children interact with their best friends. In an experiment demonstrating this, children scoring either high or low on the Children's Depression Inventory were paired with their best friends to play video games. The best friends of the children with depressive tendencies showed more negative emotions during the games than the best friends of the children who did not have depressive tendencies. Neither the children with depressive tendencies nor their best friends enjoyed the games as much the children who had low scores on the Children's Depressive Inventory and their best friends.[31]

The psychology of these children, their lowered self-esteem and external view of control of gratification, seems very similar to the patterns we saw earlier in depressed adults. Do depressed children also show some of the other thinking patterns typical of depressed adults, such as overgeneralization and a tendency to blame oneself?

Harold Leitenberg and his colleagues carried out an interesting study, which addressed this question. They presented hypothetical situations to children concerning three areas of their lives: social, academic and athletic. Following the hypothetical situations, they offered a negative thought pattern type of reaction. For example: "You call one of the kids in your class to talk about your math homework. He/she says, 'I can't talk to you now, my father needs to use the phone.' You think, 'He/she didn't want to talk to me.'" And, "Your cousin calls you to ask if you would like to go on a long bike ride. You think, 'I probably won't be able to keep up and people will make fun of me.'" The children were asked to respond to each situation using a scale ranging from "not at all like I would think" to "almost exactly like I would think."[32] The results were revealing. Similar to findings of the peer nomination study, the researchers found that most of the children did not believe that they would usually react to these situations with such negative interpretations. Negative thought patterns were not typical for young children.

The researchers reported some interesting observations. First, when negative thought patterns arose, they were most likely to arise in the social area. Young children were more likely to overgeneralize or catastrophize from incidents in their peer relationships than from events in the classroom or athletic field. Second, very young children were more prone to catastrophize and personalize mishappenings than older children. As the researchers suggest, very young children lack the experience to understand that mistakes and failures do not necessarily have dire consequences. Young children may blow the situation out of proportion. Third, and most important for our inquiry, the children who showed tendencies to overgeneralize, catastrophize and hold themselves responsible for bad outcomes were more likely to report depressed feelings. This is the same pattern we see in adults.

These findings for children then are in some respects a mirror for what we observe in adults. Most children do not have negative thinking patterns; those who do are more likely to be depressed. Most adults do not think that way either. Those who do are more likely to feel depressed. These parallel findings recall the idea of building blocks — the impact of one stage of development on the next. The child is indeed the father of the man. The elements of adult depression are forming in the child. One sees loneliness, low self-esteem, perception of external control, a tendency to overgeneralize and catastrophize failures and blame oneself. All of these adult tendencies may be observed in vulnerable children, presumably resulting from the interplay of genetics and psychologically punishing environments. When environmental stressors become too difficult to handle, a depressive reaction may develop — even in children.

In carrying out research on the way children evaluate good and bad events, Martin Seligman and his colleagues arrived at a similar conclusion. They wrote, "children with depressive symptoms share some characteristics of adults with depressive symptoms. Both have an attributional style in which bad events are seen as caused by internal, stable, and global factors. Both may be put at risk for future depression by processing information about bad events through this insidious attributional style."[33]

The potential for depression that is developed in childhood is carried into adolescence. Biological changes that take place at puberty create profound changes in the child's life. Rapid physical and sexual maturation accompanied by increased independence from parents generate considerable uncertainty and stress. Psychological vulnerabilities that may have been created in childhood can lead to poorer skills for coping with these stresses, making adjustment more difficult. Many adolescents experience periods of mild to moderate depression.

Difficulties in relationships within one's own family are often the biggest problem for adolescents and sometimes are related to depressive episodes. Tensions in the relationship of the adolescent and parents can create problems for both parties. Problems in social relationships are another prime source of emotional discord for teenagers as acceptance by one's peer group assumes a very high place in the world of adolescence. The depressed symptoms of the adolescent are in most respects similar to those of adults. In addition to the litany of depressed symptoms we have outlined earlier, the depressed teenager is likely to have trouble with school work and get poorer grades.

Researchers studying teenagers with depressive symptoms have reported that there are some differences in the way boys and girls show their depressed feelings. Adolescent boys who are depressed are more likely than girls to appear antagonistic, unrestrained and discontented. They feel worried and alienated. They often get into trouble in school and don't do well in their school work. Depressed adolescent girls also feel alienated and angry, but these feelings usually are less observable in the girls' behavior. Depressed adolescent girls may appear passive. They may become introspective and frequently have problems with self-esteem.

Young adolescent boys are often concerned about their lack of ability in sports and not measuring up, while adolescent girls tend to be particularly sensitive to the possibility of rejection.[34] Girls who have depressive tendencies sometimes engage in excessive reassurance seeking to cope with these concerns.[35] But this behavior can be counter productive, sometimes bringing on what these girls fear — rejection. Frequent family moves with resulting dislocations and loss of friends can be challenging for both boys and girls.[36]

While problems within the family circle and difficulties relating to peers are often sources of stress in adolescence, it is important to recognize that both family and peers may also act as a buffer against stress for the teenager. The teenager who feels he or she is part of a functioning family where people feel connected and care about each other has a real advantage in coping with the problems of adolescence. Having good friends is also a very important source of support for the teenager.

There are a number of growth experiences—"developmental tasks" we think of as important in adolescence — skills that we normally expect teenagers to develop during this important phase of life. We think of such things as gaining a substantial measure of independence from one's parents, finishing high school and beginning to date. Successful experiences in adolescence promote successful experiences in adulthood to follow. Failure to develop these skills may not only be associated with a troublesome adolescence but could lay the groundwork for future difficulties.

6. Stress and Depression

It is very common for depressed moods to develop during periods of stress. Though not always the case, when depressed people are questioned about what was going on in their lives when they began to feel depressed, they often relate stories of being under stress. Both clinical observation and research evidence point to the conclusion that when people have a vulnerability toward depression, stressful events in life may trigger a depressed reaction

In describing their model of the depressive process, H. A. Meyersburg and his colleagues presented some case material that illustrates the way mounting stress can precipitate a depressive reaction. Consider Judith, a 40-year-old woman who once had a depressive episode during college but had been relatively free of problems since that time. One day her husband informed her that there was another woman in his life. He then filed for divorce. When the divorce was granted, Judith moved away, taking her three children. She felt overwhelmed by the changes in her life, experienced intense anxiety, and was unable to care for herself and her children. She was subsequently hospitalized for depression. In the hospital, she spoke about a vague, diffuse anxiety, and feeling helpless and needy.

Or take the case of Sally, a woman in her early twenties. Sally came from a family in which both parents had depressive problems, suggesting that Sally was at increased risk. The precipitating stressor in Sally's case was a romantic relationship. Sally became involved with a young man whom she found attractive, but at the same time she was frightened of sexual experience. As the relationship developed, her anxiety about physical intimacy mounted. She rebuffed him and he broke off the relationship. Following the breakup, she became severely depressed.[1]

Researchers have accumulated a large amount of data that suggests that major changes in life act as stressors and may trigger depression in those who are vulnerable. By major life changes, we mean such events as developing a serious illness, changing jobs, moving to a different part of the country, getting divorced, as was the case for Judith, having a child or losing a close friend.

Researchers have compiled lists of such events, put them in the form of a questionnaire and found that people who have been going through major life changes are more vulnerable to emotional problems including depression. A review of studies linking major life changes to the onset of depression indicated that the presence of such stressors was two to three times more common among depressed people then among controls. Studies carried out in community settings indicated that depression was preceded by major life events in about 80 percent of the cases.[2]

One of the key elements in many of these changes is loss. When a young man or woman goes away to college, for example, it is a challenging experience with great potential for personal growth, but it also means separation from long-standing sources of security—from family, friends and the familiar environs of one's formative years. Such separation can be very distressing.

Ellen's experience is a good illustration of this. Ellen was a student in one of our research projects who found the transition to a large urban university very difficult and reported she was experiencing very high stress. She had previously boarded at a small all girls' school where she had lots of friends and close-knit relationships. The small classes had allowed an opportunity for students to discuss issues with their instructors and Ellen had found the atmosphere academically stimulating. Now, her classes were held in large lecture halls, sometimes with hundreds of students. She disliked the impersonal nature of the university and missed her old friends badly.

Breakups in romantic relationships are one of the most painful of human experiences. It is the stuff that novels are made of, the basis of folk ballads and popular songs. Breaking up is also a source of countless depressive reactions. Research has demonstrated that having a network of strong, supportive relationships seems to act as a barrier against depression. The loss of such ties is difficult to cope with.[3]

The observation that the experience of loss is often implicated in depression is, of course, not a new idea. As we indicated, Freud recognized the importance of loss in triggering depression many years ago in his essay *Mourning and Melancholia* . The theme has been amplified by Bowlby and others.[4] However, it should be pointed out that there is no inevitability that loss, or other types of stressors, will bring on a depressive reaction. People differ greatly in their resiliency when exposed to stressors. Some people who experience the loss of a spouse or paralyzing injuries show little evidence of depressed reactions after the event or experience noticeable depressive problems later on.[5]

It is not only the big changes in life that increase one's risk of experiencing a depressive reaction; it is also the seemingly unremitting pounding away of everyday problems. Roland Tanck and I asked college students to look over a checklist of problems that students might typically encounter (e.g., not doing well at school, having conflicts with parents, being short of money) and to check the problems that they were currently experiencing. We found that the more problems the students checked, the higher they scored on the measure of depression.[6] One problem might not get you down, but three, or four or five?

These findings bring to mind the old adage about the straw that broke the camel's back. In a somewhat similar vein, A.D. Kanner and his colleagues developed a questionnaire that measures daily hassles, events like experiencing traffic noise, preparing meals and having to wait. The more hassles people reported, the greater the chance they felt depressed.[7]

These studies point to the role of the everyday stressors in our lives in triggering depression. And where better to look for such stressors than in our places of work, at school, in our marriages and families, and our relationships. These, our primary sources of joy and fulfillment in life, can also be causes of stress, playing a part in the development of depressed reactions.

The Link Between Stress and Depression: A Closer Look

As we explore the relation between stress and depression, we find that it becomes more complex as we probe into it more deeply. First, as we indicated, not all people react to major stressors by becoming depressed. There are biological, psychological, and social factors which we will discuss later that moderate the effects of stressors, making depressive reactions more or less likely. Second, not all stressors are alike. Some types of stress-provoking situations, and some types of circumstances, may be more likely to bring on depression than others. One aspect of a stress-provoking situation, that seems to have an important bearing on whether a person will experience a depressive reaction is the extent to which the person may have been involved in bringing on or exacerbating the stressful situation. Imagine, for example, a deteriorating romantic relationship — one on the verge of a break up. This can be very stressful for one or both parties involved. Imagine further that one of the persons experiencing this loss also feels that he or she has contributed to the problem, perhaps with hasty, harsh words that were painful to the other party. The person may feel guilt and self blame and these are depressive inducing emotions.

Researchers have tested the idea that self-generated stress tends to be more often followed by depression than stress brought on by external agencies. In a review of research on stress and depression, Constance Hammen noted that researchers have found evidence supporting this idea in studies carried out with both adults and children.[8]

A second factor is the degree to which the stress provoking situation appears uncontrollable. It is my belief that when stress reaches uncomfortable levels and *no solution is in sight to change things,* depression is more likely to occur. When depression persists and becomes a lingering event, there may be some change in focus— a shift from thinking about the external stressors to a preoccupation with oneself. The focus may change from, "The situation is awful" to "The situation is awful and *I can't function."* A kind of psychological paralysis may set in. One of the effects of this immobilization is that the person may begin to avoid the stress situation. He may take sick leave from work, drop that difficult course in school or avoid social contacts. Depression in this sense functions like a psychological defense, protecting the ego from further stress. The price exacted is pain and suffering of another kind.

Interestingly, researchers have reported that stressors which are uncontrollable tend to have a greater effect on raising cortisol levels and elevated cortisol levels have been related to depression.[9]

Here is an interesting study which seems consistent with the hypothesis that the uncontrollability of stressors is a factor in promoting depression. A group of researchers led by Carolyn Cutrona studied over 700 African-American women in selected areas of two states, Iowa and Georgia.[10] Both poor and more affluent neighborhoods were included in the study. In interviews, data were collected about negative life events experienced during the past 12 months (e.g., "Did you have a family member with a serious illness or injury?") and the symptoms of major depression. As one would expect from the findings of previous research, the number of negative events was correlated with the onset of depression. However, it made a big difference whether or not the woman was living in a poor, economically depressed neighborhood. Experiencing negative events in a poor neighborhood was much more likely to lead to depression. While there are probably a number of reasons for this finding, the researchers interpretation of their data parallels my own view of uncontrollability. They wrote, "Women who experienced multiple negative life events were more likely to report the onset of depression if they lived in neighborhoods high rather than low in economic disadvantage/disorder." And later, "Neighborhoods high on economic disadvantage offer few economic opportunities and few role models for economic success, which undermines optimism and belief in personal mastery among residents. Neighborhoods high on social disorder inhibit the formation of supportive relationships with neighbors, prevent a sense of predictability, and offer threats to physical safety. When negative life events occur in this context, their impact is intensified because the worldview of the victim probably offers little hope for assistance from others and little experience with personal efficacy."[11]

The implication of the uncontrollability hypothesis is that if a person feels he or she is able to cope with an ongoing stress situation and reduce its impact, the situation is less likely to cause serious emotional problems.

Individual Differences in Response to Stressors

As we mentioned, not everybody who experiences a major stressful event becomes depressed. This is a commonplace, everyday observation. Some people experience the worst kind of traumas; combat, natural disasters, or severe interpersonal loss. They may experience a profoundly upsetting experience, but they weather the storms and do not develop a major depression. Why? What accounts for their resiliency in the face of turmoil? And, conversely what are the factors that make one more vulnerable to react to stressful experiences of far less intensity with depression?

The findings from research suggest that there is no single answer to this question. The answers probably lie in biological differences—some people have a genetic makeup that makes them more vulnerable to depression, in childhood experience, in psychological differences in the way people evaluate stress-arousing situations, in the way they cope with these situations, and in the level of social support available.

In regard to genetic factors, recall the study of Caspi and his colleagues that showed that people carrying the short variant of the promoter region of the serotonin transporter gene were more likely to react to stressful life events by becoming depressed.[12] This study suggests that we begin the race of life unevenly in our capacity to withstand the depressogenic effects of stressors.

As we have seen in the preceding chapter, childhood experiences and parent-child relationships are important influences in molding vulnerability or resiliency to depression. In her review article on stress and depression, Constance Hammen noted that exposure to early stressors can have a significant effect on the way adults react to stressors.[13] In one of her own studies, she found that exposure to earlier adversities in life appeared to predispose her sample of adult women to react to stressors with depression. Their threshold for becoming depressed when stressed appeared to be lowered.[14]

Troubled childhoods can lead to insecure attachment patterns as adults. Such insecurities in adulthood can lead to both stresses in relationships and lack of support from others when difficulties arise.[15] Both developments favor depression.

When we consider current, ongoing psychological factors that are likely to make a difference in whether exposure to stressors will be followed by a depressive reaction, we need to take account of the way people interpret and evaluate the stress situations that they encounter. One person might see the situation as very serious, with potential dire consequences; he or she may feel pessimistic about the outcome and hold himself or herself to blame for the situation. Another person might take a more benign view of the situation, trying to look for the brighter aspects of the picture, holding out hope for better things in the future and not blaming himself or herself for bringing on the problem. Researchers interested in depressogenic cognitive styles have carried out a number of studies in which measures of dysfunctional attitudes taken in conjunction with reports of stressors experienced were related to the development of depressive episodes. While the evidence from these studies is not altogether clear, it looks as if the activation of depressive cognitive sets helps promote depressive reactions to stressors.[16]

The individual's self-esteem or lack thereof can also have a moderating effect on reaction to stressors. A strong sense of one's own strengths and capabilities can help buffer the impact of stressors. In contrast, research suggests that low self-esteem makes one more vulnerable to the effects of stressors and can be a factor in promoting depression.[17]

As a way of illustrating the effects of psychological factors in moderating the effects of stress on depression, consider the reactions of two employees working for a consulting firm. There are half-finished reports lying on both of their desks. One of the employees, Dave, thinks it's extremely important to get the job done. He thinks, "If I don't work late tonight and finish it — no matter how long it takes — the boss and my co-workers will think I'm not up to the job." In contrast, Bill's attitude is, "The work will still be there tomorrow. The world won't come to an end if it takes an extra day. If I wait until tomorrow, I'm not going to lose my job and the company isn't going to go broke."

The company may be much happier with Dave's attitude than Bill's, but if that is Dave's *characteristic approach to life,* he may be setting himself up for trouble. He may be over evaluating or inflating the importance of what he is doing — not distinguishing between what is important and what is not — and not recognizing where a maximum effort is really needed. He may also be investing too much of his self-esteem in the activity. If things don't work out, he'll take the setback harder.

Research has suggested that people who become depressed tend to inflate the importance of the problems they face, feeling there is more at stake and more to lose. Their self-esteem is more often on the line.[18] When higher stakes are placed on an outcome, insecurity and anxiety are likely to develop during the process of resolving the problem. The person is more likely *to* experience the symptoms of stress — edginess, irritability and physical complaints.

If the situation is confrontational, involving another person, there is a higher chance of the stressed individual reacting emotionally. As the confrontation mounts, anger mounts. He or she may explode in an emotional outburst or the anger may be vented later at someone else who just happens to be around. Or worse yet, for the prospect of becoming depressed, the anger may be directed inwardly, against oneself. If the problem is not resolved in a satisfactory way, which happens occasionally to everyone, more hurt and disappointment may be experienced. High stakes can lead to a greater sense of loss and lowered self-esteem. Depressed people often report that their feelings are easily hurt, that they take things hard. Part of the reason for this reaction is that they have mentally turned hills into mountains. When the hill collapses, it seems like the mountain has collapsed. Setbacks and failures have been catastrophized.

We have suggested in our discussion of the controllability of stressors that the way an individual copes with stress can make a difference in the likelihood that he or she will become depressed. When responding to stress, people who become depressed are less likely to cope with the situation by taking the kinds of concerted action needed to solve the problems. Instead of engaging in prob-

lem solving behavior or trying some coping strategies that might prove helpful in lessening stress, they often become bogged down in inaction, self analysis and rumination. Wishful thinking and avoidance sometimes provide a
defense for the faltering ego, but obviously have only limited value for the long
term.

A study carried out by Roland Tanck and myself points to the depressogenic effects of ineffective coping.[19] Using questionnaires we asked college students, "Do you find that your own life as a college student is stressful?" We
followed this question with three alternatives, "Yes— it is very stressful," "Yes—
it is somewhat stressful," and "No." Only three of our 84 subjects replied, "No."
We assessed the students on two other measures, an inventory of coping behaviors that Tanck and I had developed using factor analysis and the Beck Depression Inventory. What we found was that the students who indicated that their
lives as students were *very stressful* were more likely to score higher on the
depression measure if they had a pattern of coping with stress which we called
dysfunctional behavior. This pattern included such items as daydreaming or
fantasiszing, spending endless hours thinking about things, becoming irritable and easily annoyed, eating constantly, and becoming ineffective. The students who indicated that their lives as students were also very stressful, but did
not usually engage in this pattern of dealing with stress did not have high
depression scores on the Beck scale. There are many ways to cope with stress,
but lapsing into a passive, ruminating, irritable state seems like a way station
on the road to depression.

Finally, the availability of social support can be very important when an
individual is under stress. Having others to talk to, to share what he or she is
going through can make a big difference in weathering the difficulties that we
all will encounter at one time or another.

Can Depression Promote Stress?

The evidence is quite clear that exposure to significant stressors frequently
precedes the onset of an episode of depression. Some researchers have turned
the question around, asking whether depression might generate stress. David
Cole and his colleagues suggested that, "Depression compromises a person's
ability to function effectively, thereby increasing the occurrence of negative or
stressful life events."[20] Consider, for a moment, a person disabled from depression who nonetheless has many responsibilities. He has a wife and several children to provide for, a job with the work piling up every day, a mortgage to pay,
and bills coming in all the time. Being depressed offers a degree of escape from
this pressure; he has the protection of the "sick role," a status we all find ourselves in at one time or another when we are ill or injured; a status which
informs society that we have a legitimate reason not to carry out our usual

responsibilities. One can almost hear the reassuring words from one's family and friends, "Don't worry about a thing. Just get well."[21] However, the protection offered by the sick role is probably not as good for depression as it is for a physical illness such as a heart attack, for some people still look at mental and emotional disorders as "suspect," with the hard-to-dissuade belief that the person could straighten himself out "if he really wanted to" or if he only had enough "will power." I remember a very unsympathetic wife who told me to straighten out her depressed husband so he could get back to work and take care of her. So, pressure can mount from both within the patient and without.

The possibility that depression might generate stress has not been nearly as well studied as the more intuitive idea that stress can act as an agent to bring on depression. A recent study carried out on children and adolescents found that self reports of depressive symptoms were followed by increased stress (report of negative life events).[22] Even in this non-clinical sample of school-age children, feelings of being depressed may have generated more problems.

Stress and the Recurrence of Depression

Researchers have observed that the tendency for stress-provoking situations to precede an episode of depression was more likely to occur for the first episode of depression than for subsequent episodes. As depression reoccurred, the role of stress as a precipitant becomes less clear. In time, episodes of depression appeared to occur without the stimulus of stress. It has been theorized that the onset and then recurrences of depression creates changes in our biology — possibly at the level of gene expression — which sets a person up for further episodes of depression without obvious causes. The individual has apparently become "sensitized" and may in time experience what appears to be a spontaneous episode of depression.[23]

In an article in the *Psychological Review*, Scott Monroe and Kate Harkins described two lines of explanation that would account for this observation.[24] The first line of explanation is that the individual who is prone to depression has become sensitized so that it takes lower and lower levels of stress to trigger a depressive episode. When it once may have taken a major stressor to induce depression, in time, minor stressors can bring on an episode. The other line of explanation is that depression has become independent of stress. At this point, stressors become almost irrelevant. Depression occurs with or without the stressor trigger. In this view, stressors have lost a causal relation to depression.

While sophisticated longitudinal studies are probably needed to more fully understand what is actually happening here, the data obtained so far carry an important implication for the treatment of depression. If repeated episodes of depression produce sensitization, the treatment for the first episode of depression becomes very important. Thorough treatment of the first episode of depression leading to a complete remission of symptoms may help protect against the possibility of a spiraling sensitization and repeated recurrences. In subsequent chapters, we will discuss the approaches to therapy for depression that might be most likely to put a damper on the sensitization process.

Coping with Stress as a Means of Depression-Prevention

Because stress plays a role in the development of depressive episodes, particularly the early episodes, it makes good sense for people who are prone to depression to find effective ways to cope with stress. Coping skills can be taught in therapy. They can also be learned through self study. My recent book, *Coping with Stress: Commonsense Strategies* is an example of a source for self study. Stress management programs at one's job or stress support groups in the community offer other possibilities for controlling stress.

Prompt intervention for people experiencing severe stress can be helpful in controlling depressive reactions. In a recent study, women who were assaulted and then diagnosed as suffering from posttraumatic stress disorder were given supportive counseling or brief cognitive-behavioral therapy. Both treatments helped reduce depressive symptoms.[25]

So, if there is one clear-cut message suggested by research on stress and depression, it is to try not to let stress build up. Take what steps you can to mitigate the stress you are experiencing. The old adage about a stitch in time saves nine may well apply here.

7. Depression, Alcohol and Drugs

Alcohol is a substance that has been used and abused since the development of urban civilization in ancient Mesopotamia. Archaeologists have unearthed metallic drinking straws dating back thousands of years, which may have been used for imbibing beer.

Today, the use of alcohol permeates our society, as well as many others. As Leif Crowe and William George put it, "Its consumption provides mystical trance, holy communion, celebration and consolation, social acceptance and condemnation, prowess and impotence, languor and lust. Indeed, there is scarcely a human activity that has not been said to be both impoverished and improved by the addition of alcohol."[1]

As we all know, alcohol abuse is a widespread problem. So, too, is drug abuse, which is now high on the agenda of social problems to address. Millions of Americans are alcoholics and many more millions have serious drinking problems. Moreover, millions of Americans use illegal drugs, some of which, like heroin, are addictive.

If you talk with patients being treated for alcohol or drug addiction in hospital wards or in clinics, you will often find that these patients are or have been depressed. This is an important observation that has implications for the treatment and rehabilitation of substance abusers. In this chapter we will explore how depressed mood is linked to substance abuse.

Depression and Alcohol Abuse

Let us begin with alcoholism. There are a variety of terms that have been used to describe alcoholism. Some examples are problem drinking, alcohol addiction, alcohol abuse, and alcohol dependence. While there are shades of differences in the meaning of these terms, they do share a core of meaning. They all convey the idea that the individual's need for alcohol has reached a fundamentally different level than that of the light or moderate drinker. The light or

97

moderate drinker can have a drink or two, enjoy the relaxing of effects of the drink, and then put the bottle away for another day. The alcoholic typically cannot.

I like the term *alcohol dependence* because it has been used in the Diagnostic and Statistical Manual (DSM IV) to describe one of the principal alcohol abuse disorders and has been anchored in empirical data as well. Alcohol dependence denotes a loss of control over drinking. Indicators of alcohol dependence include withdrawal symptoms such as anxiety, shaking, and sweating; an inability to stop or even cut down drinking when one tries; giving up or curtailing social and recreational activities in favor of drinking; and continuing to drink in spite of problems brought on by the drinking.[2]

How many people are believed to have alcohol abuse disorders in the United States? A national survey carried out on over 40,000 people suggested that about 8 percent of the population had an alcohol use disorder during the 12 months preceding the survey. These alcohol disorders include both alcohol dependence and hazardous acts committed under the influence of alcohol such as reckless driving.[3]

Many years ago a noted authority on alcoholism wrote, "It is therefore a matter of clinical observation that preceding the use of alcohol there is always a depression."[4] While this assertion clearly overstates the case, there is little doubt that in many people, depressed mood and the use of alcohol are linked. The linkage, however, is complicated.

On the one hand people may drink or use drugs as a way of relieving anxious and depressed moods. Alcohol and drugs are forms of self-medication: they make one feel better, at least temporarily. On the other hand, protracted substance use can lead to changes in lifestyle that can bring on depression. In this case the depression is considered secondary to the alcoholism.

To make the distinction between primary and secondary depression clearer, compare Eileen and Dan, two patients being treated for alcohol abuse. Eileen has had a plethora of emotional problems beginning in childhood. She experienced a rocky adolescence in which she had difficulties in getting along with her father, with her sexuality and in overcoming shyness. Both in her early childhood and teenage years, there were times in which she was withdrawn and very depressed.

Eileen's father and her father's family have a tradition of heavy drinking. When family members get together to eat or talk, there always seems to be an open bottle. Eileen joined in the family drinking in her teenage years and found that it made her feel better. She felt more confident and less tense. By the time she was out of college, she was a heavy, compulsive drinker who, in her own words, was "no longer drinking for fun" but because "she needed it." Drinking had become the preferred method of relieving tension and depression.

While Eileen's depressive problem preceded her alcoholism, Dan had no noticeable depressive problems until long after he began drinking. During high school Dan used "to party" with his friends. In his circle it was a matter of prestige to see how drunk you could get on weekends. The pattern of heavy drinking stayed with him after graduation and continued into his adult years. Drinking first cost him his job because of absenteeism and later his marriage. By the time he joined Alcoholics Anonymous, he felt hopeless about his life, was filled with remorse and guilt and was considering suicide. For Eileen, depression was primary to alcoholism. For Dan, depression was secondary to alcoholism. For some people depression precedes alcoholism and is intensified by it. Self-medicating only exacerbates the original problem.

Many alcoholic patients will report the usual symptoms of depression, ranging from poor sleep to feelings of hopelessness. A study carried out by David Clark and his colleagues using the Beck Depression Inventory suggested that the particular symptoms to look for in alcoholics, symptoms that point to depression, are guilt, self-disgust, irritability, indecision, dissatisfaction, work inhibition and loss of social interest.[5]

Just how strong is the tie-in between alcohol abuse and depression? If not all alcoholics are depressed, how many are? A number of studies have been carried out on patients *hospitalized* for alcoholism. Sometimes these patients have been given psychiatric interviews using the *Diagnostic and Statistical Manual's* criteria for depressive disorders. Sometimes they have been given self-report measures of depression. In reviewing these studies, David Lutz and Peggy Snow found that the estimates for depression among alcoholic inpatients varied considerably. Studies using the depression inventories suggested that a majority of alcoholic patients were depressed. The figures from the psychiatric interviews did not seem as high but there were still estimates that exceeded 50 percent. Because of the different methods used to assess depression and the variable results obtained, it is difficult to offer a precise figure of the rate of depression among hospitalized alcoholic patients. However, the numbers appear to be substantial.[6]

With over eight percent of the adult population estimated to have an alcohol use disorder which would put the number into the many millions, it is clear that only a small fraction of these people are hospitalized or even in some kind of outpatient treatment program. What about these people with alcohol use disorders who are not receiving treatment? Are they likely to be as depressed as the people in treatment? One would argue that the answer is very likely *no*. Everyday observation tells us that many of these people simply live with the problems caused by alcohol, often to the detriment of those close to them. Clinical experience suggests that many of them are using the defense mechanism of denial. Others become aggressive while drinking, scaring off those who might want to help them. In any event, the person's pattern of life has not been sufficiently degraded to do anything meaningful about the problem and their emotional state may still be far from rock bottom.

Some empirical data obtained in the national survey of over 40,000 people cited earlier in this chapter indicated that about 16 percent of the respondents living in communities who were evaluated as having an alcohol use disorder during the past 12 months also had a "mood disorder" of some kind.[7] Mood disorders are typically some form of depression. While this was double the figure reported by persons not reporting alcohol use disorders, it seems a good deal less than the estimates researchers have made for people hospitalized for alcohol use problems.

It is difficult to tell in how many of these people depression preceded the alcoholic problem and vice versa. To do so we usually have to depend on patients' memories about the past and we know that such memories can be faulty. It is interesting that when such studies are undertaken, the figures for depression preceding alcoholism run considerably higher for women than men. In studies cited in Lutz's and Snow's review, the figures for a preexisting depression in women were in the 25 percent range, while they were less than 10 percent for men.

A recent study which utilized a sample of 7,000 twins to obtain information about genetic factors as well as the onset of alcohol use and major depressive disorders found that the onset of alcohol use disorders tended to occur at an earlier age than major depressive disorder. Alcohol use disorders occurred in young adulthood while major depressive disorder had a more variable age of onset. The study confirmed the conclusion from earlier studies that for women major depressive disorder often preceded the development of alcohol use disorders.[8]

The tendency for depression to precede alcoholism occurs often enough in women to warrant consideration from a public health standpoint in terms of the prevention of alcoholism. The statistics suggest that alcohol has been adopted by a large number of women as a means of relieving depressed feelings. Therefore, one approach to attacking the problem of alcoholism in women is to attack the causes of depression in women. The suggestion would be for society to deal more aggressively with the underlying problems that cause emotional difficulties in women rather than simply treating the symptoms of alcoholism.

When people are asked why they drink, or even more specifically, what effect they expect from drinking, they typically give the following answers: They expect to be more sociable, and to feel more relaxed and less inhibited. They also believe it will increase their enjoyment of sex.[9] They see some downside risks in drinking, such as acting foolishly or becoming aggressive, but in general they have a pretty rosy view of how they are going to feel while drinking. For people who are light to moderate drinkers, these expectations are often confirmed and this will sustain future drinking.

The problem comes when one is tempted to push the idea a little too far. If drinking can make one feel better and relieve the feelings of tension and pressure that have built up during the day, why not drink a little more and a little earlier? You'll feel better faster. And maybe alcohol will relieve the blue feelings we all experience at times when things go wrong and we are disappointed. These plausible ideas, unfortunately, lead one down the garden path.

There are several reasons for this. Heavy drinking throws one's normal intellectual and social abilities from order into chaos. One makes a mess out of what one is doing and one often ruins social relationships. Instead of increasing sexual enjoyment, heavy drinking often makes men impotent.[10] Heavy drinking is a path to alcohol dependence. And alcohol is not particularly useful for relieving depression — other than blotting out reality entirely — for alcohol, itself, can have depressant effects.

People don't drink to feel more depressed, but that can happen, particularly for heavy drinkers. In a study carried out with alcoholics, the subjects were given adjective checklists to assess their moods before and after drinking. The scores for depressed mood were higher *after* drinking.[11] As alcohol can have depressant effects, it is of dubious value as an aid for coping with a depressed mood. Chances are that if alcohol is consumed in large amounts, it will only make matters worse. However, alcohol is inexpensive, available and people usually don't expect that to happen.

Secondary depression — the psychological effects of a deteriorating lifestyle that follows from prolonged alcohol use — may be a slow and insidious development, for the course of alcoholism itself is often protracted. Increasing dependence on alcohol doesn't happen overnight and one may exist with the problem for years before the roof finally caves in. By the time the person fully recognizes his or her alcoholic problems and enters a treatment program, a great deal of personal damage may have accumulated. J. F. Nugent and I conducted a study of alcoholic patients at a Veterans Administration Hospital, in which we asked the patients whether their alcohol problem had caused any of a number of things to happen.[12] We included the checklist of 17 items, which appears below. The percentage of the patients who responded yes are given in the column on the right.

Checklist Item	*Percentage Answering Yes*
1. Found it difficult to do my job well	49
2. Made me lose a job	38
3. Found myself in serious financial difficulties	54
4. Strained my relationship with members of my own family	73
5. Strained my relationship with my friends	43
6. Tried to conceal my using drugs from others	51
7. Got in trouble with the law	44
8. Spent time in jail	37

Checklist Item	*Percentage Answering Yes*
9. Stopped enjoying many of the things I used to enjoy	72
10. Began to find myself isolated	55
11. Found it difficult to concentrate	69
12. Began to feel tense and anxious	85
13. Began to have periods of depression	85
14. Had thoughts of suicide	27
15. Developed strong feelings of guilt about using drugs	78
16. Found I was living from day to day without planning for the future	67
17. Felt my life was in a downhill slide	75

As you can see from the percentages of patients who responded, "yes, this problem happened to me," almost all of the patients had experienced tension and depression that they attributed to their alcohol problem. Psychologically, the patients felt that they were on a downhill slide. They felt guilty, aimless, were not enjoying their usual activities and felt increasingly isolated. All of these responses are consistent with a picture of depression. Typically, family relationships had been strained. Many of the patients had tried to conceal their problem from others. A sizeable number of the patients had experienced problems on their jobs, and over one-third of the patients had lost their jobs. Almost half of the patients reported having problems with the law and over a third had spent time in jail.

The negative, depressing consequences of alcoholism emerge from these data. The real life stories that flesh out this skeleton of statistics may be heard over and over again at treatment centers and AA meetings. We also encounter such narratives in the psychology clinic. The following is an example showing the destructive interplay of depression and alcohol in the life of a young woman, Leila.

When Leila entered therapy at an outpatient clinic in San Francisco, she was recovering from alcoholism. She had been in AA for several years and had finally ceased drinking. As therapy began, Leila was tense. Her words were halting and measured and she was reticent in discussing many things that were still painful for her.

Leila was born in North Carolina and was raised by her mother, who had a chronic illness, and by her grandfather. Her father had been killed in an automobile accident when she was three years old. Her grandfather was a very strict person who raised her by the book and would tolerate no nonsense. Leila grew up to be a shy, passive person, used to being in the background. She did what she was told, though inwardly she felt resentful and spent as much time as she could away from her grandfather. In her school years she was something of a loner, never quite comfortable with the other children. Sometimes she felt lonely and rejected. The situation was only marginally improved when she went to college. She began to feel depressed. She thought about seeking help at the University Counseling Center, wrestled with the idea, but never made an appointment.

In her final year of college, she met Frank. Frank was good looking, bright, with an assertive, dominating personality. Frank was the sort of person who would "take over." He was attracted to her physically, swept her off her feet and they were married shortly before graduation. Leila and Frank settled in a rather isolated community in southwestern Texas. Frank was busy with his job and Leila found herself alone a good deal of the time. This is when she began to drink.

Frank and Leila never knew each other very well before they were married, and early on Frank began to show evidence of boredom with the marriage. Leila seemed dispirited by her surroundings and had little to say that was new and interesting. When Frank began to drift away from her and show her less attention, she became clinging, and this turned Frank off further. She became increasingly tense about the relationship. She felt uncertain, tentative, almost cowed; it seemed something like a replay of her childhood days with her grandfather. The more tense she became, the more she drank.

When their daughter, Charlotte, was born, Leila and Frank began to get along better, at least for a while. They moved first to Denver and then to San Francisco, where Frank's job put him into contact with many interesting people. Leila remained at home with Charlotte. Frank grew in the job. Leila just seemed to languish. Leila became unsettled emotionally. She felt trapped, tense and depressed. She drank heavily.

Alcohol gave her courage. She got into bloody arguments with her husband, often in front of her young daughter. However, alcohol only dulled her wits. She became incoherent, angry and emotionally out of control. Frank reacted by leaving home for days at a time and became involved with several women. Finally, he left altogether and filed for divorce.

When the marriage was shattered, Leila found herself with few resources, an alcohol problem and depression. She tried making it on her own, but lacked confidence and was drinking too much. She couldn't hold a job. She had difficulty making new friends and felt isolated. She contemplated suicide and for a while was hospitalized.

Alcoholics Anonymous helped her turn things around. In therapy she began to explore her own needs and to develop a more positive sense of her own identity. In therapy, the focus in her life changed for the first time to what she could do for herself and what she could become. She was able to get a job and to begin the slow process of building a life of her own.

Leila's story brings to mind a recent study of alcohol use and marital relationships. The study found that it was not so much the quantity of alcohol consumed by one of the spouses that led to the deterioration of the relationship, as much as it was the difference in the amount they drank. When one spouse was a heavy drinker and the other was not, look out![13]

Depression and Illegal Drugs

Let's talk about illegal drugs—the black market drugs that are sold on the street. The most widely used illegal drug in the United States and world wide is marijuana. World wide estimates provided by an agency of the United Nations for the number of marijuana abusers during the 1990s exceeded 140 million people. Studies suggest that marijuana use disorders in the United States have been on the increase over the past decade.[14]

Marijuana has certain pharmacological depressant effects. Research has been carried out on a variety of animals—squirrels, monkeys, cats and rats looking at the effect of the drug on activity level. Interestingly, the effect of the drug is often biphasic; i.e., there is an initial period of excitement and stimulation, which is followed by quiet behavior in which the animals move about less and do little.[15] Similar effects have been reported with human subjects. Many people become sleepy after using marijuana and report a decline in activity.

People use marijuana because of the anticipated effects of the drug. They expect a "high" from the drug and to feel relaxed. They usually hope to attain these pleasant moods in the company of friends. Smokers report such sensations as lightheadedness, giddiness, intensified perception such as seeing colors more intensely, sexual arousal, dryness in the mouth, hunger and sleepiness. Adverse effects from the drug are not usual, but happen often enough to be of concern. Users of the drug at times experience feelings of anxiety and depression. In one study, 40 percent of the users questioned reported that they had experienced such reactions.[16]

My own research on marijuana users suggested that people who used marijuana on an occasional, recreational basis were unlikely to have concomitant emotional problems to a greater degree than nonusers. This research carried out on university students who were for the most part recreational users indicated that they did not differ very much on psychological tests from students who did not use the substance. Nor did they view their behaviors on the days they used the drug as being noticeably different from the days on which they did not use the drug. Beyond the fact that they reported they more frequently smoked cigarettes than the other students, statistically they were not particularly distinguishable from the non-users.[17]

I suspect that where marijuana users begin to look differently on psychological measures is when they began to use more powerful drugs as well as marijuana and especially if they become dependent on the drug. When we think of drug dependence, we think of a person who uses the drug frequently, for prolonged sessions, where drug use has become compulsive, and the problems brought on by using the drugs are ignored. And for some drugs, where tolerance develops for the drug, the user must search for more potent doses of the drug to produce the desired effects.

When marijuana use becomes marijuana dependence, unwelcome psychological correlates are often observed. Preoccupation with the drug may impair one's ability to perform well in school and on the job. In a large-scale study carried out under the auspices of the National Institutes of Alcohol Abuse and Alcoholism, marijuana dependence was linked to personality disorders of various kinds, anxiety disorders, and depressive disorders. Nearly half of the people who were classified as having a marijuana dependence during the previous 12 months had some kind of depressive disorder. Very interestingly, this depressive disorder was very frequently bipolar I. Nearly 23 percent of the respondents identified in the survey as having a marijuana dependence were also classified as having bipolar I disorder which is far above the rate in the population.[18] I have no ready explanation to offer for this provocative finding.

A lifestyle in which illegal drugs become a centerpiece carries with it increased risk of psychological problems. People who are under treatment for dependence on the more powerful illegal drugs currently in use in this country often report a variety of psychiatric problems including depression. As is true for alcoholism, it can be difficult to distinguish between pre-existing personality tendencies that lead to the use of these drugs and the emotional difficulties that often result from drug dependence.

Let's consider psychiatric correlates of two of the more widely used illegal drugs, methamphetamine and cocaine. Methamphetamine is a designer drug manufactured in clandestine laboratories many of which are scattered around the United States. Cocaine, derived from the cocoa plant that grows in South America is smuggled into this country. In a study of over 1000 methamphetamine users receiving outpatient treatment in Oakland, California, many of the patients reported depression, attempts at suicide, and serious problems controlling angry feelings.[19] In another study, employing a sample of Internet users, methamphetamine users tended to be more depressed and apathetic than nonusers.[20] In a third study, which used a sample of people who had been arrested and were in the criminal justice system, methamphetamine users were more depressed and more likely to have suicidal thoughts than people not using the drug.[21]

Cocaine dependence can also be accompanied by depression. In a study carried out in Texas, cocaine dependent patients who were also depressed reported more distress than the cocaine-dependent patients who were not depressed.[22] And, what has important implications for drug treatment, the depressed patients' craving for cocaine was higher and their confidence about being able to refrain from using the drug was lower.

With depression as a complicating factor in the treatment of dependence on these drugs, there have been attempts to augment treatment of both substances with antidepressant medicines. The results, to date, have not been promising.[23]

Perhaps, the most strategic place to view the psychological difficulties that arise from a life style centered on illegal drugs are the experiences of heroin-addicted patients. Their stories are both sad and instructive. Heroin is often the end-of-the-line drug when everything else has been tried. Heroin was originally developed with the best of intentions, as a "nonaddictive substitute" for morphine, which was in medical use as a painkiller. The problem was that heroin turned out to be highly addictive, producing both tolerance (the user doesn't get as much effect from the drug upon continued use, so he or she has to step up the dose to get the same effect) and physical dependence (the user needs to keep using the drug to prevent the beginning of uncomfortable withdrawal symptoms).

Heroin is a very potent pain reliever. Unlike marijuana, which may be associated with increased sexual arousal, heroin use may decrease sexual interest. The drug may have an uplifting effect on many people, can act as a tranquilizer for tension, and may detach the individual from the realities of the day. Life may take on a rosy hue until the effect of the drug wears off. It is this euphoric effect that draws many people to the drug.

When a person becomes physically addicted to heroin and stops using it, withdrawal symptoms occur. Such symptoms may include nausea, diarrhea, vomiting, abdominal cramps, profuse sweating, nervousness and insomnia. Symptoms usually diminish within a few days, but a craving for heroin may persist for years. This craving often leads to resumption of use.

Dependence on a drug such as heroin can become overwhelming. Some people who are addicted to this drug may do almost anything to again experience the sensations that they remember from past use of the drug. They will put aside all of the other memories—the misery that drug abuse has caused them in their lives—to experience the drug sensation. Hard drugs can exert a fatal attraction that reminds one of the story of the Sirens in the *Odyssey,* in which the song of these nymphs lured sailors to their deaths as their ships smashed on the rocks.

The psychological and social destruction of the heroin addict is similar in many ways to that of the alcoholic. The main difference is that it is usually quicker. There are reasons for this precipitous decline. Heroin use causes a physical addiction that requires continued use of the drug to prevent withdrawal symptoms. Unlike alcohol, which is also addictive, heroin is expensive and to sustain this drug habit costs a bundle. The victim soon has an empty pocketbook and often is induced into illegal activities, such as robbery or selling drugs, to buy more drugs. The chances of being arrested are pretty high.

Take a second look at the list of consequences we used in our research with alcoholics. We gave the list with the same instructions to two samples of patients under treatment for heroin addiction. One group of patients was hospitalized, undergoing detoxification and therapy. The other group of patients was being treated on an outpatient basis; most were on methadone maintenance. Some statistics from our study showed that the inpatients in particular had encountered very serious financial and legal problems as a consequence of drug dependency. Eighty-five percent of the hospitalized patients reported they had experienced serious financial difficulties. Eighty-two percent had gotten into trouble with the law. Sixty-seven percent had spent time in jail. The psychological consequences of addiction for these inpatients were also severe. Ninety-seven percent of the patients reported they had periods of depression. Ninety-four percent felt their lives were on a downhill slide. Eighty-eight percent reported they were becoming isolated. Forty-two percent had thoughts of suicide. At this point in time it is not possible to say with precision how many of these patients would meet the criteria for major depressive disorder, but it seems likely from these data that many of them would.[24]

As we can see from the responses to the questionnaires, almost all of the inpatients in the study indicated that depression was one of the consequences of heroin addiction. From interviews we conducted with other heroin-addicted patients, however, I have the impression that for many people who use heroin, depressive tendencies had set in earlier in life and were intensified by the lifestyle of the heroin addict.

Many of the patients interviewed had experienced a childhood and adolescence that nurtured a depressive outlook.[25] A large number of the patients had come from homes in which there was no father present, or, perhaps worse, a father who was alcoholic, indifferent or abusive. We know from research on child development that such circumstances increase the chances of depressive problems. The experience of school for many was not helpful and the jobs that were available tended to be boring and dead-end.

A growing sense of futility opened the way for drug experimentation. To many, it seemed as if there was little going for them and little to hope for — so why not go for some kicks in life? Most of the patients felt that they would not become addicted; there was a sense of invulnerability: "It won't happen to me." The consequences of addiction, however, often proved devastating, resulting in severe depressive problems. Almost all the studies that I have seen found elevated levels of depression among inpatients being treated for heroin addiction.

Drug addiction often leads to a kind of twilight existence. Addicts move surreptitiously in circles of other addicts and pushers. Many of them conceal what they are doing from their families as long as they can but the unrelenting need for the drug usually leads to family strains and financial disaster. The resulting conflict and misery can be glimpsed in excerpts from statements of the addicts themselves.

"I feel very depressed. I was unhappy with being out of work, out of money, being drug addicted. Using drugs has hurt my self-confidence. I feel I have messed up so many times in the past, I will do it again in the future."

"My wife got ready to leave me. I attempted suicide."

"I feel super depressed. Things piling up, bills, family things-makes me worried and depressed. Life on drugs made me go through more hell and frustration and more sickness than it's [possible] to imagine."

"I couldn't trust myself when I was strung out."

"The problem has been a constant struggle for my wife ... I get disgusted at myself in preparation stage, but once I am high, I don't give a damn."

"I felt I was going down, down, down. I had to get off of it."

"Living the life of an addict is really hell. After you've become hooked it's pure hell. An addict may be smiling on the outside-but inside he's crying — it's a thing that bites and bites."

8. Coping with Depressed Feelings

Now that we have completed our inquiry into the nature of depressed moods and states, it is time to ask what you can do about them. What steps can you take to help reduce the risk of becoming depressed? And, how can you cope with depressed feelings when they occur? In addressing these questions, we are going to first look at what a person can do to deal with his or her own depressed feelings. Next, we will look at the way family and friends can help. Then, we will look at what mental health professionals may offer in the way of medicine, psychotherapy and other treatments. Finally, we will examine some alternative medicine approaches that appear promising.

When we discuss self-help in preventing depression, we are largely talking about gaining increased control over your life. To move in this direction may require both changes in thought patterns or mind-sets and changes in behavior. In this process you should begin to view life in more positive terms, to recognize that you can bring changes into your life, and that your efforts can make a difference in the way you feel.

If you have read my book *Coping with Stress: Common-sense Strategies*, you will probably notice some overlap with the ideas and suggestions that will be offered in this chapter. This is almost inevitable because stress and depression are closely linked. An action that may be helpful in the control of stress may also be helpful in coping with depression.

Setting Rewarding and Reachable Goals

In looking at some of the ways you can gain more control over your life, let's begin with the question of setting rewarding, yet reachable goals. Consider these questions: Do you have goals for the near future–for the next weeks or months? Do you have longer range goals—for the years ahead? Take a few moments and try spelling out what you would like to accomplish, both in the near term and in the more distant future. Now consider, are these reasonable goals, things that you have a decent chance of achieving? If they are, fine. But if they seem unrealistic, where does that leave you? You may be setting yourself up for more failure and disappointment, which may lead to the question, "What's wrong with me?" The result may be a further erosion of self-esteem.

A woman came to see me in therapy. She was 45 years old. She had average ability. Her college grades had been mostly Cs. She told me she was thinking about applying to law school. Realistically, the chances are that she would have a hard time both getting into and through a law school and would be pushing 50 if and when she got her degree. Further, it is questionable how competitive she would be in the job market at that point. One doesn't like to discourage aspirations, but if she had chosen a more attainable goal, it would have increased the chances of her experiencing success rather than disappointment.

There is a wonderful song in the musical *The Man of La Mancha* called "The Impossible Dream." You may remember both the song and the play, based upon Cervantes's story of Don Quixote. The lyrics of the song speak about reaching unreachable goals. Now, there are people who are made of sturdy enough stuff to try this, who can tolerate endless frustrations in the search of deeply rooted ambitions. One thinks of artists like Van Gogh, who painted masterpieces that no one would buy, actors who lived from hand-to-mouth while trying to make it on the stage or the minor league baseball player who couldn't make it into the big leagues, but never quit trying.

I have always encouraged patients who believe that they have the talent to do something to go ahead and give their dreams their best shot so they will not spend life wondering what they might have been. But I also advise them to keep a dash of realism — not to end up tilting at windmills like Don Quixote.

While unrealistic goals can lead to disappointment and depressed reactions, the extreme alternative of setting goals that are very low, unchallenging and raise little risk, can also lead to a life of frustration and unrealized potential. A life of self-selected mediocrity can be bitter and depressing.

There are, of course, many reasons that people aren't able to do things that challenge them and afford them the opportunity to develop their full potential. Job openings may not be available. The person may lack education or economic resources, or be burdened by heavy responsibilities for the care of family members. However, for many people, selecting a restrictive lifestyle is a result of psychological factors. Fear of failure and taking risks has kept many people locked into situations that offer little fulfillment. The result is often dependency, frustration and depressed mood.

Goal setting that is unrealistic on the one side or unchallenging on the other raises the potential for problems. Ideally, when we set goals, we would like them to be desirable, challenging, yet attainable. It should be not only what we want to achieve, but the sort of things that our talents, resources and personal characteristics give us a reasonable chance of bringing to fruition.

Clearly, some self-evaluation is required in goal setting. There are important questions to consider. What are the things you really want? What things do you do best? What are your weaknesses? Do you have the patience and persistence necessary to follow through to achieve what you want? Do you have problems like fear of failure or difficulties in asserting yourself that might interfere with reaching your goals? If such issues are troublesome for you, perhaps you may want to discuss them with a counselor or therapist.

Analysis of the goals themselves and what is necessary to achieve them is also important. Consider career decisions as an example. Do you know the kinds of training that are necessary to get into the type of work that you would like to do? Do you know what future job opportunities are likely to exist in this line of work?

When you think about career goals, you might want to research such questions. It may be helpful to talk to people who are working in the field. Also, look over the resources in the public library. Ask the librarian for *The Occupational Outlook Handbook* which is loaded with information. If you are unsure about your aptitudes and interests, you may find it useful to call the counseling center at your local college or university. They may offer vocational counseling and have interesting tests to help you more objectively evaluate yourself.

Taking a Look at Where You Are

If you have been feeling depressed, chances are that you could profit from making a general reassessment of what's going on in your life. I have to introduce a word of caution, here, because people who are depressed tend to put a negative spin on their situations, viewing their lives more pessimistically than is often warranted. So, in making an assessment, it is prudent to talk things over with people who you have confidence in — people who can react to your ideas and offer another perspective. Consider a minister, a counselor, a therapist, someone whom you trust and feel comfortable with. Listening to the reactions of another person is helpful for most people and can be particularly important if you are prone to depression.

The idea in this assessment is to identify what is going right in your life and what is not. Ask yourself what are the things that bring satisfaction to your life and what are the sources of stress and unhappiness. This task is something like taking personal inventory, but it is also a beginning of diagnosis. Your objective is to determine where it is desirable to make changes in what you are doing.

Be specific in your thinking. If you say, "I don't like my job," it may be that there are only *some aspects* of your job you don't like. Perhaps it is a co-worker who is giving you a problem or it may be one of your duties that you particularly dislike. When you pinpoint things, it is easier to discuss making possible changes. Remember, people who get depressed have a tendency to overgeneralize. The fact that there are some problems does not mean everything is bad.

Frequently the problem that is upsetting you will be in human relationships. For example, you may find yourself in a situation where you care a great deal about another person, but there are things about that person that you find irritating. Ambivalence — having both positive and negative feelings toward another person — is part of the human experience. Can you pinpoint the negatives, the things that are bothering you? Ask yourself how significant these negatives are in the total context of the person. If they appear to be minor blemishes in a person who is otherwise more than okay, this realization can lead to a change in your thinking. You may conclude that there really isn't a problem, that things are basically all right. Maybe what is needed is a little tolerance and forbearance on your part and these apparently troubling issues will vanish like a puff of smoke. After all, in seeking the company of others and especially a romantic partner, you were not looking for someone who is a clone of yourself. Why not accept and enjoy the differences between you? On the other hand, if these issues that are troubling you are profound, perhaps it is time to begin to think about taking steps to change things.

In pinpointing the things that are upsetting you — the situations that are creating stress in your life — you may look at your environment (your home life, your place of work, your relationships) and you may also look at yourself. Are you doing things now that you would like to be doing differently? Ask yourself, where would you like to see changes in yourself?

Changing Patterns of Thinking

When we talk about changes, we include both changes in thought patterns or mind-sets and changes in behavior. Sometimes just looking at situations differently can make a difference in whether you are likely to feel depressed.

I have discussed research that indicates that the way a person evaluates a situation makes a difference. If you tend to inflate the importance of events, to magnify what is at stake, then you may be setting yourself up for an overreaction. The trick is to be able to distinguish between what is *really important* and what is *not*. If you act as if everything falls in the former category, then be prepared to ride on an emotional roller coaster and have your self-esteem beaten down like a rug at spring cleaning. When you sense you are about to get riled up over something that is trivial, stop and ask yourself, "What am I doing?" Surely there are enough important things in your life to be concerned about without going bonkers over things that don't really matter.

A woman with a teenage son developed an acrimonious relationship with him, putting both of them under a lot of unnecessary stress by making repeated issues out of such things as the way he decorated his room with rock star posters, the way he dressed and the way he sometimes procrastinated in doing chores like mowing the lawn. The relationship would have been a lot smoother had she acknowledged that the important things in his life were going well-he got good grades in school, stayed clear of drugs and had many friends. What the mother needed was a larger measure of tolerance, an understanding that other people can do things in a different manner from her and her world will not fall apart.

I have also mentioned being hung up on comparisons with other people as a thinking pattern that promotes depression. One of my favorite examples of these comparison traps is a patient who came to see me who was the operator of a photocopy business. The man had practically no formal education. He worked very hard in his business, putting in long hours, and made an excellent income. I thought he had done very well, having started and successfully run a small business. When I ventured this opinion to him, he shook his head forlornly and replied that he was a failure. In explaining his feelings, he told me about a man who had a similar business three blocks away. It was a larger, more attractive shop that offered more services and had more machines. The other shop was doing more business and making more money than my patient's shop and he felt demoralized by this.

We grow up in a world of comparisons. As children and adolescents we are defined by others as being bigger or smaller or smarter or not so smart or more attractive or less attractive, and so on. While such comparisons are inevitable in the way we are raised, it does not mean that we have to bound by such notions in our adult thinking and live this way. There is an alternative approach. This approach is to carefully define your own goals—goals that are desirable and attainable for yourself—and go after them. The measure of your success is the extent to which you attain your goals. What other people decide to seek in life is their concern, and need not be a gauge for your own evaluation of success.

If you measure yourself against what everyone else is doing, it's almost impossible to win. If you have your own goals in life and meet them, you can feel you are doing what you want and can experience a sense of satisfaction. It's all in the way you define success. My patient's attitude was self-defeating. Even if he had owned the larger of the two photocopy shops, there would always be someone else who had a larger one.

In discussing thinking patterns that need changing, let's recall another source of difficulty: perfectionist thinking. Do you have this tendency? Here are a few signs:

You are chronically dissatisfied.
Nothing is ever good enough to please you.
Things have to be ordered just so-nothing can be out of place.
Everything has to be done on time.

Your house and yard must look like a museum.

You find faults with everybody.

You obsess about the quality of your work.

You seldom finish anything because "it isn't good enough." Your motto is, "Don't do anything unless you can do it right."

People tell you that you are a nitpicker.

If you find yourself nodding your head and saying, "That's me, all right," you have a problem.[1] What can you do about it? As a beginning, try to recognize these patterns in your thoughts and behavior when they occur. Recognition of a tendency toward perfectionism is an important step in doing something about it. Then take a good look at your behavior, or better yet, what such behavior is doing to you and the other people in your life. As you reflect on this, you will probably find that your perfectionistic standards are interfering with your ability to get things done and with your feelings of satisfaction from what you are doing. It is also turning off other people and causing them problems.

This may be a hard idea to accept and you could be inclined to argue, "Well, isn't it important to do things well?" The answer is sure. Making a solid effort and turning out high-quality work are very important values. To be hung up on an error-free existence, however, is something else, a burden one would not wish on anyone. If you are a perfectionist, loosen the screws on yourself and others. Try being more tolerant and less critical. See if you and everyone else are not a little more relaxed and a lot happier as a result.

Reinforce Yourself Instead of Kicking Yourself

We could title this section, "give yourself a break." Many people who become depressed are much more inclined to get down on themselves for making mistakes than to pat themselves on the back for doing something well. It is something like a football game where the fans boo when you fumble the ball but don't cheer when you score a touchdown. Consider this: positive reinforcement builds up self-esteem, nonconstructive criticism tears it down.

When you do something well, tell yourself that you "did OK." When you accomplish something that you've wanted to do, smile and give yourself some credit. When you've done something especially satisfying, how about going out and celebrating? Do something you really like or buy something you've always wanted. How about that new sweater or jacket? It will help you move away from the idea that life is nothing but a series of negatives.

A psychologist, E. M. Heiby[2] developed a measure that assesses the frequency of self reinforcement. Not surprisingly, researchers have found an association between low scores on this measure and symptoms of depression.[3]

Reinforcing yourself is one of the ways of moving toward a more optimistic perspective about your life. Another mind-set that will help nudge you in this direction is to give yourself the benefit of the doubt when something goes wrong. When things go awry, too often depression prone people look inwardly and stop there. The conclusion may be almost automatic, "It's my fault."

The conclusion may be true, it may be partly true or it may not be true at all. We live in a complex world where cause and effect is seldom very clear. How many things are *totally* under your control? Not many, if you think about it. You depend on other people to do things in a very interrelated society. When someone else fails to come through, it may affect your ability to do what you're trying to do. What do you do when someone else screws up? Or consider all the uncontrollables in life. Can you control traffic, the weather, catching a virus, your boss's temperament, the state of the job market? If something goes wrong, there may be some very good reasons for what happened other then something you did. Let's suppose you did make a mistake on something. Before overreacting and lapsing into a sea of gloom, ask yourself these questions: Do you know anyone who doesn't make mistakes? Is the mistake you made catastrophic? The answer is likely to be no to both questions. So, pick up the pieces and move on.

When you do have negative experiences, it is vital that you do not overgeneralize. As we have indicated, many people who become depressed have a tendency to turn negative experiences into calamities. In contrast, the person who remains emotionally intact often finds a way to shrug it off. Her reaction may be, "C'est la vie," or "So what?" She limits the impact. She does not get down on herself; rather, she searches for the next opportunity, recognizing that success is likely to come only if she keeps trying. The person who resists depression may not only brush aside the negative experience but downgrade its importance. Defense mechanisms rationalize failures away. This may seem unrealistic, but it offers protection. While you may not always be able to put the best face on a negative experience, to avoid becoming depressed try not to put the worst face on it. It helps if you keep your sense of perspective and don't overgeneralize.

Changes in Behavior

Changing attitudes and thought patterns are important steps in protecting oneself against the onset of depressive episodes. Equally important are changes in behavior. In your assessment of things that you would like to do differently, you probably spelled out some specific changes you would like to make. Let's talk about getting started.

One way of approaching change is to adopt a strategy of small wins.[4] This strategy recognizes that you can't do everything at once, and to try too much too soon can set you up for more experience of failure. If you've been depressed, you don't need any more of that. In a strategy of small wins, you begin with a defined goal and start taking steps toward realizing it. When you've taken a step in the right direction and experienced some success—"a small win"—reinforce yourself.

A woman who was feeling depressed came to see me. She reported that one of her biggest problems was feeling lonely. Too many nights she had nothing to do and no one to see. The weekends were particularly depressing. After a few therapy sessions, she agreed to join a club where she would have an opportunity to meet people. Finding out about clubs and organizations that might interest her was an important first step. She did this by looking through the notices posted at her public library. As she was an outdoors-type person, she chose a local hiking club that went on outings on the weekends. She called the number listed on the notice and with some anxiety attended her first meeting. She found that the people were nice and she enjoyed the walks. On her third outing, she met an interesting man and began dating him. She wasn't sure whether the relationship would pan out, but she is making friends and her loneliness is fading. My patient told me that at each step toward becoming more involved in the club, she felt a little anxious. There is a certain amount of risk involved in starting new undertakings. But risk taking is necessary if you are going to make changes. And if you are depressed, changes are usually necessary.

A careful, step-by-step approach minimizes risks and anxiety that might be aroused. A strategy of small wins builds confidence and provides the opportunity for larger successes. My patient who joined the hiking club experienced some stress in the process of becoming a member and making friends. Going through this discomfort was necessary to attain an important objective-dealing with her loneliness. Many people who are prone to depression already have too many stressors in their lives, stressors they can't handle, so care and timing are important when a person who is depressed contemplates adding new activities. But these steps are important as they can rebuild confidence and rekindle hope, both of which are important psychological bulworks against depression. A poet once put it well, "Each forward step we take we leave some phantom of ourselves behind."[5]

Overcoming Resistance to Change

Change is sometimes a difficult thing to bring about. You'll often find resistance to making needed changes both in yourself and in others. I mentioned that change involves taking risks. The anticipation of risks elicits anxiety, and anxiety can be very uncomfortable. An all-too-easy way to terminate anxiety is to call a halt to what you are planning to do. Of course, that leaves you right where you started from, in a malaise.

You might use rationalizations to prop up a decision not to carry your plan through. Can you hear the inner voice, "I didn't really want to do that anyway. Besides, it wouldn't have worked." People who are depressed often have a negative perspective and it is very easy to convince themselves that anything they try won't work. After all, hasn't their history been one of failure? Why should they expect anything different?

It can be very hard to break through a demoralized attitude. Encouragement from family and friends can be helpful and so can the actions of an energizing therapist. Still, the bottom line comes down to the person who is feeling depressed. If you want to feel better, you have to start doing things. Reading books such as this is an indication that you want to make changes and is a positive sign that you can. Beginning steps, small wins and confidence building are the orders of the day.

Many of the sources of stress that make life difficult involve our relationships with other people. Stress on the job often involves your relationship with your boss or conflicts with other employees. Stress in the home life usually involves other people. And stress in romantic relationships can be an important, and at times, overwhelming concern.

To make changes in the way people interact can be a difficult undertaking. When you express the wish to introduce changes in a relationship, the idea that is generated is, "something is wrong." And if you do not handle the situation adroitly, the other person may then think, "You're accusing me of doing something wrong." This notion can trigger an emotional reaction of defensiveness. You may encounter hurt feelings, avoidance, the silent treatment or indignation. One can almost hear the denials. "I did not! I am not!" The anger that is provoked may lead to retaliation. "You're the one who is at fault." The attempt to reduce stress has only resulted in increased levels of stress.

The possibility of this all-too-familiar scenario is enough to discourage many people from even trying to suggest changes. However, if the current situation is making life unlivable, you have little choice but to try. Diplomacy is often the best bet. One approach is to say something like this: "You know, I've been under a lot of stress. I've been feeling bad and I'm trying to make a few changes to see if it can help. Can you help me in this?" In this context, it makes it a little harder to refuse.

One of the ways to lower resistance in others is to ask for their input, their ideas. If some of the things they suggest make sense to you, incorporate these ideas into an overall package that includes your own ideas. Propose the overall package as a joint plan and see if you and the other party or parties can agree to the plan. A process like this where everyone's ideas are considered seriously, and where an agreement can be reached, has added force and staying power.

Many people who become depressed have problems in asserting themselves, in making known what they want to do and what they don't want to do. Such people often have a hard time in saying no. This reluctance to communicate one's true wishes adds to the difficulty of making needed changes. The alternative of not speaking up, of accepting a bad situation, of course, merely prolongs the situation that help bring on the depressed reaction.

There are books, even courses, on assertiveness training. The goal of assertiveness training is usually to learn how to state your wishes in a clear, convincing manner without being argumentative, and if you don't want to do something, you practice saying no. You learn how to give a simple reason for your decision without becoming bogged down in lengthy explanations, which may only weaken your case. Being able to be assertive when you need to be is an important tool is making the kind of changes you wish to make. If you have a problem being assertive, it is a skill you can learn.

Start with Exercise

When people come to see me and tell me that they are feeling depressed, one of the first things I often recommend is that they start an exercise program. I always ask them to check with their doctors first to be clear about their physical condition and to find out what level of exercise is safe and appropriate — what is well within their capabilities.

Within these guidelines, I don't think it really matters very much what type of exercise you choose, whether it's tennis, riding an indoor bicycle or walking. The latter is usually a safe and satisfying way to begin. Imagine a daily routine that includes a pleasant walk in the park, or along city streets with interesting shops and lots of people, or perhaps a tree lined suburban road. Some people find that just being in a pleasant setting, enjoying the beauties of the natural world is therapeutic. The poet John Keats wrote about immersing oneself in nature when downcast. In his poem, *Ode on Melancholy,* he wrote,

> But when the melancholy fit shall fall
> Sudden from heaven like a weeping cloud,
> That fosters the droop-headed flowers all,
> And hides the green hills in an April shroud;
> Then glut thy sorrow on a morning rose,
> Or on the rainbow of the salt sand-wave,
> Or on the wealth of globed peonies ...

Whether it is a park, a suburban road, or a modern health spa — whatever you prefer as a setting — find a place that's safe and pleasant, then *move*. In a word, exercise is the thing!

The reason I suggest starting an exercise program as a first step in combating depressed feelings is that there is considerable research evidence that indicates that exercise has an antidepressive effect. Three different types of studies have been carried out, all with positive results. The first type of study is a randomized controlled trial in which subjects are assessed for levels of depression, then given various intensities of exercise levels in laboratory settings and assessed for changes in depression. The second type of study is epidemiological in design, in that samples of people in the community are assessed in surveys for self reported exercise levels and levels of depression. The third type of study uses people who are being treated for clinical depression. Once again their self reports of exercise and their levels of depression are assessed, sometimes in longitudinal designs over a period of years.

A recent report of a randomized controlled trial carried out in a laboratory setting found that exercise appeared beneficial in reducing symptoms of depression and that higher levels of exercise were the most beneficial.[6] Community studies generally found a correlation between self reports of exercise and lower levels of reported depression.[7] The same is true for correlational studies of depressed patients.[8] While none of these studies would indicate that exercise is a cure for depression, all of these studies suggest that exercise can be helpful.

Some of the reasons for the beneficial effects of exercise may be physiological, but there are important psychological benefits as well. Among the psychological effects is the fact that you can see that you are accomplishing something and you will make measurable progress in accomplishing more. For example, if you are riding an indoor bicycle, you can ride increasingly longer distances. This can give you a psychological lift. Exercise is a good way to reduce tension. Moreover, exercise tones you up. You feel better, you look better, your wind and stamina are better. You feel more alive.

When you select an exercise program, it is important to choose something you really like to do. Don't start a regimen of doing sit-ups if you hate sit-ups. A pleasant routine of exercise is most likely to be antidepressant.

Look Better, Feel Better

Exercise may help you look better, and for many people, that in itself may make them feel better. Studies have shown that people who feel better about their appearance tend to have brighter psychological outlooks.[9] This is particularly true for adolescents and young adults where appearance is usually highly valued. Body dissatisfaction in young adolescent girls can be predictive of subsequent depressed mood as they transition through adolescence.[10] It's not so much the way a person looks in the eyes of other people that tends to be depressogenic, it's the way one feels about one's self. Looking better in your own eyes is the objective and that is something almost everyone can try to do.

If one is pleased about the way one looks, it can help boost one's confidence and self-esteem. For many people, shaping up to look better can be part of an overall therapeutic plan of behavioral change to cope with depressed feelings. Shaping up may include weight loss, if weight is a problem, and toning up one's body.

Some therapists have suggested to their depressed patients to consider buying new clothes. For many people, an attractive wardrobe has a place in looking better and feeling better about oneself.

Mirror, mirror on the wall.

Who is looking better these days? C'est moi!

Introduction of Pleasant Activities

Could you list five or six activities you really enjoy? Taking walks, going to the movies, swimming, going to a party, listening to music, whatever. Take a few minutes and come up with your own list. All right, how many of these things are you doing now? If you're not doing some of these things, wouldn't it make sense to start? A life with no fun is depressing.

In planning changes in your life, see if it is possible to give a higher priority to these activities. If you can, you will probably find that this will cause a shift in the negative-positive balance in your daily life. You will have more things to look forward to and this is likely to elevate your mood.[11]

In thinking about this idea, try not to put it into a "must-do" framework. These activities should be things you *want to do,* not things you feel you have to do. Viewing such activities as ordered or imposed will only take the joy out of them. Just start doing some of the things you've always liked doing and do them at a pace you find right for you.

Developing Meaningful Social Relationships

Much of what is meaningful and important in life is having friends and loved ones, feeling a sense of connectedness with other people. Many people who report depressed feelings feel lonely. They don't have many friends; they often feel isolated. When things go well, they may not have people with whom to share their good tidings. When things go badly, they may have no one to reach out to.

Social support — the caring and responsiveness of others when one is experiencing difficulties — can be a significant buffer against stress. The support of others can help deflect and mitigate the deleterious effects of stress which for many people may help ward off or at least tone down depressive reactions. People who can count on the support of others during difficult times have an advantage. Indeed, a study carried out on patients being treated for depression in Australia found that more than half of the people studied believed that a lack of social support was instrumental in maintaining their depressive state.[12]

While the perceptions of these patients probably overstates the case, as depression is a complex, multilayered phenomenon, there is little doubt that being able to talk to people whom you feel are accepting and understanding is an asset in dealing with a range of mental and emotional difficulties, and this certainly includes both anxiety and depressive disorders. Studies carried out in such disparate countries as the United Kingdom, Sweden, and Japan suggest that the association between social support and better mental health holds across cultures and may be universal.[13]

Most of us recognize the importance that friends play in our lives and people who are lonely and depressed perhaps appreciate this truth even more keenly. However, many depressed people have had difficulties in building friendships in their lives. They may feel qualms and uncertainties about how to meet new people and make friends however, many of these people have difficulties in building such relationships in their lives.

Making friends is not always easy to do, even when you're young and in school and it probably doesn't get any easier as you find yourself separated from the people you grew up with in an ever-larger and often fragmented society. You might recall the example of my patient who rather systematically examined the notices of community organizations and joined a hiking club. This is certainly a reasonable approach. In metropolitan areas, there are usually plenty of groups like this to choose from. The recreation department in the suburban community in which I live offers classes in activities ranging from archery to yoga. Churches offer social activities. Some community colleges are becoming Mecca's for adults seeking to upgrade their skills and pursue their interests. When you get involved in such activities, you increase the opportunities for making new friends. And, of course making friends through sites provided on the Internet is now an everyday occurrence.

Research indicates that many people who become depressed do not have fluent social skills. They may not present themselves well or feel at ease with other people.[14] This can increase the difficulties of developing satisfying friendships. The point has to be made, however, that social skills, like most other skills, may improve considerably with practice. Isolating oneself to avoid discomfort and discouragement will not afford the opportunity to make this improvement and establish these vital connections.

Some thoughts about making new friends for people who are feeling depressed. When you meet new people, projecting gloom and low self-esteem will probably turn them off. You will probably have more success if you can get out of yourself and the problems that have been consuming you and focus your attention on what other people are saying. There is an added benefit to this. One of the surest ways to make new friends is to be a *good listener.*

If you project the feeling that you are really interested in what the other person is saying, you will find yourself in increasing demand. Think of each person that you meet as a special individual who has a unique story to tell, with experiences and ideas that might be interesting to learn about. If you follow this advice, you might be tempted to ask people a ton of questions. This really isn't necessary. A few general questions are usually enough. And one thing to avoid are pointed questions. Such questions can make people defensive.

At a party, a man asked a woman who taught at a high school experiencing some bad problems, "Isn't it awful working there?" The woman became uncomfortable and soon broke off the conversation. The man might have phrased the question, "How do you like working there?" Chances are the conversation would have continued.

In projecting an attitude that you are interested in what the other person is saying, you will probably find it helpful to maintain some eye contact, to nod your head occasionally to indicate that you are paying attention, and — perhaps most importantly — to remember what the other person is saying so that your comments and reactions reflect this. Referring to names, places and ideas that a person has brought up tells the person that you are really tuned in.

It's easier to make and keep friends if one maintains a latitude of tolerance both towards others and oneself. If you look at almost any individual through a microscope, you can usually find something that is "wrong." As we indicated earlier, perfectionism in the choice of friends is about as useful as perfectionist demands on oneself. One may end up without friends.

The starting point in making friends is the attitude that people are different, most people are interesting and good social relationships can enrich your life. Can some people be irritating and a pain in the neck? You bet! But the alternative to trying to develop lasting friendships is isolation, loneliness and increased risk of depression.

Finding a Support Group for Depression

Social support is not only useful in buffering the effects of stress, it can play a significant role in helping a person move through the recovery process for both physical and emotional illnesses. This idea has been institutionalized into networks of support groups scattered around the country to help people cope with various kinds of disorders. For people experiencing depression and bipolar disorder, the Depression and Bipolar Support Alliance (DBSA) coordinates a grassroots network of more than 1000 support groups. Each group is peer-led, has a professional advisor, and welcomes both people who experience depression and bipolar disorder and their loved ones. DBSA support group meetings provide an opportunity for participants to share their experiences and learn from each other in an atmosphere of mutual acceptance. Contact information for local support groups can be obtained from the Alliance by telephone or from the organization's web site, www.DBSAlliance.org.

Many people who join support groups find that being in the group helps them cope with their depression. Participation in group meetings can play a significant role in helping people with depressive disorders through the illness.

One participant in a support group for depression sponsored by the Depression and Bipolar Support Alliance put the matter succinctly, "These meetings work miracles. They save lives and they give people hope. It's like watching a flower bloom sometimes."[15]

Bibliotherapy: Some Useful Homework

Bibliotherapy is a common-sense idea. If you have some understanding of a problem, you can deal with it more effectively, and what better way to learn about a problem in depth than reading about it. The idea has lead to books and pamphlets about a whole range of physical and emotional disorders, including depression. This book is an example.

Now, a book about a disorder such as depression can range from simply providing information to attempting to directly assist the reader in treating the problem. The present book takes a position somewhere between these points of view; we try to provide both information about depression and ideas that may help in the management of the problem. In no way, however, is this work conceived as a substitute for the professional treatment of depression.

The idea that books and their successors (computer programs) may function as a partial or even complete substitute for face to face professional treatment dates back into the 1980s and probably before. An issue of the *Psychological Bulletin* in 1978 provided a review of self-help behavior therapy manuals.[16]

Two of the earlier books that were written for general readers with the intent of being helpful in a therapeutic context, *Feeling Good* by David Burns and *Control Your Depression* written by Peter Lewinshon and his colleagues have been studied for their possible effectiveness in helping people with depression. The first book presents a cognitive approach to dealing with depression while the later book presents a behavioral approach. We shall discuss these therapeutic approaches to treating depression singly and in combination in a later chapter. Suffice it to say for the moment, that a study carried out by Fred Scogin and his colleagues on a sample of older depressed people showed that reading either of these books over a period of a month was related to decreases in depression measures.[17]

Most of the participants in the study seemed motivated by the task; they reported that they read nearly the entire book assigned to them. While noting the possible benefits of bibliotherapy for depression, the researchers commented that asking people to engage in bibliotherapy on their own (without the backup of trained people) could present both ethical and practical problems.

The potential problems that might ensue by leaving people on their own without the backup of a trained professional has not deterred researchers from developing programmed instruction to help people cope with their depressions. These programs offer computerized versions of cognitive-behavioral therapy. An example of these programs is mood GYM, developed by Australian researchers Kathleen Griffiths and Helen Christensen.[18] The program has been well studied and evaluated and is currently available on the Internet (http://moodgym.anu.edu.au) without cost or restriction. Providing an automated form of cognitive-behavioral therapy, the program has been used both by interested individuals and in Australian schools under the supervision of a teacher. Mood GYM uses five modules and a workbook that contains a series of exercises. The program teaches such skills as cognitive restructuring and assertiveness and self-esteem training. The authors point out the program could be particularly useful in rural areas where there is a scarcity of trained psychotherapists.

What can one expect from bibliotherapy? If you read pamphlets or books which emphasize information, you will probably become a lot more knowledgeable about depression, although this may not translate directly into your feeling less depressed.[19] A recent study carried out in Germany, however, did suggest that knowledge about depression might help lessen the chances of recurrence of the disorder, so this is still an open question.[20] The computer programs which try to influence perceptions and behaviors which promote depression seem more likely to have a direct impact on depressive symptoms. A review of evaluation studies conducted on several of these programs concluded that they were helpful.[21] There is a caveat, however. The user must take the task seriously, following through on the tasks presented. A dilettante approach to using these programs is likely to yield little or nothing in the way of benefits. Also, one must keep in mind the possibility of problems arising, if one proceeds on this task, alone, and without any knowledgeable backup.

Maintaining a Good Balance in Your Life

We have discussed adding more pleasant experiences in your life and increasing your social activities. These steps are likely to have an antidepressant effect. Implicit in this advice is the notion that all of us have a kind of optimal balance point in our lives—a balance between our various needs—whether the needs be for love and affection, for being with friends, for creative activities, to work on a job, to spend time with children, to exercise, or to spend quiet time alone or in religious observances. Each person's balance of activities is different, depending on how strong one's needs are in different areas. Regardless of the nature of our activities, it is important to try to maintain our different activities at levels that keep us reasonably close to our optimal balance.

Putting all one's eggs into a single basket and letting everything else go is a recipe for emotional distress for many people. If you live for your work or for that passionate love affair, you are putting yourself at risk if something goes wrong. Ask yourself, "If things go badly, what will you have left?" If you take some pains to keep a balance of meaningful activities in your life, you should have a cushion if disappointments happen in one area of your life, a cushion that will help sustain you while you try to fix the things that have gone wrong.

Maintaining a balance in activities helps keep good things happening in life and guards against developing a victim or martyr mentality, which may happen when one is consumed by a single, overriding role in life. When there is more in your life that is gratifying, the chances of experiencing overwhelming disappointment and depression are less. So, set a proper balance for your activities and try not to get too far away from it. If you find yourself becoming too one-sided in your behavior, take steps to bring yourself back to the balance of activities that works best for you.

To briefly recapitulate, the self-help plan I have outlined consists of a number of interrelated ideas. These ideas include (1) setting reasonable but satisfying goals, (2) examining the pattern of your daily activities to identify sources of satisfaction and stress-provoking situations, (3) recognizing maladaptive thought patterns which promote problems, and changing these to patterns that promote more positive emotional health, (4) making changes in your life to increase your level of satisfaction, and (5) creating a more optimal balance among your daily activities.

The types of actions I propose are drawn from research and clinical experience and are not unique to this writer. Similar ideas for ways of better handling the pressures of daily life have been advanced by other writers. For example, an article by Donald Jewell and Maureen Mylander is very much along these lines.[22]

What I am suggesting represents movement toward a more problem solving approach to life. Remember that people who become depressed often react in dysfunctional ways, such as catastrophizing situations. These dysfunctional responses can be steps on the path to depression. A path away from depression requires a different approach, beginning with a careful examination of what has gotten you into trouble and then taking steps to move in new and more constructive directions.

Dr. Arthur Nezu and his colleagues used a problem solving approach in successfully treating depressed patients. They believed, as I do, that it is important to help depressed individuals identify the situations that are causing, or have caused, stress in their lives and to increase the patient's effectiveness in coping with these situations. They developed an interesting program that teaches problem solving skills to patients to help them deal more effectively with future problems. [23]

James Mahalik and Dennis Kivlighan raised the interesting question of what sorts of persons are likely to profit from using self-help manuals for depression. They carried out a study on mildly depressed students using a self-help manual that laid out a seven-week therapeutic program. The researchers also gave the students personality tests. The investigators found that persons who were "realistic types" seemed to benefit more from the program. The researchers also suggested that persons, "who persevere in situations that are challenging and require effort succeed in self-help programs that ask its user to go it alone."[24]

Having said this, there is generally little reason for people to try to work their way through a depression on their own. Support groups for people with depression are widely available as well as professional help. The self help strategies that we have described here may well work better in the context of this support.

9. Some Counsel for the Family and Friends of a Depressed Person

In earlier chapters, I discussed how family and friends can be the sources of stress that trigger a depressive reaction. Paradoxically, we also saw how family and friends can be a buffer, helping to shield a vulnerable person from experiencing a depressive reaction. Let's see if we can unravel this seeming contradiction.

Difficulties in interpersonal relationships are among the more significant stressors that we encounter. These stressors may arise in a parent-child relationship where the child suffers at the hands of an unaffectionate, neglectful or abusive parent. Sometimes, the shoe may be on the other foot. Consider the stresses generated in parents whose teenage children become involved in drugs or delinquency. The stresses of romantic love with its passions, disappointments and breakups sometimes are overwhelming. The stresses of a bad marriage can lead to an emotional debacle for both parties.

When relationships are destructive, they are part of the problem in depression. When they are not, they are part of the solution. Fortunately, most of us have relationships that have a lot of good in them. We are not talking about perfect relationships; we are talking about relationships where there are *positive bonds,* and whatever difficulties exist are manageable. Perhaps the critical factors are a *feeling of belongingness* — a feeling that these are my people — and a *sense of support* — a sense of assurance that they are here for me in times of trouble.

The concept of bonds is basic to human security. Remember the attachment that infants develop as a basis for beginning their explorations of the unknown environments about them. The need to be related to others remains with us in varying degrees for the rest of our days. People who have close, positive relationships tend to be happier and healthier. Married people are more likely to live longer than single people. If good relationships are a prophylaxis for depression, the question becomes, "How can we best utilize such relation-ships to assist those who are vulnerable to depressive problems?" Or put very simply, "How can family members or good friends help?"

The first key to being helpful is to understand. Understanding begins with being knowledgeable about depression. Here is a brief checklist of some impor-tant things to keep in mind about depression.

1. Remember the symptoms of depression. Understand the difference between transitory depressed mood and depressive disorder. If depressed symptoms *persist*, there is a problem that needs attention.
2. Remember that there are different types of depression. While most depressions are unipolar, some people have bipolar disorder. The symptoms of bipolar disorder are different and the treatment is different.
3. Keep in mind that depression often has a genetic basis. Some people have inherited vulnerabilities and are more likely to react with depression than others. Remember that the mechanisms for depression are in part biological, including disturbances in the action of the neurotransmitters in the brain.
4. Remember that stressors often trigger depression.
5. Keep in mind that support from friends and loved ones is very good medicine for depression.

Knowledge about depression is most useful when it is translated into *alert-ness* that there is a problem in your family or with your friends and that some-thing needs to be done. When you recognize very clear signs of depression in persons close to you, it may prove helpful if you can find out what mental health resources are available in your community so you can offer reasoned advice when the opportunity seems appropriate. Find out about the availabil-ity of psychiatrists, psychologists, clinical social workers, mental health clinics and depression support groups.

When things are clearly going wrong, you can suggest going for a profes-sional consultation, perhaps starting with the family doctor. If the troubled person feels unsure, consider volunteering to go along with the person. The important thing is that you do whatever you can *reasonably* do to ensure that the person who needs help gets it. If you make a suggestion that someone should consult a professional for a depressive problem, you may well run into resist-ance. You may hear responses like, "I don't need help," or "Nobody can help me, there's nothing anyone can do." These statements may reflect the confu-sion, hopelessness and inertia that are part of the depressive problem.

One approach to dealing with such resistance is to first make it clear that you recognize the pain and suffering that the person is going through and what a difficult problem it is. Try to communicate the idea that, "I understand that you're going through a lot of distress and I want to help." Then, you might state that there are a variety of treatments available that are effective for most people who have depressive problems. Explain that there are different kinds of medicines and short-term psychotherapies that have proven useful. One of these treatments may help him or her feel better.

Alertness on your part as a member of the family or close friend should extend beyond recognizing the need for outside help and suggesting that the person seek it. When a person is severely depressed, alertness also means keeping an eye open for potential signs of self-inflicted harm. The possibility of suicide is a very troubling idea, but you must be aware of it. While no one can predict with any certainty when a seriously depressed person might make a suicidal attempt, there are a number of signs that suggest the possibility of one. Here are three signs that are particularly worrisome.

1. The person expresses feelings of hopelessness. He or she sees the future as bleak and sees, "no way out."
2. The person talks openly about suicide. There may be statements like "I can't stand this pain anymore" or "I won't be around."
3. The person has made a previous suicide attempt.

The first sign suggests a state of thorough demoralization. Charles Neuringer painted a portrait of such demoralization in describing a group of women who threatened suicide after experiencing a personal crisis.

> They felt life to be duller, emptier, and more boring than the other women did. They also seemed less interested and responsive to people and to events than did the other groups. They felt angrier than the other participants; they had less interest in their work and were more dissatisfied with it than were the other women. Their thought processes were experienced as slow and sluggish, which was not true for the other participants. They felt that thinking was a great effort and that their ideas were valueless .... The high-lethality women felt more anxious than the others. They also felt more guilt-ridden and were less self-approving than the other women. Their feelings of inadequacy and helplessness were greater than those of the other participants. They also felt more depressed and weary than the other women.[1]

No matter how careful family and friends try to be, there is always a chance of self-inflicted tragedy. A survey of psychologists revealed that about one-quarter of them had a patient who committed suicide while under their care. The emotional effects of this tragedy on the psychologists were severe. The effects on members of the family can be devastating.

As a general rule, it seems unfair to hold anyone responsible for another person's suicide. A therapist may see a patient for an hour or two a week. Members of the family have a multitude of other responsibilities. It is virtually impossible to prevent a suicide by someone who is determined to carry out the act, unless the person is hospitalized and kept under 24-hour surveillance. The crucial thing would be to know when to hospitalize, and we simply do not have the scientific basis to allow us to know this with certainty.

If a patient exhibits signs of suicide, then family consultation with the attending physician and/or therapist seems warranted. A decision by the patient and the therapist for *voluntary hospitalization* may be in order. Hospitalization would last until the crisis is over and the high risk of suicide has abated.

If there is a high risk of suicide and the patient is unwilling to be hospitalized, a very difficult situation emerges. The options are to live with a high risk or to set into motion the coercive power of the state to hospitalize the patient against his or her will. This can be a very unpleasant dilemma; it is not only a wrenching emotional experience but places one in a briar patch of ethical and legal thorns.

Maverick psychiatrist Thomas Szasz once suggested that it is questionable for mental health professionals to get into the business of suicide prevention, suggesting that, "Forcibly imposed interventions to prevent suicide deprive the patient of liberty and dignity" and "the use of psychiatric coercion to prevent suicide is at once impractical and immoral."[2]

I think one has to recognize that the thought of suicide in depressed people comes near the bottom of a psychological well, probably exacerbated by biological dysregulation. It is not a condition in which one expects to find rational decision making. A few weeks of time and treatment may make the world look very different to the patient. The argument for intervention is to allow this change of attitude to happen.

Learning about depression and community mental health resources, and becoming alert to signs of depression in those who are close to you are constructive steps to take in being of help to loved ones or friends who are experiencing a depressive problem. Recognition of strains and stressors in the home environment is another important area where family members may be particularly helpful. Try to become aware of any environmental problems and interpersonal strains that are exacerbating the stress levels of the patient. If there are chronic hassles in the home situation that are irritating the patient, can something be done to defuse them? Stress-free environments are not reasonable goals, but lowering levels of stress certainly are. If a member of the family is doing something roughly equivalent to beating on a drum all day long, maybe you can do something to stop it. A more peaceful environment may be a good idea for everyone.

It may be a time to look inward, too. Is there anything you might be doing that is exacerbating the problem, something that is causing stress for the patient. Give it some thought. If there is, would it be possible to make some changes?

As a person who is concerned about depression in a friend or loved one, you might have as one of your objectives to increase your *sensitivity* to the concerns, thinking processes and feelings of the person. What this comes down to in large part is better listening, paying attention to what is said and trying to put yourself into the shoes of the other person so you can better understand what is happening. When you do this, the other person will sense that you care and you will have increased understanding of the problem.

In interactions with a depressed family member, The Depression and Bipolar Support Alliance (DBSA) suggests that in times of crisis, not to take a loved one's actions or hurtful words personally or to use phrases like, "snap out of it." As a general guide, DBSA urges patience and respect for the patient's boundaries.[3]

The emphasis on respecting the patient's boundaries strikes me as particularly important because some studies have reported the counterintuitive finding that a family's social support can sometimes have a detrimental impact on people recovering from depression.[4] It is not clear why this is so. It may be that an excess of interactions may lead the depressed person to feel he or she is being forced back into situations and roles that in the past were difficult or confining. I hesitate to use the term "smothering" because I have not seen the evidence to support this idea, but I can well imagine that for some people recovering from depression, too much attention might be as big a problem as too little. In some situations, it can be a difficult judgment call for the patient's family, a delicate balancing act.

If the depressed person is undergoing psychotherapy, the spouse may be asked to come in for one or more sessions. Many therapists like to do this, as it enables them to see the patient's behavior from another perspective. As family problems and particularly marital conflicts can play a role in triggering depressive episodes, it often makes good sense to try to deal with these problems as part of therapy. If these difficulties cannot be resolved to a reasonable degree, the chances are high that there will be further episodes of depression in the future. Interestingly, marital therapy itself, in which the focus is on both parties, can sometimes be as effective in treating depression as therapy focused on the depressed person.[5]

If it becomes clear in therapy that changes are needed in the patient's lifestyle, there may be an opportunity for you to participate in making these changes. For example, exercise usually has antidepressive effects. How about starting a walking or jogging program or some other exercise program on a regular basis with the patient? As we have emphasized, it should be exercise that is approved by the family physician and something you both enjoy.

There may be a need to introduce more pleasant activities into the patient's life. When the time seems right, you can help in arranging that dinner out, that ride in the countryside, that visit with friends or whatever the two of you feel is fun and not too stressful. These activities should be paced into the recovery process as part of a plan to establish a more balanced lifestyle.

As you do these things, it is important to recognize signs of resistance and not to push too hard when you detect them. Go with what works and build on successes. A little praise on your part when there has been progress may help keep things moving along.

The behavior of depressed persons turns off many people; the sad expression, the tears, the stream of self-deprecatory comment, the pessimism and hopelessness can be difficult to take. There will be times when you may be tempted to throw in the towel and give up trying to help. Try not to do that. Remember, most people who are depressed usually get better. Some people get better even without medication or therapy. Moreover, drugs and psychotherapy are both proven means of helping patients overcome episodes of depression. It is important to keep in mind that even when things look bleakest, the odds for most people are that the symptoms will abate and the afflicted individual will become a good deal better.

While not giving up is the marching order of the day, the spouse and children of a depressed person may have to take steps to protect their own mental health during the depressive episode. Living with a person who is depressed can be very difficult. Studies of the families of depressed patients have found that family members are likely to encounter a variety of difficulties stemming from the depressive illness. Family members may experience restrictions in social and recreational activities, a tightening of the family budget and interpersonal strains.[6] The patient's spouse may not know how to cope with a husband or wife who may be withdrawn and sad and sometimes says things which are unkind. Many spouses worry about their husbands' and wives' conditions. Will they get better? What will the future be like? Spouses may find their lives burdened by having to take on extra responsibilities in the home and in child care. And the children, themselves may shows signs of stress. They may become more difficult, do less well in school or have problems sleeping. It can be a big load for the spouse, and if the depressive episode is protracted, it is little wonder that the spouses of depressed patients often develop emotional problems and frequently show signs of depression, themselves. In carrying out research on persons living with depressed individuals, James Coyne and his colleagues observed, "Overall, 40 percent of the respondents living with a depressed person in the midst of an episode were sufficiently distressed themselves to meet the criterion for needing psychological intervention."[7] Subsequent studies have confirmed the tendency for the spouse of depressed patients to develop depressive symptoms.[8] With this kind of risk, it is prudent for the spouse and children to do things to protect themselves from being overwhelmed by the problem.

Some obvious suggestions are getting away from the house at times, and doing things that the individuals enjoy. Perhaps it is spending time with friends, going for a walk, or taking in a movie. The objectives are to keep one's own routines as normal as possible during the illness and to divert oneself from the problem to keep it from reaching overwhelming proportions. You can't help the distressed member of the family if you are going under yourself. Caretakers need a safety valve too: few people are emotionally indestructible.

If there are young children in the family, the intact spouse has the responsibility of insulating them from the more emotionally destructive effects of the illness. It is not going to do the children any good to spend a lot of time with a parent in the depths of a depressive episode. Try to find things for the children to do when things are bad. Look for means of getting them out of harm's way. When the situation improves, the children can be helpful in the recovery.

Perfectionism and guilt are psychological factors that probably contributed to the depression of the patient. Perfectionism and guilt are equally unlikely to benefit the people caring for the patient. It may be helpful to know that at times, the best of therapists make mistakes in their conversations with their patients. They may wish that they had picked up on something the patient had said or responded to the patient somewhat differently. The patient's spouse or caregiver is facing a difficult situation. Trying to be sensitive and patient are important virtues here. But having unrealistic expectations about one's own behavior and feeling guilty about coming up short is not going to help one's self or the depressed patient. It is a case where the old cliché of trying to do the best one can fits very well.

10. Seeking Professional Help: Changing Patterns

I would like to begin this chapter by telling again a story I related in the first edition of this book. The story was a brief account of how a man, Jack, experiencing what was eventually diagnosed as major depressive disorder, found his way into treatment for the disorder.

When Jack's wife, Erica began to notice his symptoms, she didn't know what to make of them. Jack had trouble falling asleep at night. When Erica awoke at night, she saw him lying there wide awake. Sometimes he would get up and pace the floor. In the morning there were circles under his eyes; he looked exhausted. Jack used to be a big eater, but now his appetite had dwindled. Breakfast was no more than coffee and it seemed that he hardly touched his dinner. Jack looked sad and at times he brooded. He complained of headaches and stomach cramps. He said he had no energy to do anything and worse, he didn't seem interested in doing anything. They used to go bowling every Friday night and visit her mother on Sunday. Now he didn't want to do either. And his interest in her sexually had almost disappeared.

Erica knew something was wrong, but didn't know what it was or what to do about it. She confided in her sister Robin, who suggested that Jack see a doctor. When Erica broached the idea to Jack, he resisted it, but she kept at it and finally Jack consulted his physician, Dr. Sutherland. Dr. Sutherland was in the midst of a very busy day. He listened to Jack for a few minutes and thought Jack sounded like a "croc," a patient with lots of complaints without any physical basis for them. Dr. Sutherland ordered some routine lab tests. When all tests proved negative, he suggested that Jack take a few days off from work and see if he felt better. In his brief examination, Dr. Sutherland did not identify the problem for what it was: depression.

Jack's short vacation helped only a little. When he began to have difficulties on his job and wanted more time off, Jack spoke to the counselor in the personnel office at work. She talked with Jack several times, and then recommended that he consult a therapist. She gave him the names of a psychiatrist and a psychologist who had worked with other employees in the company who had emotional problems. Jack was able to get an early appointment with the psychologist. When Jack began therapy he became one of some ten million people who made a visit that year for professional mental health care.

Jack's story took place some time ago. Things have changed since then, and continue to change. Let's pose some questions about the changing patterns of professional care for mental and emotional disorders.

1. You can see that there was a delay between the time Jack first developed symptoms and the time he began to receive treatment for his depressive disorder. Are such delays still common today?

In a recent large-scale interview study, it was found that most people with psychiatric disorders will eventually receive treatment, but delays, sometimes very long delays are not uncommon.[1] People with depressive disorders are more likely to enter treatment sooner than people with anxiety disorders, impulse-control disorders, or substance abuse disorders, but delays in receiving treatment for depression sometimes extend into years rather than weeks or months.

2. Are physicians still the gatekeepers for treatment of depressive disorders?

Yes. While Jack saw his family doctor first, and without success, for many people, perhaps a majority, their primary care physicians facilitates the beginning of treatment for mental and emotional disorders. Not only is the physician's office frequently the entry point for beginning treatment for mood disorders such as depression, the family doctor is frequently the sole provider of treatment. With the rising acceptance of antidepressant drugs, there has been an increasing likelihood that the primary care physician will be the only professional to work with the patient. Recent data suggest that the practice of primary-care physicians treating depression on their own using antidepressant medicines—without referring the patient to a mental health specialist is the most frequent way that depression is treated in America today.[2] It should be stated that such physicians are more likely to treat cases of depression on their own which are less severe.

3. Are primary-care physicians more likely today to recognize and identify depression than they were in Dr. Sutherland's day?

Very likely. There has been considerable education about mental health issues for physicians. One study suggested that primary care physicians identify about two out of three cases of major depression which isn't bad, although this leaves a very large number of people who are missed and may go untreated.[3] The primary care physician is probably more likely to miss the case that is less overtly symptomatic. It is obviously important for the primary care physician to take the time to engage the patient about what is happening in his or her life, if the physician is going to go be able to pick up on less severe depressive symptoms.

4. Do primary care physicians experience roadblocks when they want to refer patients to mental-health specialists?

A recent study reported that this is often the case.[4] Interestingly, pediatricians seem more likely to experience problems in making referrals for their young patients to mental health specialists than primary care physicians who work with older patients.

5. How do primary care physicians and mental health specialists differ in terms of their treatment of depression?

When compared to the time spent with a mental health specialist, the time spent in visits to a primary-care physician for depression is likely to be brief. This difference reflects the fact that mental health specialists schedule extended times (typically, fifty minutes) for their patients while visits to primary care physicians are often considerably shorter. In addition, the primary care physician relies primarily on medications, and is usually not trained to do psychotherapy.

6. As Jack eventually did, can a person who is feeling depressed go to a mental health specialist without referral from a primary care physician?

Usually yes, unless the patient has a medical insurance plan that disallows this. If the individual is in an HMO, he or she may experience difficulties in going to a therapist who is not affiliated with the HMO. Interestingly, the use of psychotherapy alone, without medication has been in decline since the 1990s.[5] In contrast, the use of psychotherapy in conjunction with antidepressant drugs has been on the rise. This is true whether the therapist is a psychiatrist who prescribes the drug or a psychologist or clinical social worker who provides therapy while the family physician typically writes a prescription for antidepressant drugs.

Research suggests that, overall, most people in the United States today who have a mental or emotional disorder are not receiving treatment for the disorder.[6] The situation is probably better for depression because antidepressant medicines have won wide public acceptance and are now routinely dispensed by primary care physicians. Researchers, however, have questioned the adequacy of treatment of depression solely by the primary care physician suggesting that it falls short of what is needed.[7] In particular, for people who are seriously depressed, antidepressant drugs may not be enough. In this context, it is useful to recall the studies linking stress to depression which found that this link weakens over time as the depression reoccurs and the depression tends to occur without stressor-triggers.[8] The inference from these data is that it is important to treat depression thoroughly the first time its surfaces in the hope that this may help prevent recurrences. For many depressed patients, thorough treatment of depression may require more than antidepressant medicines. It may require the insights provided by psychotherapy.

Let's consider some of the typical barriers that people may encounter which can reduce the chances of their receiving fully effective treatment for depression. First and often foremost is the cost of treatment. Psychotherapy is expensive. Insurance plans may limit the number of treatment sessions that the patient may receive and many patients may need more than the stipulated number of visits to adequately address their problems. In addition, a very large number of Americans, perhaps 45 million have no health insurance at all. People who cannot afford to pay for psychotherapy or for that matter repeated visits to a primary care physician may not receive anything close to adequate treatment for their depressive disorder.

The belief that mental and emotional disorders carry with them a stigma has not disappeared from American culture. While this perception is not as strong and widespread as it was years ago, even today many people would not want it known that they are seeing a psychiatrist or a psychologist. In a recent study, a majority of the people surveyed reported that they would still feel at least somewhat embarrassed if other people found out that they were seeking help from a mental health professional.[9] Holding a stigma-related view of mental illness or feeling that others may hold this view would engender reluctance to seek help.

The availability of a competent mental health professional varies from place to place. People who live in urban areas often have a substantial number of mental health professionals to choose from. However, those who live in small towns or rural areas may not have anyone available who could offer such services. Interestingly, research suggests that people experiencing depression who live in rural areas are more likely to find themselves hospitalized for the disorder.[10]

Finally there are cultural factors. The acceptability of seeking professional help for mental and emotional illnesses varies somewhat within the many ethnic strands that make up American society. The studies of David and Stanley Sue, for example, suggested that the stigma associated with mental illness may run higher among Asian Americans then among their Anglo counterparts.[11] Be it cultural factors or economic factors, or both, professional mental health services are underutilized by both African-Americans and Hispanic Americans. Among African-Americans, this is particularly true for the very young and elderly.[12]

The good news is that despite such barriers, increasing numbers of Americans are receiving treatment for mental and emotional disorders and this includes depression.[13] While many people who need treatment for depression still find themselves outside the system of professional care, the trend is in the right direction.

It is now time to turn to a detailed examination of the treatments now being offered by primary care physicians and mental health professionals for depression. We will begin with antidepressant medications.

11. Antidepressant Drugs

Antidepressant medicines are the most widely used treatment, today, for depression. Many millions of prescriptions are written for these drugs each year both in the United States and abroad. For many people antidepressant medicines are the only treatment they will receive for their depressive disorder. Other people will use these drugs in combination with psychotherapy. Antidepressants work well for many depressed people but not for many others. Important as these drugs are for the treatment of depression, they are not a cure for the disorder and at present are far from an invariantly successful treatment for controlling depressive symptoms.

A few preliminary words about our discussion of antidepressant drugs. We will not attempt to offer an exhaustive review of all antidepressant drugs currently on the market, complete with details of the chemistry involved, warnings about all known drug interactions and a complete list of possible side effects. There are a number of excellent references, such as the *Physician's Desk Reference* available in many public libraries which can provide detailed information about individual antidepressant drugs for those who are currently using them or are considering using them. In addition the National Library of Medicine's *Medline Plus* available on the Internet presents very readable concise information for users of specific drugs.

What we shall try to do here is to provide an overview of what antidepressant drugs are all about. We will describe something of the history of how antidepressant drugs were discovered, their presumed mechanisms of action, their efficacy in the treatment of depression, and some cautions about their use.

The discovery that certain drugs may have antidepressant effects has a history of about 50 years. If there is a bottom-line to the story of these drugs, it is that they are not magic bullets. They do not work with the effectiveness of an antibiotic clearing up a bacterial infection. Antidepressant drugs do not cure depression. For many, if not most users, they will probably not eliminate all of the symptoms of depression, and if they do, the effects may not be permanent. Having said this, they can alleviate the symptoms of depression for perhaps half, or somewhat more than that of the people taking them (depending on the studies you look at) and can bring about a remission of symptoms in perhaps a quarter of the users.[1] So, while antidepressant drugs can make an important difference for many depressed patients, they may be of little help for many others.

As a generalization, antidepressant drugs do not vary that much from one to the other in terms of their efficacy in treating depression. In clinical trials comparing antidepressant drugs, one drug is likely to be about as effective as another in relieving depressive symptoms and all of these drugs are likely to show some advantage when compared with a placebo— pills that look like real medicine but contain no active antidepressant ingredients. Interestingly, there have been studies in which antidepressant drugs have not performed better than placebos, but these trials are unlikely to be reported.[2]

While antidepressant medicines do not differ appreciably in their efficacy when compared in sizeable groups of research subjects, some antidepressant medicines are better tolerated than others. They have fewer side effects and hence are easier to live with over extended periods of time. In addition, it is always possible that one type of antidepressant drug might work better for a given individual than another. Switching antidepressants in the hope of achieving better results is not uncommon and research suggests that this can be an effective strategy for many patients.[3] Increasing the dose is another common strategy when no results are obtained. Combining certain antidepressant has also been tried. If none of the above strategies appear promising, then psychotherapy is the best alternative for mild to moderately depressed people. For severely depressed people, hospitalization may be required, and if both medication and psychotherapy fail, electroconvulsive therapy remains a viable option.

The Tricyclics

My description of the discovery of antidepressant drugs is based largely on David Healy's excellent book *The Antidepressant Era*. Judging from Healy's account, the discovery of the first class of antidepressant drugs that entered widespread public use, the tricyclics, was something of a helter-skelter process. After the discovery of the antipsychotic drug, chlorpromazine in 1952, there was renewed interest in looking at the possible uses for other chemically similar compounds. One of these compounds, iminodibenzye, synthesized way back in 1898 and subsequently discarded because there were no apparent uses for it was, so to speak, gathering dust in the basement of the pharmaceutical company, Geigy. In the 1950s it was resurrected for study, but once again no immediate uses were uncovered. The drug was tried on schizophrenic patients. However the effects, if anything, seemed to be adverse. Interestingly, some of the patients given the drug appeared to develop a form of mania. Healy describes how when one of the patients given the drug escaped from a hospital and rode into town on a bicycle in his nightshirt, singing loudly, trial of the drug on schizophrenics was discontinued.

This experience, however, led to the idea that the drug could have an elevating effect on mood. Accordingly, the drug was tried out on 40 depressed patients. For some of the patients the positive effects on mood were dramatic.

One of the central figures in the discovery of the antidepressant effects of the drug which was given the name *imipramine* was a Swiss born psychiatrist named Roland Kuhn. Kuhn gave the drug to several hundred patients and found that for many patients imipramine not only elevated the patients' moods, it had positive effects on their activities and social interactions. The drug also had positive effects on the patients' sleep and appetite. Kuhn described his findings at a meeting in 1958 and his work was reported in an issue of the *American Journal of Psychiatry*. The drug was marketed under the brand name Tofranil.

Imipramine is a tricyclic, so named because of its molecular structure which includes three rings of atoms. Tricyclics are believed to be effective in relieving depressive symptoms because they inhibit the reuptake of the neurotransmitters, norephinepherine and serotonin.[4] Following the release of imipramine, a number of different tricyclics were offered by the pharmaceutical industry to the public. Some examples are amitriptyline, desipramine, nortriptyline, doxepin, protriptyline, and dothiepin. These drugs were effective in relieving depressive symptoms in many depressed patients.

Here is an example of an early study that investigated the efficacy of the initial antidepressant marketed, imipramine.[5] A research team led by James Kocsis wanted to evaluate the effectiveness of this drug in treating depression. For their study they recruited subjects from among adults who sought outpatient treatment for depression at two medical centers, one in New York, the other in Maine. The subjects were screened by psychiatrists to make sure they met the currently established criteria for chronic unipolar depression and had not been on antidepressant medications during the preceding six months.

All patients who were accepted into the study were given placebo tablets for two weeks. These tablets had the same appearance as the imipramine tablets but had no therapeutic action. At the end of two weeks, the patients were randomly assigned either to continue with the placebo or to receive imipramine. In a "double blind" design, neither the patients nor the evaluating psychiatrists knew who had been given the medication and who had been given the placebo.

After six weeks, the patients were reevaluated. The patients who showed a substantial improvement in their depressive symptoms were called "responders." The patients who did not were called "nonresponders." The results: 59 percent of the patients given imipramine and 13 percent of the patients given the placebo were characterized as responders. The study indicated that imipramine can be an effective antidepressant with many patients, though clearly not with all.

The tricyclics have now been well researched. The statistics for efficacy of the tricyclics vary somewhat according to the criteria used in the clinical trials. Some researchers looked at stipulated decreases in scores on the Hamilton rating scale, an observer-based assessment of depression while other researchers used the more stringent criteria, the absence of depressive symptoms—true remission. One would not expect the drugs to show as well using the latter criterion. A review of studies conducted on tricyclics and other antidepressant drugs published in 1999 indicated that about 58 percent of the patients were improved, which is similar to the figure reported by Kocsis and his collegues.[6]

The Trouble with Tricyclics

Tricyclics helped many people who were experiencing depression, but the medications were far from being a magic bullet for the disorder. First, tricyclics did not work for large numbers of people. Second, there is a time lag between first use of the medicine and benefits from taking the drug. It might be a week or as much as a month or even more before the medicine becomes fully effective. For people with mild to moderate depression, this time lag might present little problem. However, for people who are severely depressed, particularly those who are suicidal, weeks of waiting for effective treatment could entail real risks.

The third issue was adverse effects (side effects) from taking the drugs. Most drugs have adverse effects, some occurring infrequently, even rarely, others occurring all too often.

Here are some of the more common side effects of tricycles; dry mouth; blurred vision; constipation; and difficulties with urination.

And there is a long list of less frequent side effects. These include drowsiness, confusion, dizziness, increased heart rate, sexual dysfunction, increased appetite with weight gain, sweating, weakness, nausea, and muscle twitches. For some people, these uncomfortable side effects proved too much of a burden and they simply discontinued the medicine.

Tricyclics have the potential for overdose. The dose needed to obtain a therapeutic effect is fairly close to what can be a toxic dose. Overdosing on these antidepressant drugs was not uncommon. A report in the *Emergency Medicine Journal* noted that overdoses of tricyclic antidepressants are among the most frequent causes of drug poisoning observed in emergency rooms.[7]

Monoamine Oxidase Ihibitors

The second class of antidepressant drugs, monoamine oxidase inhibitors (MAOIs) were developed and marketed in the same general time frame as the tricyclics. As was the case for the tricyclics, the researchers investigating the use of these drugs were not initially looking for an antidepressant. The discovery of the antidepressant effects of these drugs was largely serendipitous.

In his book, Healy traces the discovery of the MAOIs to basic research carried out in England in the late 1920s and early 1930s. Researchers at Cambridge University and other sites discovered an enzyme that was named monoamine oxidase (MAO) that could break down chemicals used in the body now recognized as neurotransmitters. These chemicals included epinephrine, norepinephrine, dopamine and serotonin

This basic research was followed years later by discoveries made by researchers working in the Hoffman-la-Roche laboratories in New Jersey. These researchers synthesized a chemical called *iproniazid* which had the very interesting property of inhibiting the breakdown of these neurotransmitters.

Based on previous research with tuberculosis drugs, this new drug looked as if it might be useful in the treatment of tuberculosis. Accordingly, the drug was given to TB patients to see if it might be useful in healing tuberculosis lesions. What the researchers found that while the drug did have possible usefulness in treating tuberculosis, it also had the effect of elevating the patient's mood and behavior. It looked as if the drug might be an antidepressant.

Studies of the drug were carried out in France and in America. The research of Nate Kline, a professor of psychiatry at Columbia University who also directed the research facility at Rockland State Hospital led him to conclude that use of the drug was associated with remarkable improvements in psychiatric patients. Kline played a pivotal role in bringing the antidepressant effects of MAOIs to public awareness.

MAOIs are believed to impact depression by inhibiting the activity of monoamine oxidase, thus preventing the breakdown of neurotransmitters such as serotonin and norepinephrine. The use of MAOIs would leave more of these neurotransmitters available in the synapses between neurons.

A number of MAOIs have now been developed. These drugs differ in their selectivity of action. For example, one of the newer drugs, moclobemide is more likely to target the form of monoamine oxidase that depletes serotonin.

MAOIs currently approved for the treatment of depression are isocarboxazid, phenelzine, selegiline, and tranylcypromine.

The Trouble with MAOIs

If there are problems with tricyclics, there are still bigger problems with the MAOIs. As a starting point, there is a long list of possible side effects that might occur from the use of these drugs. A Mayo Clinic Internet posting on MAOIs listed a total of 23 possible side effects. However, side effects are just the beginning of the story. The biggest concern for many people using MAOIs are possible drug interactions, not only with other medicines but with certain foods that they might be accustomed to eating. The users of MAOIs should be very careful what they eat. Eating restricted foods while using MAOIs can precipitate a sharp rise in blood pressure (a hypertensive crisis) that could lead to a stroke.

Here is a *partial* list of foods that should be avoided entirely or restricted in amounts when using MAOIs: Aged cheeses, beer, caffeine in excessive quantities, certain kinds of beans, liver, pickled foods, yeast extracts, and wines. People using MAOIs should consult with their physicians to be certain that they are fully aware of what foods and drinks they should avoid completely and what foods and drinks they should restrict in quantity. Accurate information is the first line of defense.

Among the medications one should avoid while using MAOIs are over-the-counter decongestants, other antidepressants, and the herbal, St. John's wort. It is always a good idea for MAOIs users to check with their physician or pharmacist before using any new prescribed or over-the-counter medicine.

Here is some good news for people using MAOIs. The Food and Drug Administration has approved a new means of administering the MAOI, Selegiline (trade name Emsam).[8] Instead of using a pill, the drug is absorbed through the skin into the bloodstream by means of a three layered transdermal patch. Using the patch rather than the pill reduces the risks of the drug interacting with food. The FDA notes that for the lowest dose of the drug (6 mg for 24 hours), the drug can be used without the usual dietary restrictions for MAOIs. Currently, the FDA advises patients who require higher doses of the drug to continue to observe the usual dietary restraints. The cautions for interactions with other drugs were not altered in the FDA release. The FDA noted that using the patch may produce some redness on the skin.

Studies suggest that the MAOIs, phenelzine and tranylcypromine are particularly effective in the treatment of atypical depression — depression that is characterized by such behaviors as oversleeping and overeating.[9]

Selective Serotonin Reuptake Inhibitors

When the antidepressant properties of the tricyclics and MAOIs were first uncovered, there was some skepticism expressed in the pharmaceutical companies developing these drugs that there really was a sizeable market for antidepressant drugs. Whatever remained of such skepticism must have vanished like a puff of smoke into a bright blue sky when the selective serotonin uptake inhibitor fluoxetine was released. Marketed under the brand name *Prozac*, the drug skyrocketed into public awareness. The name Prozac became part of everyday language.

Prozac was licensed in the United States in 1987. However, it was not the first of the SSSRIs to be marketed. I believe that the honor belongs to Fluvox-amine (trade name Luvox), marketed by Luvox-Faverin in Europe in 1983. Still, it was Prozac developed by David Wong and his colleagues at Eli Lily that got the ink. Peter Kramer's best-selling book *Listening to Prozac* and an appearance of the drug on the cover of Newsweek help make Prozac part of the popular culture.

After the success of Prozac, a number of other SSRIs were developed and approved by the Food and Drug Administration. The list includes citalopram (e.g., trade name Celexa), escitalopram (e.g., trade name Lexapro), paroxetine (e.g., trade name, Paxil) and sertraline (e.g., trade name, Zoloft). Why the pop-ularity of the SSRIs? Was it simply a matter of media hype or were these drugs actually more efficacious and better tolerated than the tricyclics?

A meta-analysis of randomized controlled trials involving over 10,000 patients found no overall difference in the effectiveness of the two classes of drugs. And if anything, the studies suggested that the tricycles were more effec-tive for hospitalized, presumably more seriously depressed patients.[10]

For an illustrative study investigating the efficacy of SSRIs, consider this study of the SSRI, citalopram. Over two thousand outpatients in both psychi-atric and primary care settings were given the drug. After using the drug for approximately eight weeks, the researchers reported a response rate of 49 per-cent, with remission rates of about half that.[11]

Based on such reports, the edge for the SSRIs over the tricyclics is not efficacy. Rather, it is that for many people, they are better tolerated than the tricyclics. The reports of adverse affects in the randomized controlled trials are not as high as for the tricyclics, and people using these drugs are less likely to discontinue use of the drug than is the case for the tricyclics.[12] The same patterns have been reported for patients seen by primary care physi-cians.[13]

Does this mean that SSRIs are free from side effects? No. Far from it. The use of SSRIs are linked to a number of complaints such as nausea, drowsiness, insomnia and anxiety.

Many of the antidepressant drugs can have adverse effects on sexual desire, performance, and satisfaction. Among the antidepressant drugs, the SSRIs prob-ably have the most notorious reputation for engendering these effects. While the statistics vary somewhat from study to study, the frequency with which these effects are reported tend to be uncomfortably high. A study carried out in the United States on men and women questioned in primary care clinics found that adverse effects for sexual behavior were reported by about 40 per-cent of those using SSRIs. The figures for a similar study carried out in Spain were even higher, in the 60 percent range.[14] For a great many people sex is a very big part of life, so these side effects can be a big problem. Many of the peo-ple questioned in the study carried out in Spain said as much.

Some cautionary notes about the use of SSRIs.

1. SSRIs have been linked to reports of suicidal thinking in children and adolescents. Although it is not yet clear that SSRIs actually cause suicidal thinking in children, as a precautionary note the Food and Drug Administration has ordered warning boxes on SSRIs informing people about this possibility.[15]
2. The use of SSRIs during pregnancy remains somewhat controversial. These drugs can cross the placenta and have the potential to affect the developing child. Some recent studies, however, have reported that using SSRIs during pregnancy did not lead to an increase in major deformities in the baby.[16]
3. One of the rare effects of SSRIs is to cause bleeding. People who have a bleeding disorder should notify their physicians before taking these antidepressant medications.[17]
4. When discontinuing an SSRI, it is important to check with your prescribing physician. Abrupt discontinuation of an SSRI can precipitate a variety of unpleasant symptoms such as agitation and insomnia which may persist for a few weeks or even longer.

Perhaps a summary statement for the SSRIs would be that they are effective in reducing depressive symptoms for many (roughly half, perhaps more, once again depending on the studies one looks at) of the people who use them, are better tolerated than the first generation of anti-depressants, the tricyclics, have some adverse effects, particularly on sexual behaviors which for many people can be a particularly significant problem.

The Newer Antidepressants

While serotonin has been the major target for antidepressant drug research, the neurotransmitters norepinephrine and dopamine have always been good secondary targets. And, indeed drugs which inhibit the reuptake of these neurotraansmitters have been shown to be effective in treating depression. Bupropion (trade name, e.g., Wellbutrin) which inhibits the reuptake of both norepinephrine and dopamine is now in very wide use, with prescriptions numbering in the many millions. One of the biggest advantages of bupropion is that it is far less likely to cause sexual dysfunction than the SSRIs. To treat sexual dysfunction caused by other antidepressants, some physicians will substitute bupropion for these drugs or simply add bupropion to the current antidepressant.[18]

Serotonin, Norepinephrine Reuptake Inhibitors

Venlafaxine (brand name Effexor) and duloxetine (brand name Cymbalta) are two of the drugs called SNRIs which act to inhibit the reptake of both norepinephrine and serotonin. Duloxetine has only recently been approved by the Food and Drug Administration (2004) so there is less experience for the use of the drug in everyday clinical practice than for the SSRIs. In our comments about the SNRIs, it should be understood that these promising drugs are not that far off the shelf, so our remarks will be tentative.

It is not yet clear how the SNRIs compare with the older SSRIs in terms of efficacy. A meta-analysis suggested that the newer SNRIs may have an advantage over both the SSRIs and the tricyclics.[19] However, I have seen studies in which venlafaxine was compared with an SSRI and the two drugs had about the same effect on depression.[20] A recent study found no difference in the efficacy of Duloxetine and the SSRI escitalopram.[21] Clearly, more research is needed to establish whether these newer drugs are more efficacious than the earlier drugs. Still, these drugs look interesting and could provide possible alternatives for people not responding to SSRIs

Both drugs have a range of side effects. Duloxetine, for example, may cause nausea, dizziness and tiredness. The discontinuation of either medicine precipitously could engender problems. Once again, consultation with one's prescribing physician is important.

Medicines for the Treatment of Bipolar Disorder

The pharmacological treatment for bipolar disorder is different from that of unipolar depression. It is not a good idea to treat bipolar disorder with an antidepressant alone, because the antidepressant when used alone may precipitate an episode of mania or hypomania (a less intense form of mania).

Mood stabilizers are used both to control acute episodes of mania and to try to maintain more even mood over the long haul. Of the drugs used to stabilize mood in bipolar illness, the first one that comes to mind is lithium. Lithium is a popular name for the chemicals *lithium carbonate* and *lithium citrate*. Lithium compounds are found in some rocks, in the sea and in sparse quantities in the tissues of plants and animals. As a drug, lithium carbonate is taken orally in the form of a capsule or tablet. Some trade names for lithium carbonate are Eskalith, Lithane and Lithobid.

An Australian physician, John Cade, used lithium successfully as a treatment for mania in the late 1940s, but his work was not fully exploited until many years later. A major problem with lithium was that if the drug were used at too high a dose, it could have very dangerous effects. When the problems relating to drug safety were resolved, the drug was approved by the FDA for psychiatric use and is now in widespread use.

Lithium has been the most commonly used medicine for bipolar disorder. The chemical can be effective in reducing manic episodes. The National Institute of Mental Health's publication *Medications for Mental Illness* notes that while lithium should have some effect within five to fourteen days, it may take considerably longer than that, weeks or even months to fully control the symptoms.[22]

The response of people with bipolar disorder to lithium is variable. For many people with bipolar disorder, lithium works very well in maintaining stable mood; for many others, lithium is helpful but not fully effective in controlling mood swings, and for still others, it may not be helpful at all.

Because the difference between an effective dose of lithium and one which is toxic is not all that large, care must be taken that the patient remains on the proper dose. Periodic blood tests are required to monitor the amount of lithium in the blood. In addition to monitoring lithium levels in the blood, thyroid functioning should be monitored as well.[23]

Lithium has its share of side effects. These include drowsiness, fatigue, weakness, increased thirst, frequent urination, weight gain, and hand tremors. Some of these symptoms may subside with continued use of the drug.

There are additional cautions the lithium user should be aware of. It is important for lithium users to maintain an adequate level of sodium in their blood. Reduced sodium levels can lead to a buildup of lithium in the blood which can lead to toxicity. While most people get plenty of sodium in their normal diets, this could be a concern for people who are using lithium and are also using diuretics or are on restricted sodium diets as part of their treatment for high blood pressure. Situations which could reduce sodium levels such as engaging in vigorous exercise on a hot day, simply living in a hot climate, or experiencing a bout of diarrhea which can be dehydrating pose potential risks for lithium users. These contingencies should be discussed fully with the prescribing physician.

In *Medicines for Mental Illness*, The National Institute of Mental Health noted that, "Doctors either may not recommend lithium or may prescribe it with caution when a person has thyroid, kidney, or heart disorders, epilepsy or brain damage...."[24] Lithium use by pregnant women could increase the risk of congenital malformations in their babies.[25]

So, it should be clear that lithium is not one of those pills that one can take casually and put out of mind. While lithium can help stabilize mood swings and in so doing help people with bipolar disorder experience more normal lives, it is a drug that requires both monitoring by the prescribing physician and knowledge on the part of the user about possible problems.

Because of its unpleasant side effects or because of reasons such as the patients' feeling they don't need the drug anymore, a large number of patients stop using the drug. This could leave many bipolar disorder patients vulnerable to the onset of mood swings. Fortunately, there are other useful drugs to try.

The main alternatives to lithium for stabilizing mood are certain anticonvulsive drugs used to control seizures. Valproic acid (trade name, e.g.,

Depakote) is an anticonvulsant that has been widely used to control bipolar disorder. In *Medications for Mental Illness*, the National Institute of Mental Health noted that valproic acid is as effective as lithium in controlling the disorder and may be superior to lithium in controlling rapid cycling bipolar disorder.[26] Adverse effects that sometimes happen from using the drug include gastrointestinal symptoms, headache, double vision, dizziness, anxiety, and confusion. As there is a possibility that the drug may cause liver dysfunction, liver function tests should be carried out periodically to insure that this problem is not developing. The use of this drug by teenage girls and young women could raise their testosterone levels which could lead to a variety of unpleasant consequences including obesity and amenorrhea.[27]

A second anticonvulsive drug that appears to be effective in controlling episodes of acute mania is lamotrigine (trade name, Lamictal). A third drug in this class recently approved by the Food and Drug Administration for use with bipolar patients is carbamazepine extended-release (trade name, Equerro).

If the use of a mood stabilizer, either lithium or an anticonvulsive proves ineffective in controlling an episode of mania, there is another pharmacological option to try: atypical antipsychotics. Several of these drugs have been approved by the Food and Drug Administration for the treatment of bipolar illness. These include olanzapine (trade name, Zyprexa) quetiapine (trade name Seroquel), risperidone (trade name, Risperdal), aripiprazole (trade name, Abilify), and ziprasidone (trade name, Geodon). Studies of the efficacy of atypical antipsychotics (e.g., olanzapine, quetiapine) indicate that they are effective in reducing manic symptoms.[28]

Possible side effects associated with the use of atypical antipsychotics include weight gain, drowsiness, constipation, dry mouth, blurred vision, and sexual dysfunction. And importantly, the Food and Drug Administration requires all of these drugs to carry a warning label about possible risks for hyperglycemia and diabetes.

So, the prescribing physician has a variety of drugs to select from that can be effective in controlling manic episodes and or maintaining stable moods over time. Finding the best combination of medications to control bipolar disorder is important and requires judicious selection, careful monitoring of the patient, and sometimes switching medications.

As an illustration of the sometimes uncertain road one travels in finding the right medicines, consider the case of Ben, a man in his mid–20s, living in a large Midwestern city. Ben was diagnosed with Type I bipolar disorder. Ben was 15 years old when he had his first episode of manic behavior. His manic symptoms were so florid, bordering on psychotic that his parents decided to hospitalize him. At the hospital he was put on three drugs, a mood stabilizer (valproic acid), an atypical antipsychotic (risperidone), and an antidepressant (fluoxetine). It took about 10 days for the symptoms to begin to abate. When he was discharged from the hospital and returned home, he felt over-medicated, sluggish and occasionally showed symptoms of his disorder. In view of his condition, his parents decided not to send him back to school; instead, they arranged home schooling for him. During this time, he continued using the three medications. His physician decided to switch him from the mood stabilizer, valproic acid to lithium. Ben did not like being on lithium because of its side effects and in time he discontinued all of his medications.

Ben was fortunate in that for a period of several years his bipolar symptoms went into remission and he was able to finish school. Later on, however, he had renewed outbreaks of mania, and he was again put on medications. In time, he tried the mood stabilizer, lamotrigine and the atypical antipsychotic Aripiprazole. Ben found that he tolerated these medicines quite well and was able to live a more normal life. He went to college and now holds a full-time job.

Recent reviews of studies comparing the efficacy of some of the drugs used to treat bipolar disorder (lithium, lamotrigine, valproate semisodium, olanzapine, quetiapine) in preventing relapse of symptoms, concluded that all of these drugs were more effective in preventing relapse than a placebo.[29] However, the use of lithium was more likely to be followed by the patient discontinuing use of the drug because of adverse effects.

As we end this chapter, I think it is fair to conclude that while antidepressant drugs are not a panacea for the treatment of depression, they do represent an important advance in the treatment of the disorder. This conclusion is supported not only by research, but by a vast amount of clinical experience in the use of these drugs in everyday clinical practice. We should close, however, by tempering this conclusion with a few additional words about the use of antidepressant drugs with two special populations— young children and adolescents and pregnant women.

In regard to children and adolescents, there is evidence that the use of antidepressant medications is associated with increased risk of suicidal thinking. The Food and Drug and Administration has issued a black box warning that if young people are given antidepressants, they should be carefully monitored for signs of worsening depression and possible suicide. This is an excellent admonition, but at times it may be unrealistic. The burden of monitoring the child or adolescent will usually fall largely on the parents. Circumstances may render effective monitoring of their child very difficult, if not impossible. The child may live in a single-parent home in which the resident parent has a full time job. In many homes where there is a two parent family, both mother and father may be working. And in the best case, monitoring the thoughts and behavior of an adolescent can be difficult. Because of these difficulties and the attendant risks that antidepressants pose for suicidal thinking, if there are alternative treatments for depression available such as psychotherapy, it makes sense to consider these first.

What happens when a child or adolescent is taken to the family doctor is judged to be depressed and there is no child psychologist available? A pediatrician related a story to me of such a case. He was faced with the dilemma of accepting the risks of increasing the possibility of suicidal ideation by prescribing an antidepressant, or doing nothing which could also result in very serious consequences for the child. It was not a happy choice.

In regard to the use of antidepressant drugs during pregnancy, I would like to pass on some advice offered by the National Institute of Mental Health in the pamphlet *Medicines for Mental Illness.* "Because there is a risk of birth defects with some psychotropic medications during early pregnancy, a woman who is taking such medication and wishes to become pregnant should discuss her plans with her doctor. In general, it is desirable to minimize or avoid the use of medication during early pregnancy. If a woman on medication discovers that she is pregnant, she should contact her doctor immediately. She and her doctor can decide how best to handle her therapy during and following the pregnancy."[30]

12. Psychotherapy

Antidepressant drugs have proved helpful for many people in dealing with depressive problems. However, for some of these people, the side effects of the drugs are quite uncomfortable. Moreover, there are many people who are not helped appreciably by these drugs. Fortunately, there is an alternative approach to the treatment of depression, which is drug free. This approach is psychotherapy.

The evidence to date indicates that psychotherapy can be an effective treatment for mild to moderate unipolar depression. There is, however, still some controversy in regard to the effectiveness of psychotherapy for cases of severe depression.

Drugs act to inhibit the reuptake of neurotransmitters to achieve their effects. Psychotherapy has its impact on thoughts, feelings and behavior. Psychotherapy can have significant effects on a person's attitudes and lifestyle, helping him or her better cope with the interpersonal and environmental stressors that tend to trigger depression. The singular advantage of psychotherapy is that it can teach the patient important things about himself or herself that can be useful in making adaptive changes in perceptions and behaviors.

While almost all of us are familiar with medicines, many people have only a vague idea of what psychotherapy is. One's image of therapy may be something like the cartoon character of a bearded analyst holding a small notebook, sitting behind a patient who is reclining on a couch, listening to the patient talk at length about what is on his or her mind. While this picture may once have been close to the mark, it is not typical today.

The poet Elizabeth Barrett Browning wrote a memorable sonnet that began, "How do I love thee? Let me count the ways." If she had counted as many ways as there are ways of doing psychotherapy today, her brief sonnet would have turned into a multipaged epic.

A few decades ago the choices in psychotherapy consisted of not much more than several varieties of psychoanalysis and client-centered therapy developed by Carl Rogers. How the situation has changed! Let me quote from an article by Alan Kazdin: "Although at any given time it is difficult to pinpoint the precise number of techniques in use, surveys have revealed tremendous growth. In the early 1960s, approximately 60 different types of psychotherapy were identified. By the mid–1970s, more than 130 techniques were delineated.... By the late 1970s, growth continued to encompass more than 250 techniques .... A more recent count has placed the number of existing techniques well over 400.[1] While it has not yet reached the point where there are as many brands of therapy as there are therapists, there is certainly a variety of approaches for a therapist to use. Such diversity creates choices for people who are seeking help. The situation, however, may be confusing.

Let me try to clarify this situation. First, it is important to recognize that most therapies have significant elements in common. For example, most therapists provide a supportive atmosphere for the patient: They are interested in the patient and his or her well being. Also, the relationship that develops between therapist and patient is important in almost all therapies. Moreover, almost all therapies have an effect on the restoration of morale. The patients usually experience a regeneration of hope. They become more enabled and energized and can begin to do things for themselves, which has the effect of rebuilding confidence.

Second, you will find that many therapists are not doctrinaire. They take an eclectic position, picking out what seems to work best for their patients from what is available in the different therapeutic techniques. Moreover, many therapists continue their education after graduate or professional school, learning new, innovative techniques. It may be helpful to briefly describe some of the major approaches to therapy that are being used today to treat depression. Three of the better known and most influential approaches are (1) *psychodynamic therapy,* in which the focus is on intrapsychic conflicts, (2) *cognitive-behavioral therapy,* which focuses on thought processes and behavior and (3) *interpersonal therapy,* which focuses on human relationships.

Psychodynamic Therapy

Psychotherapy as we know it began with Freud and his invention of psychoanalysis. Psychoanalysis is both a complex theory about human personality and a technique for treating emotional disorders, particularly those disorders that have been labeled as neuroses or neurotic behavior. Therapies that draw heavily on Freud's psychoanalytic theories are usually referred to as psychodynamic therapies.

Psychodynamic therapies focus on conflicts within the person. Typically these conflicts have their roots in childhood experiences, and often in parent-child relationships. The roots of these conflicts are not usually accessible to the patient. Much of the troubling material is believed to be out of the patient's awareness, or in Freud's term, *unconscious.* In order to resolve the conflicts that underlie the patient's current symptoms, it is important in psychoanalytic therapies to bring this material into the open. The analyst works with the patient to bring these ideas to light and shows the patient how they relate to her or his current problems.

In classical psychoanalysis, making what is unconscious known is accomplished by such techniques as free association and dream analysis. In free association, the patient speaks about whatever is on her or his mind, trying not to hold back anything or to suppress any idea. The patient's flow of ideas tends to form links with unconscious materials. In dream analysis, free association is used to work back from the dream content to the unconscious materials that are believed to have given shape to the dream. In the procedure, the patient is asked to freely associate to different parts of the dream.

During therapy, the analyst will try to stay in the background and allow the patient to talk freely. She or he listens attentively, trying to pick up clues about the conflicts that are causing distress in the patient. From time to time the analyst will interpret the patient's narrative, linking current materials to events of the past and offering some explanation of what has happened in the patient's life.

One of the important ideas in psychodynamic therapies is the concept of transference. Transference is a replay or revival, in a current relationship, of conflicts that remain unresolved from earlier experiences, particularly those involving parent-child relationships. A basic tenet of psychodynamic therapy is that the feelings and thoughts of these prior relationships arise again in therapy, with the therapist finding himself or herself in a position very much like the parent. Feelings of love, anger or dependency that develop toward the therapist are part of this transference. Transference is felt to be an essential part of therapy, but the process should be resolved by the time therapy is terminated.

Freud's approach to therapy was originally developed to deal with such emotional disorders as hysteria and obsessive-compulsive behaviors. He later turned his attention to depression in *Mourning and Melancholia,* pointing to the experience of loss and internalized anger as important aspects of the problem.[2] Over the years a number of writers in the psychoanalytic movement have expanded on Freud's thinking about depression. These writers include Karl Abraham, Otto Fenichel, Edith Jacobson and Leopold Bellak.[3] Bellak presented a rather comprehensive list of the issues he believed psychoanalytic therapists should pay particular attention to in treating depression. The list includes problems relating to self-esteem, a severe super-ego, aggression turned against the self, feelings of loss, feelings of disappointment, feelings of having been deceived by others, dependence on positive input from other people, an excessive need to be loved and the use of denial as a defense mechamsm.

Bellak's list suggests the kinds of issues one might anticipate being addressed in a contemporary psychoanalytic approach to depression. These problems are clearly important, but could take considerable time to cover in therapy, particularly in psychoanalytic therapy, which traditionally proceeds at a slow pace. However, Bellak believes that if the therapist is sensitized to these issues, effective therapy for depression can be carried out in a relatively short period of time. Typically, the therapist will approach these issues by exploring the life history of the patient, considering recent incidents that triggered the depression, and pointing out common denominators between the past and present to improve the patient's understanding and insight.

Some psychodynamically oriented therapists interested in the possibility of radically shortening the course of treatment but still drawing on the legacy of Freud's ideas have developed various forms of *brief dynamic therapies.* In these therapies, the therapist does not try to deal with all of the patient's personality problems; rather, the therapist and patient focus on an important problem area. They attempt to deal with this problem in a limited number of sessions, usually less than 20. Within these restrictions, the therapist will view symptoms from a psychoanalytic or modified psychoanalytic framework and use some of the techniques of psychoanalysis. The therapist may analyze defense mechanisms, show how current symptoms have their roots in early childhood experiences, and interpret relationships in terms of transference.

A Case Study of Psychodynamically Oriented Therapy

We are going to present a case study of psychodynamically oriented therapy of a severely depressed patient. Although treatment by antidepressant drugs or brief psychotherapy are the norms today for most depressed patients, there are times when a clinical judgment is made that long term, intensive therapy offers the best chance for a successful outcome. This is such a case.

The case was provided by clinical psychologist Donald S. Jewell. Jewell offers an interesting, somewhat different perspective on the long-term treatment for depression. While generally speaking, people entering short-term therapy who are less depressed seem to benefit more from therapy than people who are more depressed, Jewell believes this may not necessarily be the case for people who enter long term treatment. Motivation to persist in treatment becomes an important factor in whether such treatment will be effective. Jewell hypothesizes that people who have been experiencing the acute stress of depression will be more inclined to stay with the treatment and deal with the difficult emotional issues that are likely to arise. The idea that the time of acute pain in depression is a strategic point to begin intensive therapy is an intriguing hypothesis that merits testing in research.

The patient treated was extremely depressed and overtly suicidal. Often, the choice that is made for such patients is to hospitalize them and try a course of electroconvulsive therapy. In this case the decision was made to try intensive psychoanalytically oriented therapy. As we shall see, the decision proved to be a good one. Here, then, is the case as presented by Jewell.

Jay is a 39 year old professional referred to me because of increasing suicidal ideation. He is extremely bright, did well in academics, but is an underachiever in his professional life. He has attempted suicide three times in his life. Each episode occurred during a period of transition, graduation from college, moving from home, and passing his professional board exam. The last attempt would have been successful had he not been discovered by chance by a friend. His everyday childhood consisted of endless terrorizing by a paranoid schizophrenic father and lack of protection from a passive and frightened mother. The house was a pathway of flea market debris with barely room to turn around in and guns which were held to Jay's head with threats of what would happen to him if anyone found out the nature of things.

When Jay related this tale of horror it was with composed, modulated, feelingless tones. It was as if he were reading someone else's case history, suicides, death threats and all. He told me that he was on three different medications and complained that he woke up every morning wanting to kill himself and it was getting worse. It was clear that Jay was very depressed.

I told him that it was "great" that he was able to tell me these things, an indication of increasing personal strength. He was trying to overcome his depression and becoming more in touch with himself and that it was time to get off the medication which had not been effective in resolving his depression. I said I would arrange to meet with the psychiatrist I worked with to begin weaning him off the medication and that I wanted to hear all he had to say about the suicidal thoughts. I suggested the more he cut back on the medication, the more we might learn about his feelings. When I said this to him, be looked at me as though the therapist was crazier than the patient, so I spent some time talking with him about the nature of depression.

Jay was immediately seen in individual therapy with a view to discovery in terms of the impact of his nightmare childhood and the impact of this on his present day living. After some time in therapy, he moved into a men's group in conjunction with the individual therapy. This gave him a place to experiment with new ways of both understanding and dealing with some of the misconceptions of his old life.

The path we embarked on was not an easy one for either therapist or patient. There were times when I lost sleep about how close to the edge we came. This was especially true when we hit periods of transition in the therapy, i.e., a new discovery in historical development or a current failed romantic relationship. On the other hand, transitions were interspersed with comments like, "I woke this morning and for the first time that I can remember I didn't want to kill myself" or "every time I go through one of these changes, I feel like someone has a gun to my head." This was followed by an amazed stunned look and, "Oh my God what did I say!"

Today, Jay still has occasional suicidal thoughts. He has added another graduate degree. He no longer lives with his mother. He is looking for a position commensurate with his abilities and is now seeing a girlfriend. This, after two years of hard work. In my experience, if you have been depressed for 35 years, you are unlikely to turn around in 12 visits to a therapist or even with a pill, or two, or three.

Cognitive Therapy

In contrast to traditional psychodynamic therapy, which delves deep into the personality and may take years to complete, cognitive therapy is usually carried out in a matter of weeks or months. The basic premise underlying cognitive therapy is that depressed emotion is triggered in large part by maladaptive thought patterns. The objectives of cognitive therapy are to work with the patient to identify maladaptive thought patterns and then to help the patient change these patterns— to begin to think in ways that are adaptive rather than disabling. In his book *Cognitive Therapy and the Emotional Disorders,* Aaron Beck spoke of the challenge to psychotherapy as one of giving the patient effective techniques to overcome his or her faulty perceptions. The therapist reaches the patient's emotions through the patient's cognitions. Beck proposed that by correcting faulty beliefs, the excessive, emotional reactions will be diminished.[4]

We have previously discussed some of the typical maladaptive thought patterns found in patients experiencing depression, including over generalizing, perfectionistic and black-and-white thinking. The patient may not be aware of these tendencies, and if he is, may not see anything wrong in thinking this way. He may not see that these patterns are causing trouble. The therapist attempts to discover these thoughts and help the patient understand his or her role in the depressive problem.

In the early stages of cognitive therapy, the therapist tries to elicit from the patient any automatic thoughts that the patient has been experiencing. Later, the therapist will attempt to weave these fragmented thoughts into more general patterns— the views that the person has about him or herself, his or her life and the outside world. As an aid in therapy, the therapist may ask the patient to keep a diary to record thoughts that occur during feelings of depression. The therapist will discuss the material in the diary during the therapy hour.

In cognitive therapy, the therapist might ask questions like "Before you started feeling sad this morning, what were you thinking about? What was on your mind?" Or, "When you were lying awake last night and couldn't get to sleep, imagine you had a tape recorder, recording your thoughts. Try playing some of that tape back for me. What would it sound like?" The questions may vary, but the objective is to bring out the patient's thoughts, particularly those automatic thoughts that are believed to trigger and sustain depressed mood. To illustrate a cognitive therapy approach, here are some excerpts from a case reported by Jeremy Safran and his colleagues. The client, a 25-year-old male, was being treated for depression, apathy and procrastination. At the time of entering therapy he had been thinking about applying for admission to a university, but found himself unable to get moving. During the stage of therapy illustrated here, the therapist was concerned with uncovering the thought processes that were supporting this pattern of immobilization.

The client told the therapist that he planned to have his transcripts sent to the university; instead, he found himself lying in bed, thinking of telephoning the transcript office but not doing so. The therapist asked the client to recall how he was feeling at the time and to relate any images or thoughts that seemed relevant. The young man described how he imagined the people in the transcript office would react to his call. "I see a picture of some of the people that I have to contact to try to get something moving on this and I see them hating me. They see me as a nuisance." He imagined that he would receive a curt, unpleasant response, something like, "Sorry you've got your answer and that's all there is to it." On afterthought, he added that this fear was probably ridiculous.

The therapist commented that the fear was real for the client. The client agreed that it was indeed very real. As the session continued, the therapist asked him to elaborate on his imagery. "Like I'm lying here in bed and the thought occurs to me 'this is what I've got to do. I've got to phone this woman.' Ah ... it's funny, after describing all this, suddenly it doesn't seem as surprising to me, that what happens is that I stay in bed for another hour."

The client later observed, "Yeah. I can see when I was lying there in bed thinking ... 'I should call the transcript office,' the other part of me was saying 'No way ... I'm not going to call that woman.'" The therapist asked whether he could make a case for not calling the woman. The client replied, "You bet I can!" He then related automatic thoughts, catastrophizing the scenario. He saw the woman as threatening and himself as powerless and helpless. "And suddenly, it's like I'm wrong and she's in the right. I can imagine her saying 'I'm going to call the principal,' and it's like I've got to hang up and run and hide."

The therapist observed that it was like he was a powerless child who had done something wrong. The client agreed, "Yeah, I'm in the wrong. And I'm gonna get squashed like a bug. And 1 have no defense, no defense at all."[5]

The interchange had elicited a group of automatic thoughts suggesting a self-image of a powerless child victimized by powerful and threatening adults. As therapy continued, other tendencies of the client — to seek the approval of others and not to express his own anger became clearer in light of this fundamental perception of powerlessness and his exaggerated fear of retaliation. In later sessions, the therapist was able to work along with the young man to take a more critical look at these debilitating ideas and successfully challenge them. One of the techniques of cognitive therapy is to challenge the maladaptive beliefs — the basic assumptions of the patient that are believed to underlie the depression. An effort is made to break through the patient's closed systems of thought, to open up the patient's thinking so that he or she can entertain new information and alternative ways of looking at problems. The process of challenging the patient's beliefs is not unlike a Socratic dialogue and sometimes can have the flavor of a debate. The therapist may bring up facts and counter examples that tend to question and contradict the negative mind sets of the patient.

At times, the actions of a cognitive therapist resemble those of a lawyer for the defense of the patient, and particularly his or her self-esteem.

Cognitive therapy is compatible with a number of elements of behavior therapy such as teaching patients relaxation techniques and activity scheduling to increase the frequency of pleasant activities. A hybrid form of therapy (cognitive-behavioral therapy) emphasizing both cognitive and behavioral change is now widely practiced and has been widely used both in the treatment of depression and anxiety disorders.[6]

Interpersonal Therapy

Like brief dynamic and cognitive therapies, interpersonal psychotherapy (IPT) is designed to be time limited and can be carried out in a few months. IPT provides an alternative focus to the treatment of depression, moving away from the patient's psyche and belief systems to his or her interpersonal relationships. Since we know that interpersonal stresses often trigger the onset of a depressive episode, it makes sense to consider these problems in treating depression. IPT endeavors to help the patient develop more effective ways of coping with the interpersonal problems that appear to have played a role in bringing on the depression.

The therapist tries to identify the interpersonal problems that are of central importance to the patient; then the therapist helps the patient deal more effectively with the problems. The IPT therapist is particularly sensitized to look for problems in the following areas: grief, interpersonal disputes, changes in roles and interpersonal deficits such as loneliness.

With regard to grief, the therapist looks for indications of abnormal grief — reactions to loss that have not been resolved in a reasonable period of time. The therapist tries to help the patient facilitate the mourning process and free himself or herself from a crippling attachment to someone who has gone.

With regard to interpersonal disputes, the therapist looks for possible problems with the patient's spouse, children, other family members, coworkers and friends. If significant disputes are uncovered, the therapist and the patient will try to work out plans to better resolve the disputes. The plans might involve changing the patient's expectations about the people involved or trying to improve communication with the other people.

There are many role changes or transitions that may be associated with the onset of depression. Think of such changes as leaving for college, getting married, becoming a parent and changing jobs. As indicated earlier, such changes often generate stress, and high levels of stress can trigger depression. The therapist looks for difficulties that have occurred during these role transitions. As the therapist explores these changes, he or she looks for losses of familiar support in the patient's life, how the patient has managed emotions such as anxiety or anger that have been aroused by the transition and whether the patient has experienced loss of self-esteem. The therapist also assesses the types of new social skills that may be required to cope effectively with the changed situation. The therapist tries to help the patient put the old role in perspective, as well as to acquire the skills needed in the new role.

With regard to loneliness and social isolation, we know that loneliness and depression are highly related. In helping the patient cope with this problem, the therapist explores the patient's past and present relationships and employs techniques such as *role playing* to diagnose specific difficulties the patient may have in communicating and relating to others.

Role playing is a technique in which the therapist and patient engage in a spontaneous drama. The therapist and patient each take a part (role) in a situation in which they make up their lines as they go along. For example, let's say that therapist Debra Carter is working with a patient, Don, who has great difficulty asking a woman for a date. Dr. Carter may play the part of the woman Don is interested in. She and Don will engage in a dialogue in which he asks her out. Dr. Carter may critique Don's performance, helping him to sharpen his approach. Practice in role playing may improve Don's skill and confidence.

In the book *Interpersonal Psychotherapy of Depression,* the developers of this technique provided case examples illustrating the way IPT is carried out. One example, the case of Ellen F. described a woman whose central problem involved role transition.[7] Ellen had been in an unhappy marriage for about ten years. She had married at age 17, in part as a way of escaping an over intrusive mother. Her husband turned out to be an alcoholic who when intoxicated could be both verbally and physically abusive. Ellen had an abortive affair, which proved disastrous, precipitating her suicide attempt. Ellen wanted to end the marriage but found herself incapable of doing so. She hoped therapy would help her take this step.

After beginning therapy she asked her husband to leave the house; he proved more than willing to do so, having complaints of his own. Therapy then focused on helping Ellen manage the transition out of marriage. The therapist helped her identify new social relationships to fill the vacuum left by the shattered marriage, helped her deal with her fears of being alone, and helped her understand that her own self-worth should not depend on having a man to call her own.

Therapy also strengthened her resolve not to reconcile with her husband when he came back and asked her to try again. She realized that being lonely for a period of time was better than the misery that she had been through.

During therapy, Ellen widened her circle of friends and began dating again. When therapy ended she had not reached the point where she had achieved a comfortable life, but she had made a difficult transition away from a destructive situation.

Effectiveness of Therapy

How effective is psychotherapy in the treatment of depression? Are some approaches to therapy more effective than others in treating depression? Does the competence of the therapist make a difference in the outcome of therapy? Are there characteristics of the patient that make a difference in whether therapy will be effective? These are some of the questions that researchers have posed and are seeking to answer in clinical studies. These questions are important both to the practitioner of therapy and to the person in need of therapy.

In conducting research to answer these questions, investigators must exercise considerable care in the way they design and carry out their studies to ensure that their results are as clear-cut as possible. For example, in studying the effectiveness of therapy, researchers are careful to ensure the following:

1. All patients included in the study are clearly diagnosed as depressed. The selection of patients is usually based upon a clinical assessment such as is provided by the Hamilton rating scales.
2. The patients selected for inclusion in the study are randomly divided into two groups: One group receives therapy; the other group is usually put on a waiting list for treatment and serves as a control group.
3. Measures of depression are taken before therapy begins, at the end of therapy and at a subsequent follow-up time.

The gold standard for these evaluation studies is a randomized, controlled clinical trial.

Many studies have now been carried out comparing patients given psychotherapy with patients serving as controls. Inasmuch as idiosyncratic factors and research allegiances to a particular form of therapy can affect the results of any given study, meta-analyses examining the overall trends from a variety of studies provide the most reliable evidence for the efficacy of a treatment that we have available today.

Because of the energy the proponents of cognitive-behavioral therapy have put into evaluating this technique, we have more evidence for the efficacy of cognitive-behavioral therapy in treating depression than we have for any other therapeutic approach. In brief, meta-analyses have found that cognitive-behavioral therapy is an effective treatment for adult depressed patients and for children who are depressed as well. Using the conventions established in meta-analysis research for assessing the size of an effect, the effect of cognitive-behavioral therapy on depression has been described as large.[8]

A recent meta-analysis of 13 studies looking at the efficacy of interpersonal therapy in treating depression also found positive results. As is true for cognitive-behavioral therapy, interpersonal therapy appears to be an effective treatment for depressive disorders.[9] Interpersonal therapy appears to be effective for both adults and adolescents.[10]

The efficacy of brief psychodynamic therapy for treating depression is more problematic. I have criticized the research efforts of proponents of psychodynamic therapies for not carrying out the research necessary to objectively evaluate the effectiveness of their therapeutic procedures. I am pleased to acknowledge that for the proponents of brief psychodynamic therapy, the situation is changing. There is now some evidence available to evaluate the efficacy of brief psychodynamic therapy for depression. Having said this, there remains much work to do. Carefully conducted randomized clinical trials for psychodynamic therapy are still relatively hard to come by. While early meta-analyses produced inconsistent results, recent analyses of data suggest that brief psychodynamics therapy can be an effective treatment for depression. Psychodynamic therapy has been used to successfully treat depression in both children and adolescents.[11]

So, the evidence is strong that both cognitive-behavioral therapy and interpersonal therapy are effective treatments for depression and there is developing evidence that this may be also true for brief psychodynamic therapy. In addition there is now evidence that cognitive-behavioral therapy can be an effective alternative therapy when an antidepressant medicine proves wanting.[12]

Although a great many depressed people have been helped by psychotherapy, as is the case for antidepressant medications, not everyone responds to psychotherapy. And, while there is ample evidence that psychotherapy is effective in the treatment of depression, there still remains some question as to *how* effective. When a person is improved, what precisely do we mean? Do people who are treated by psychotherapy achieve the same level of well being as people who were not depressed to begin with? The answer is probably no. While improved, people who are treated for depression are still likely to experience higher levels of depressive symptoms than "normal" people.[13]

To use a very rough analogy, therapy for depression in some respects is like treatment for chronic diseases such as heart disease or arthritis. Treatment for such conditions helps control symptoms and prevent flare-ups of the problems. Likewise, in psychotherapy for these diseases, one may not find a magic bullet that cures the problem of depression in the same way an antibiotic wipes out a bacterial infection. After psychotherapy, the person prone to depression usually feels a lot better and should be in a better position to effectively manage himself or herself, which will reduce the chances of further symptoms. But underlying genetic vulnerabilities remain and the problems in the environment that triggered the depression may also remain. There is a clear potential for further problems.

Having shown that the major types of psychotherapy offered today appear to be effective treatments for depression, researchers turned to the question of directly comparing different types of therapies. Is one approach to therapy for depression more effective than another? This is a very practical question for anyone considering therapy; one would like to know which approach is most likely to be beneficial.

In "comparative outcome" studies, patients are randomly assigned to one of the several types of treatments under investigation. Particular care has to be given so that all types of therapy are carried out in the clinical trials in the manner in which they are designed to be carried out. Evaluation measures may include psychological testing and clinical assessments such as the Hamilton rating scale.

To date, the tentative conclusion from comparative outcome studies is that there is not much difference between the therapeutic approaches that have been tested in terms of their effectiveness in treating depression. In an important paper, B. E. Wampold pointed out that the important thing is not what kind of therapy is offered, but whether the therapy has a rational basis for addressing depression. Therapies that target depressions are likely to work roughly equally well.[14]

There are some practical consequences to the observation that different forms of psychotherapy do not differ appreciably in their efficacy of treating depression. People looking for help can pay attention to the qualities of the individual therapist and how they relate to the person without worrying too much about the technical aspects of therapy. Also, prospective patients can select an approach that is short term and feel some confidence that they will be helped. There is little evidence at this point to indicate that a person is likely to profit more by undergoing long-term, deep therapy to deal with an ongoing depressive problem. A person may want to choose long-term, intensive therapy for other, more fundamental reasons, but it is not usually necessary for the alleviation of depressive episodes. If proponents of long term, intensive therapy could demonstrate in controlled research that the effects of such therapy are more robust — that there is less chance of a recurrence of depressive symptoms — a stronger case could be made that it is the treatment of choice.

Let's talk about the individual therapist. Doctors, lawyers and teachers differ in how competent they are and this can make a difference in what you get from them. A good lawyer may win your case for you; a bad one may lose it. In much the same way, a skilled therapist is more likely to do more useful things in therapy than a less skilled therapist. Observations of ongoing therapy indicate that a skilled therapist is more likely to help patients explore issues and problems and to do so without arousing the patient's hostility or causing unnecessary distress. Researchers have reported a relation between the competence of the therapist and the extent to which a patient improves during treatment for depression.

As the skill of a therapist can make a difference in the outcome of therapy, the question that must inevitably arise is how does one find a good therapist? This is not an easy question to answer, but here are some ideas. Probably the most useful benchmark in choosing a therapist is how effective he or she has been with previous patients. Unfortunately, this kind of information is unlikely to be available in a systematic way. No one takes polls of this situation. However, it is possible to ask around. If someone has been to a therapist, you should be able to find out whether the person felt the therapist was helpful and what the therapist was like as a person.

If you cannot get a likely name from a friend, then your next best bet may be the referral services of the local professional associations for psychiatrists, psychologists and clinical social workers. The referral services will usually give you several names of people who are licensed practitioners. They may also have background information about each person, which will allow you to make some inquiries. If you decide to call one of the names, see if you can talk briefly with the therapist on the phone to gain a sense of what he or she is like and whether you feel comfortable talking with the person. You should also ask about fees. If they are way out of line, you might want to try someone else. A sky-high fee does not guarantee a better therapist.

Some other possible sources of referral are community mental health associations and the psychology, psychiatry and social work departments of local universities. You will also find listings in the Yellow Pages of your phone book.

Let's now turn our spotlight away from the therapist and onto the patient. Are there characteristics of patients that may make a difference in whether therapy is likely to prove helpful? Certainly one of the most important factors is how depressed the patient is when he or she enters therapy. People who begin therapy feeling mildly or moderately depressed are more likely to emerge from therapy in decent shape than people who are severely depressed.[15] Individuals whose personal and social resources are in better condition to begin with are likely to do well.[16]

Personality factors and the ease with which one can attach oneself to other people can affect the way one will respond to different types of therapies. People with serious problems in forming attachments (attachment avoiders) may find interpersonal therapy too threatening and may do better with cognitive-behavioral therapy.[17]

Finally, the patient's attitude can make a difference. If the patient has a positive attitude about psychotherapy — a willingness to believe that it can help — the chances are better that it will help. This "expectation factor" is not only important in psychotherapy, it plays a role in almost all kinds of human healing processes. Hope and belief are important in the treatment of physical problems as well as emotional problems.

Comparisons of Psychotherapy and Drugs

Studies comparing antidepressant drugs with psychotherapy began in the late 1970's. Patients given cognitive therapy were compared with patients given the first generation of antidepressants. The results of these initial studies suggested that cognitive therapy was at least as effective as antidepressants in treating depression, perhaps even better.[18]

After these initial studies were reported, it was felt that a larger scale study was needed to provide a more definitive answer to the question of drugs versus therapy for the treatment of depression. Under the aegis of the National Institute of Mental Health, a collaborative study was undertaken at three different sites: the University of Pittsburgh, the University of Oklahoma, and George Washington University. Two hundred fifty unipolar depressed outpatients were randomly assigned to one of four treatment conditions: cognitive-behavioral therapy, interpersonal therapy, an antidepressant drug, imipramine plus clinical management, and a pill-placebo control plus clinical management. Clinical management provided patients with support, encouragement, and advice and as such constituted supportive therapy. Post treatment evaluation of the patients revealed little difference among the three groups of treated patients which seems more or less in line with the findings of previous studies. However, an analysis conducted on the patients who had been most severely depressed at the onset of the study, found that those treated with the antidepressant drug seemed better off than those receiving psychotherapy.[19]

The results relating to severe depression were received as gospel by some in the mental health community who proceeded to downplay, if not dismiss the usefulness of psychotherapy for the treatment of severe depression. For example, the United States Government's Agency for Health Care Policy and Research stated, "For severe and psychotic depressions, there is strong evidence for the efficacy of medication and little or none for the efficacy of psychotherapy alone."[20]

"Not so," replied the proponents of psychotherapy. They argued, justifiably that one study is hardly definitive. They pointed to inconsistencies in the results of the collaborative study and cited other studies which found no advantage for drugs over psychotherapy or an advantage for psychotherapy. An examination of the raw data from four separate studies, including the collaborative study, was carried out by Robert DeRubeis and his colleagues at the University of Pennsylvania. The researchers concluded that cognitive-behavioral therapy faired as well as antidepressant medication in the treatment of severely depressed outpatients.[21]

So where does this leave us? Unfortunately, with an unresolved, and at times heated debate. Partisans espousing one position or the other published articles in the scientific journals which were followed by rejoinders attacking the technical merits of these articles. Moreover, it has been observed that the findings of a particular study seemed to bear a relation to the allegiance of the researcher. While ideally, science is supposed to be neutral and dispassionate, it is possible that a proponent of one type of treatment of depression may do things which unconsciously bias the results of the study. What seems needed are more large scale collaborative studies involving many researchers to nail down convincing answers. Replication is one of the hallmarks of good science. And, clearly replication is needed here, because these findings have affected practice guidelines for patient care. Without such replication, it seems premature to draw firm conclusions about the relative efficacy of drugs versus therapy in the treatment of severe depression.

How should these mixed results affect a patient's choice of available therapies? Here is my take on this question. For patients suffering from mild and moderate levels of depression, it seems clear that either antidepressant drugs or psychotherapy are potentially useful treatments, at least in the near term. For people suffering from severe depression, it makes sense that the patient be put on an antidepressant as soon as possible. Because antidepressant medicines sometimes take weeks to be effective, it makes equally good sense that if the patient is not hospitalized, he or she should have a consultation with a psychotherapist at the earliest opportunity. Severely depressed patients need all the help they can get and as soon as they can get it.

Combining Psychotherapy and Antidepressant Drugs

The foregoing studies placed the psychotherapeutic community and the advocates of antidepressant drugs in what appeared to be an adversarial relationship. However, a cooperative relationship makes more sense for both groups of mental health professionals and their patients. One area where such cooperation has been manifest is the study of the efficacy of combining psychotherapy and medicine in the treatment of depression. Since antidepressant drugs and psychotherapy appear to act in different ways to lessen depressive symptoms, one might reasonably expect that a combination of treatments would be more effective than either used alone.

A number of studies have been undertaken to evaluate combination treatment for depression, dating back to at least the 1980s.[22] The conclusion of the early studies was that while the use of combined treatment may have some benefits, it did not produce the substantial improvement that one might have hoped for. I have recently looked at half a dozen recent reports evaluating the effectiveness of combined treatment and the conclusions of the earlier studies seems to generally hold. Improvements in depression symptoms can be detected from the use of both medicine and psychotherapy, but the improvements noted are not typically robust and dramatic.[23] Even with these less than stellar results, for people who are not responding well to a single modality of treatment for depression, I would recommend a trial of combined treatments, as in many cases, it could be beneficial.

As a final word, I should note that patient noncompliance with treatment is a problem for both pharmacological and psychotherapeutic approaches. Many patients will stop taking their antidepressant drugs either because the medication isn't working, they experience side effects, or just simply decide to stop. At the same time, a significant number of patients referred to psychotherapy may not follow through with seeking care or will stop coming to the therapist before maximum benefits are obtained.

Cost factors may be involved in the patient's willingness to adhere to a treatment program. Even short-term psychotherapy (say, a course of a dozen visits) can be expensive. Use of prescription drugs for an extended period may not prove to be that inexpensive of an alternative. For patients with liberal health insurance benefits, such costs may be a minor factor, but for many people, it is not.

Successful completion of initial treatment seems to have value in preventing a recurrence. An incomplete recovery from a major depression episode is a predictor of future depressive problems. Patients who show signs of depression after treatment are more likely to experience subsequent depressive symptoms than patients who are symptom free after treatment.

13. Hospitalization for Depression and the Use of Electroconvulsive Therapy

When should a person be hospitalized for the treatment of depression? As a general rule, hospitalization should be considered when the patient's symptoms are unmanageable through outpatient care. Two clear-cut cases of this are when the depression includes psychotic features such as delusions and when the patient is overtly suicidal.

Many depressed people think about suicide; some talk about it. When a person is openly suicidal, there may be little choice but to consider hospitalization. It may be impossible to adequately monitor the person's behavior and protect her or him against self-harm outside of a hospital setting.

The decision to hospitalize may be made in the psychiatric emergency service in the hospital or by the patient's psychiatrist (if he or she has one) in consultation with the patient and/or the patient's family. In making the decision, the attending psychiatrist will likely consider a number of factors such as the likelihood of self-harm, the severity of psychotic symptoms if present, the capability of the patient for self-care, the degree of impulse control, and the severity of the depression.[1]

Psychiatric hospitals can provide care and safety for the severely depressed patient. Throughout the United States there are both public and private psychiatric hospitals. The National Mental Health Information Center in Rockville, Maryland, has compiled lists of these hospitals.[2] In addition, you can probably obtain information about hospitals in your area by calling your state's mental health agency. Judging from the brochures that inundate private practitioners, some of the private psychiatric hospitals look very attractive, resembling resorts more than the infamous asylums of the not-too-distant past.

Psychiatric hospitals may offer several modalities of treatment for depressed patients. These include medication, individual and group therapy and electroconvulsive therapy. With regard to psychotherapy, you may find increased emphasis on group therapy in hospitals. The patients are all gathered together under one roof, which can reduce or eliminate scheduling problems. In addition, group therapy is cost effective for a hospital; one therapist can work with a number of patients simultaneously. Group therapy can be of particular benefit to patients whose problems have to do with difficulties in interpersonal relations. One learns to relate by relating and group therapy provides a relatively safe training forum in which to learn.

Electroconvulsive therapy, more popularly known as "shock treatment" or "shock therapy," is a procedure used to treat severe depression, as well as other mental illnesses such as schizophrenia, that involves the use of an electric current to induce a seizure similar to what one sees in epilepsy. The procedure, which has generated a lot of controversy over the years, can have a significant therapeutic effect on depression.

Electroconvulsive therapy has it roots in experiments conducted in Europe in the earlier part of the twentieth century in which insulin and metrazol were used to induce seizures in schizophrenic patients. These seizures led to at least temporary improvements in many of the patients. The procedure in which electric current is used for a few seconds to induce such seizures was developed in the 1930s by the Italian researchers Ugo Cerletti and Lucio Bini. Because electroconvulsive therapy was about all that was available at the time to treat severe mental illness, the procedure was widely used. In time it was recognized that electroconvulsive therapy seemed to be particularly beneficial for patients suffering from depressive disorders.[3]

In these early days when electroconvulsive therapy was coming on board as a treatment for psychiatric disorders, the procedure had a very bad reputation. And this reputation was fully deserved. The procedure might be carried out without anesthesia, and this may still be the case in some countries. Moreover, there was no way to stop the often violent, jerky muscular reactions that ensued. Broken bones were commonplace. And there was memory loss, particularly of the recent past. Sometimes one's memory returned, but sometimes it did not. And perhaps most damning to the procedure's image were accounts of hospitalized patients being given the treatment without their consent as a means of controlling their behavior.

While the reputation of electroconvulsive therapy in its early days of use was probably better than that of an alternative procedure, frontal lobotomy, which was an even more desperate venture to deal with what seemed to be an intractable psychiatric disorder, electroconvulsive therapy was still thought of as a last resort, and subsequent depictions on television and in films such as One Flew Over the Cuckoo's Nest just added to its unsavory image. To add to the unsettling view of the procedure, no one really knew why it worked when it did. A sociologist who had been working in that period on a study of the reactions of the family to mental illness in one of its member suggested wryly to me that it worked "because it scared the hell out of the patient."[4] The implication was that anything was better than going through electroconvulsive therapy and the patient would do whatever it took to avoid it.

Happily, the administration of electroconvulsive therapy has improved dramatically over the years. Short acting anesthesia is now routinely given to the patients so that they can sleep through the procedure. A muscle blocker such as succinylcholine is used to immobilize the muscles and prevent the once feared fractures. Oxygen may be administered to the patient. And there have been refinements in the ability of the medical team to monitor what is happening to the patient's brain.[5] Still, with all of these improvements in technique, as late as 1985, a consensus statement issued by a group of experts convened by the National Institute of Mental Health called the procedure the most controversial in psychiatry.[6]

Here, briefly, are some of the pros and cons for the use of electroconvulsive therapy for depression. On the positive side, favorable response rates are at least as good as antidepressant medicines, and probably better. The procedure has helped many patients who were unresponsive to medications.[7] When nothing else seems to work for a big-time depression, electroconvulsive therapy has a good chance of being effective. Proponents of electroconvulsive therapy see it not only as a last resort treatment, they recommend its use at an earlier stage in the treatment for severe depression. The argument is that if it works well later why not try it sooner?

Let's consider some of the negatives. There are a number.

Sending electric shocks in the brain and producing an artificial seizure such as one sees in epilepsy is a scary idea, no matter how much it is soft peddled. The patient may be reassured that the death rate for the procedure has dropped precipitously to now where it is roughly similar to childbirth and that the confusion he or she will most likely feel after awakening will go away along with the headache and nausea, that memory loss will most likely be transitory, and that there is no compelling data that indicates the procedure may cause damage to the brain. Such reassurances may help calm the fears of the patient and then again they may not.

We still don't know why electroconvulsive therapy works.

The patient may lose some memories. Such lost memories will most likely be about the recent past, but memory losses that plunge deeper into time are possible. Research suggests that lost memories are more likely to concern impersonal events such as the events one might hear about on the nightly television news rather than the events that are part of one's personal life.[8]

Currently, electroconvulsive therapy is usually administered in the hospital, sometimes on an inpatient basis, sometimes on an outpatient basis. It takes a team of skilled professionals which includes a psychiatrist and an anesthesiologist to carry out the procedure. Compared to other ways of treating depression, electroconvulsive therapy is difficult to carry out and expensive.

Electroconvulsive therapy affects the cardiovascular system. For example, it may cause significant decreases in pulse and blood pressure. While these effects are usually transitory, and can be counteracted by drugs, the cardiovascular system needs to be constantly monitored during the procedure. If the patient has a heart problem, it is prudent that his or her cardiologists be brought into the decision making process.[9]

As is true for other types of treatment for depression, electroconvulsive therapy is not a magic bullet. A single treatment may do little. Typically electroconvulsive therapy is given three times a week for a series of six to twelve treatments. For many if not most patients the beneficial effects of electroconvulsive therapy are likely to dissipate over time. It has been recommended that following a course of electroconvulsive therapy the patient should be put on a regimen of antidepressant drugs. Another possibility that has been suggested is to continue electroconvulsive therapy treatments periodically.

With these pros and cons, the bottom line still seems to be that if a patient has a severe and seemingly intractable depression, and particularly if he or she is suicidal, electroconvulsive therapy is probably the best option now available. Chances are that the treatment will help the patient considerably. To use electroconvulsive therapy under less compelling circumstances seems to me questionable if other possible treatments have not been exhausted.

A few notes about electroconvulsive therapy

1. Because anesthesia is involved, the patient will be asked to fast before beginning the procedure
2. The patient may be asked to temporarily discontinue the use of lithium as lithium could affect the seizures.[10]
3. The medical team will have to decide whether to place the electrodes delivering the shock in a bilateral position (on either side of the head, at the temples) or position both electrodes on the same side of the head. The bilateral position is the usual choice because it seems to work better, although there may be more impairment of memory.
4. The medical team will also have to determine the dose of electricity administered. In making this decision, they may use the age of the patient as a guideline, utilize previous experience with the patient, or attempt to titrate the dose in a kind of trial and error procedure. The goal is to induce a seizure that lasts at least 30 seconds. This is considered the minimum time for the procedure to be therapeutic.

As is true for other approaches to treating depression, researchers have tried to tweak the procedures involved in electroconvulsive therapy to improve its efficacy. Recently, for example, researchers working out of Duke University Medical Center added a different anesthesia to the preoperative regimen for electroconvulsive therapy called ketamine for which there was suggestive evidence that it may have antidepressant properties on its own.[11] The researchers added ketamine to the mix of preoperative meditations and then carried out electroconvulsive therapy with rather dramatic results which they reported in the following case study.

The patient was a 54-year-old man who had been severely depressed for several months. His appetite was very poor; he lost 35 pounds. He had difficulty sleeping at night, took little personal care of himself, and thought about suicide. The patient was described as profoundly withdrawn. On occasion, he became physically aggressive. His depression was complicated by psychotic features. The man had been using lithium and an antidepressant. But these did not seem to help him. As the patient had been given electroconvulsive therapy in the past, this seemed like the best bet to deal with his very severe symptoms.

Following a single treatment of electroconvulsive therapy augmented with ketamine, the researchers reported that the patient responded in a very dramatic and unexpected way. Eight hours after the treatment was completed the patient began to show major signs of improvement. He began to interact with other people, had an increased appetitive and slept much better. The improvement continued without further treatment over the next days. The researchers observed the case was notable in that it showed that an episode of severe major depression accompanied by psychotic features responded immediately to one treatment of bilateral electroconvulsive therapy that included the use of this different type of anesthesia. One case of successful treatment, of course, proves very little, but it does suggest an avenue of research that needs to be further explored.

14. Alternative Treatments for Depression

People sometimes treat their depression using methods which are not under the control or supervision of their physician or psychotherapist. These methods go beyond some of the self-help strategies we have previously talked about such as talking with friends or exercise which many people would view as not really under the rubric of medicine, alternative or otherwise. These "alternative methods" may be sought out by an individual as specific treatments for depression which he or she can use with or without a physician's or therapist's authorization or blessing.

Surveys indicate that millions of people in the United States—and I suspect many more millions around the world use one or another form of alternative medicine in dealing with physical and emotional problems.[1] Sometimes techniques of alternative medicine are used to complement conventional, traditional medicine and sometimes they are used in place of conventional medicine.

The National Center for Complementary and Alternative medicine was founded to study the safety and effectiveness of alternative medicines. There was a clear need for such an institute because many claims have been made for alternative medicines, especially dietary substances which have not been rigorously evaluated. It is important for consumers to know whether alternative medicines offered in the marketplace are safe and effective. One of the ways that the Center for Complementary and Alternative Medicine evaluates alternative medicine is to convene a panel of experts drawn from universities and medical schools, asking the panel to review existing research and present its conclusions. My reading of several of these reviews is that these expert panels tend to be guarded in drawing conclusions and may not offer clear-cut guidance about whether to use an alternative medicine approach.

My own view is that the standards for evaluating the safety and efficacy of alternative treatments for depression should be equivalent to the standards for evaluating the products of the pharmaceutical industry and the work of psychotherapists. The standards should be equivalent, but not arbitrarily higher on the belief that alternative approaches are not really medicine. We have discussed allegiance biases in carrying out and interpreting scientific research. These are very real and hard to overcome because scientists are human beings with their own hopes, needs, and disciplinary biases. In evaluating what has been written about alternative medicine, we must watch out carefully for both pro and con biases towards alternative medicine. In my view an ideal panel of reviewers might be one which includes both those who swear by alternative medicines and those who swear at them.

This admonition about the need to be open-minded does not in any way diminish the need for rigorous research on alternative medicines. In a 1998 review of complementary therapies for depression E. Ernst and his colleagues at the University of Exeter noted that the quantity of rigorous scientific data supporting the efficacy of complementary therapies for depression was extremely limited.[2] The situation has clearly improved but we still have a long way to go.

The list of what constitutes alternative medical treatments is not constant and unchanging. New possibilities for treatment arise from time to time and as the National Center for Complementary and Alternative Medicine points out some alternative treatments become widely accepted and enter the domain of traditional therapies. The National Center for Complementary and Alternative Medicine classifies current alternative treatments into five : (1) alternative medical systems such as traditional Chinese medicine, (2) mind-body interventions techniques such as meditation which are believed to enhance the mind's capacity to affect bodily function and symptoms, (3) biologically based therapies which utilizes substances found in nature such as vitamins and herbs), (4) manipulative methods which include chiropractic manipulation and massage, (5) energy therapies such as the use of electromagnetic fields.

In our discussion of alternative treatments for depression we will consider five possible treatments, most of which fit into the Center's system of categories. The alternative treatments for depression we will consider are meditation, massage therapy, the herb St. John's wort, the use of omega-3 fatty acids, and bright light therapy. Most of these approaches have shown some promise in research as possible treatments or adjunct treatments for depressive symptoms.

Meditation

Meditation has a number of different meanings. One might think, for example, of a young man reflecting on the events of his life. But what we are thinking about here is a deliberate mental process, arising in the main out of Eastern religions and spiritual traditions in which a studied effort is made to focus one's attention. Probably, the most well-known form of meditation is focusing on an image in the mind's eye, or on a repetitive sound or phrase sometimes called a *mantra*, or on one's breathing. One popular form of meditation used in America today is Transcendental Meditation. In its publications, The National Center for Complementary and Alternative Medicine notes that Transcendental Meditation (TM) "originated in the Vedic tradition in India. It is a type of meditation that uses a mantra, a word, sound, or phrase repeated silently to prevent distracting thoughts from entering the mind. The intent of TM might be described as allowing the mind to settle into a quieter state and the body into a state of deep rest."[3]

Another type of meditation that has attracted much attention is mindfulness meditation. This type of meditation originated in Buddhism. The National Center for Complementary and Alternative Medicine notes that mindfulness meditation, "Is based on the concept of being mindful, or having an increased awareness and total acceptance of the present. While meditating, the meditator is taught to bring all her attention to the sensation of the flow of the breath in and out of the body. The intent might be described as focusing attention on what is being experienced, without reacting to or judging that experience." Mindfulness mediation is thought to help the individual learn to experience the thoughts and emotions of daily life with greater balance and acceptance.[4]

In a review article of electrical and neuroimaging studies of meditation, B. Rael Cahn and John Polich describe meditation as practices which, "Self-regulate the body and mind, thereby affecting mental events by engaging a specific attentional set."[5] They view meditation as a subset of the techniques used to induce relaxation or altered states such as hypnosis. In their view the key to all of these practices is the, "Regulation of attention."[6]

To help in the focusing of attention, The National Center for Complementary and Alternative Medicine notes that most types of meditation encourage the individual to find a quiet location with as few distractions as possible, to adopt a specific comfortable position whether it is sitting down, standing, or even walking and to maintain an open attitude, "Which means letting distractions come and go naturally without stopping to think about them. When distracting or wandering thoughts occur, they are not suppressed; instead, the meditator gently brings attention back to the focus. In some types of meditation, the meditator learns to observe the rising and falling of thoughts and emotions as they spontaneously occur."[7]

Meditation has a quieting effect on the body. Meditation can reduce heart rate and blood pressure and cortisol levels, the so-called "stress hormone." As Cahn and Polich note, "A considerable body of research supports the idea that meditation training can mitigate the effects of anxiety and stress on psychological and physiological functioning."[8] Studies of the brain using the electroencephalograph show that meditation also affects the electrical activity of the brain; among the changes observed are increases in theta and alpha band power and decreases in overall frequency.[9]

These changes in the body and brain are accompanied by short term psychological effects which have been described as a, "Deep sense of calm peacefulness, a cessation or slowing of the mind's internal dialogue, and experiences of perceptual clarity...."[10]

Although it is clear that meditation can be an effective stress reducer, it is not as clear that by itself, meditation is an effective treatment for depression. We do not have enough evidence yet to be certain on this point, one way or the other. Almost all of the research I have seen using meditation as a treatment for depression uses mindfulness meditation. At first look, the case for using meditation as a potential alternative medicine treatment for depression would not appear as promising as it is for anxiety and stress related disorders. Many depressed people appear lethargic and dispirited and one might wonder how meditation would help them. One could certainly make the case that when the depressive picture includes agitation or is accompanied by a comorbid anxiety disorder which happens frequently, meditation might prove beneficial. One could also hypothesize that controlling stress could be helpful in treating the depressive problem. Indeed, a study reported by Kabat-Zinn and his colleagues showed that a stress reduction program emphasizing mindfulness meditation had a long lasting impact in reducing both stress and depression levels of anxiety disorder patients, a number of whom were also diagnosed as having major depressive disorder.[11] It would be interesting to see whether meditation, by itself, might be useful in patients whose depression is in remission to see whether it might be helpful in preventing recurrences.

In the treatment of depression, mindfulness meditation has sometimes been used as part of a therapeutic package along with other more traditional therapies such as cognitive therapy. At first blush, the combination of mindfulness meditation and cognitive therapy may raise some eyebrows for as Mark Lau and Shelley McMain pointed out in a review article there are some seeming contradictions in the approach of these two techniques.[12] If you are living with a dysfunctional belief such as, "Nobody really likes me," a cognitive therapist might try to alter this belief to one that is not disabling such as, "some people may not like me, but that's true for almost everyone. It's unrealistic to expect everyone to like you." Rather than attempt to challenge the idea in the dialogue of therapy, mindfulness meditation would ask you to experience this dysfunctional belief as part of your stream of consciousness, and in a non-judgmental way, accept the thought — but recognize that that's all it is, a thought — not a reality. Mindfulness meditation allows one to decouple the thought from other aspects of your experience and not allow it to become a central part of your beliefs.

While these techniques may seem somewhat at odds, researchers have combined the two approaches into a form of therapy called *mindfulness based cognitive therapy* (MBCT).[13] MBCT has been developed into an eight week course integrating mindfulness meditation and cognitive therapy. A recent exploratory study of the efficacy of this combined treatment carried out on patients in primary care settings who were experiencing symptoms of depression and anxiety yielded positive results. Depression scores declined following treatment.[14] However, it is not possible to say at this point, how much mindfulness meditation contributed to the results as the therapeutic package included a number of different elements.

How efficacious is mindfulness meditation by itself as a treatment for depression? The amount of research that has been carried out on this problem is currently insufficient to render anything like a definitive conclusion. A recent meta-analysis carried out on the available research that used measures of anxiety and depression yielded equivocal results. The researchers concluded that mindfulness based stress reduction did not have a reliable effect on depression.[15]

Because of the paucity of research on this question, I would suggest a Scotch verdict: the efficacy of this treatment for depression is as yet unproven.

Massage Therapy

As was true for meditation, massage therapy has a long lineage. In a review article evaluating the effects of massage therapy, Christopher Moyer and his colleagues noted that the practice of massage therapy was recorded as far back as 2000 B.C. Physicians in ancient Greece such as Hippocrates, Celsus, and Galen discussed massage as a therapeutic treatment.[16] Interest in massage as a form of therapy was rekindled in the 19th century and has flourished in recent years.

In practice, the client receiving massage therapy usually disrobes, and then loosely covered by a sheet or a towel lies down on the massage table. Sometimes, massage is given to a fully clothed individual seated in a chair. The massage-therapist will then apply pressure, strokes or perhaps vibrations to the various parts of the client's body. Many varieties of applying massage to the body have been developed over the years and these have been given different names, such as Swedish massage, deep tissue massage, and trigger or pressure point techniques. The time given to massage treatment may vary from a few minutes to over an hour.

Surveys carried out in the states of Connecticut and Washington have found that the great majority (85 percent) of today's practitioners of massage therapy are women.[17] Most of the clients are self-referred rather than referred by a physician. Most of the clients who come to see massage therapists for help in dealing with muscle-skeletal problems, particularly problems with their backs, shoulders, and necks. While far fewer people seek massage therapists for relief from psychological distress than for physical complaints, the benefits of using massage therapy for psychological distress are clear. As massage therapy can be quite relaxing, it is a natural fit for reducing stress and stress-related disorders. In carrying out a meta-analysis of studies looking at the effects of massage therapy on a variety of stress-related indicators, Moyer and his colleagues concluded that massage therapy tended to reduce heart rate, blood pressure, and self reported levels of anxiety.[18]

As was true for meditation, the rationale for using massage therapy as a treatment for depression is not as clear cut as it is for treating stress and stress related disorders. However, there are circumstances where stress reduction in the treatment of depression makes intuitive sense. As was the case for meditation, the rationale for using massage therapy for depression seems reasonable when the depressive picture includes agitation or is accompanied by a comorbid anxiety disorder or where current levels of stress have brought on or are exacerbating the depression.

What if we are dealing with a relatively uncomplicated case of major depression disorder or dysthymic disorder? Is there clear-cut evidence to indicate that massage therapy would be useful in these cases? I have not yet seen a definitive study in this regard, but there is some research evidence which suggests that massage therapy could indeed be useful in helping people who feel depressed.

Most of the research studying the effects of massage therapy on depression has been carried out by the Touch Research Institute of the University of Miami School of Medicine. In some very intriguing studies in which serotonin levels were assessed in urine samples, the researchers noted an average 28 percent increase in serotonin following massage therapy.[19] If massage therapy does in fact increase serotonin levels, there would be a rational basis for believing massage therapy might be beneficial for depressed mood. And the studies carried out by the Institute suggest that this is the case.

Moyer and his colleagues carried out a meta-analysis of 10 studies carried out by the Institute in which a measure of depression was included in a battery of tests to study the effects of massage therapy. It is important to note that in none of the studies were the subjects selected as a group of clinically depressed patients. Rather, the subjects included groups of headache patients, adults with hypertension, and patients with Alzheimer's disease. With these samples of patients massage therapy proved very effective in lessening depressed mood. As Moyer and his colleagues noted, the average patient who had undergone multiple sessions of massage therapy experienced, "A reduction of depression that was greater than 73 percent of comparison group participants."[20] This effect would be similar to what one might expect using psychotherapy. While these effects are impressive, it should be recognized that the subjects were not selected as clinically depressed patients.

One of the more direct tests of the effectiveness of massage therapy on depression was reported in a study carried out by researchers at the Touch Research Institute using 84 depressed pregnant women as subjects. One group of the women received massage therapy in 20 minute sessions administered by a "significant other" each week for 16 weeks of pregnancy, starting during the second trimester. Another group of women received training in progressive muscle relaxation. Not only did the massage therapy have an immediate effect on the women's reports of both anxiety and depressed mood, by the end of the study these women had higher serotonin levels. Interestingly, the women given massage therapy experienced lower incidences of prematurity and lower birth weights.[21]

One of the problems in evaluating the effectiveness of massage therapy — and this difficulty is shared by almost any intervention technique — is ruling out the effects of the extra attention the subject is receiving simply by undergoing the treatment. In the study of pregnant women just cited, it is difficult to say how much of the benefit resulted from the specific effects of massage — and how much from the attention — in this case intimate attention of a loving partner.

The same point might be made with an interesting study carried out in Korea. Women, recruited from a community health center were tested on a variety of measures including depression, and then taught a self administered form of foot massage.[22] The women practiced this massage technique both at home and in the clinic. After six weeks, the women's depression scores were clearly improved. Was it the specific form of massage that produced the effect (which would be very intriguing as this is a self-administered technique) or was it the added attention the patients got from the nursing staff during training and practice?

One way of teasing out the effects of extra attention is to compare massage therapy with another treatment and better yet a sham treatment that functions as a placebo. In a recent study carried out at Stanford University, massage therapy was compared with another treatment, active acupuncture and a "control" version of acupuncture. The patients, 61 pregnant women with major depressive disorder were initially assessed for depression, then randomly assigned into one of these three treatment groups (massage therapy, active acupuncture, active control acupuncture), then assessed again after eight weeks. The women who received active acupuncture had the best response (69 percent were judged to be improved) while only 32 percent of the women given massage therapy were judged so. The women given massage therapy did not do any better than the women given the sham acupuncture treatment.[23]

Where does this leave us? Clearly, there is a need for additional carefully controlled studies using clinically depressed subjects in which massage therapy is compared with both potentially useful treatments and sham treatments. Until we have such data, it is difficult to fully assess the potential usefulness of massage therapy as a treatment for major depression. Because massage therapy is a well tolerated, usually benign technique it may be worth trying to see if it is helpful, particularly where the depression is linked to ongoing stress. Actions which help keep stress under control could be beneficial in the long range treatment of depression and there is enough evidence from the studies carried out at the Touch Research Institute to believe that massage therapy could have a positive impact on depressed mood. Above all, massage therapy is a low risk treatment that can have widespread positive effects.

St John's Wort

St. John's wort (Hypericum perforatum) is a yellow-flowered plant that is native to Europe and was subsequently transported to America. The plant is a perennial that grows wild in both continents. It is considered noxious when eaten by livestock and its growth has been controlled by both the use of herbicides and the introduction of beetles that feast on it. The name St. John's Wort stems from a tradition of harvesting the flowers on or by St. John's Day which is June 24th. The flowers were hung in the house in the belief that they would ward off evil.

The medicinal use of the herb has a long history. In its publication, *St. John's Wort and the Treatment of Depression* the National Center for Complementary and Alternative Medicine notes that in ancient times physicians wrote that the plant could be used as a sedative, and to treat burns, insect bites and wounds.[24] Currently the major medicinal use of the plant as a medicine is in the treatment of depression. To use St. John's wort for this purpose, extracts from the plant can be purchased in the form of capsules or may also be brewed into an herbal tea.

How effective is St. John's wort in treating depression? The answer to this question is not altogether clear. Some studies have found the herbal to be effective. Others have not. At one end of the spectrum of these variable results is a recent study carried out in Brazil in which 72 patients suffering from mild to moderate depression were randomly assigned to receive either St.John's wort (900 mg per day), an antidepressant, fluoxetine (20 mg per day) or a placebo. Only 12 percent of the patients receiving St. John's wort achieved remission status. The patients receiving the antidepressant did better, 35 percent achieving remission. But hold on! The patients receiving the placebo did better than either. Forty-five percent were classified as being in remission.[25]

While the study did not shower kudos on the two would-be treatments for depression, there are positive findings from enough other studies to caution us not to throw out either the plant or the pharmaceutical as ineffective. However, such negative results should make one skeptical of extravagant claims that either of these substances is the end-all and be-all treatment for depression. As we have said, no one has yet found a magic bullet to treat depression.

A meta-analysis of clinical trials of St. John's wort as a treatment for depression published in the *British Medical Journal* in 1996 found that the herb was indeed more effective than the placebos. As over 1700 patients were included in these clinical studies, one would have to give this meta-analysis credence. It would appear that St. John's wort is an effective treatment for depression. Two subsequent meta-analyses have confirmed this conclusion. However, a collaborative study funded through the National Institutes of Health found that the herb was ineffective in treating people with major depressive disorder.[26]

So, where does this leave us? How about perplexed? Relying principally on the results of the collaborative study, The National Institutes of Health voiced the position in the publication *St. John's Wort and the Treatment of Depression* that the herb, "Is not a proven therapy for depression."[27] It was further stated that, "Recent studies suggest that St John's wort is of no benefit in treating major depression of moderate severity."[28] These statements seem rather dismissive of the herb as a therapy for depression. The implicit recommendation is that people who are depressed should try something else, presumably a pharmaceutical antidepressant. What the publication failed to mention, however, is that in the collaborative study cited as a basis for dismissing St John's wort, an antidepressant, seratline, was also used as a comparative treatment, and on the principal outcome measures used, it, too, fared no better than the placebo in treating depression. The publication, however, did not conclude that antidepressant medications are unproven therapies for depression.

And most interestingly, in a recent study carried out in Germany, 251 outpatients diagnosed with acute major depression were randomly assigned to receive either St. John's wort or the antidepressant, paroxetine. The patients given St. John's wort evidenced over a 50 percent decrease in their depression scores which was somewhat more than that achieved by the patients given paroxetine. So, the herbal treatment was at least as effective as the antidepressant and better tolerated.[29]

Clearly, St. John's wort does not have a track record of proving effective in every study testing its efficacy. But, the same could be said about antidepressant medicines and psychotherapy. That is one of the reasons we use meta-analyses, to look through a series of studies for overall trends. So far, the meta-analyses for St. John's wort have looked good.

Because there seems to be enough evidence accumulated to indicate that St. John's wort could well be effective in ameliorating depression, many people who are experiencing depression may want to try it. This might be particularly true for people who have a preference for "natural medicines" over pharmaceuticals or like the fact that it is an over-the-counter substance not requiring a prescription, or that the herbal may be less expensive than the pharmaceutical. If one decides to make a trial of the herbal, what things should one look out for?

We must preface any cautionary statements with the overall conclusion that St. John's wort seems to be generally well tolerated. Postmarketing surveillance studies of thousands of users find the incidence of side effects not only appears to be quite low, but seems to be considerably lower than for pharmaceutical antidepressants.[30] St. John's wort, of course, can have side effects. These include fatigue, dry mouth, dizziness, diarrhea, nausea, and increased sensitivity to sunlight. It is important to recognize that the herb also interacts with some pharmaceuticals, including antidepressant medicines and some anti-cancer drugs. If you are currently using any medicine, it is a very good idea to check with your physician and pharmacist before trying St. John's wort to make sure that using the herbal will not interact with your current medicines.

Because St. John's wort is an herbal and therefore not regulated by the Food and Drug Administration in the same way as pharmaceuticals, it is prudent to buy only products from a trusted and recognized manufacturer of herbal products.

There is also another less constraining caveat. At this point, we simply don't know what it is in the plant that does what it does. Scientists have amassed a list of suspects, constituents of the plant (e.g., hyperforin) which might produce the antidepressant effects, but the conclusions of two recent papers are that we don't really have enough information yet to be sure of what is producing the antidepressant effects.[31]

Omega-3 Polyunsaturated Fatty Acids

Omega-3 polyunsaturated fatty acids (PUFAs) are long chain acids found in the oils of some saltwater fish, especially salmon, tuna, and herring. Some other sources for these acids are flaxseed and canola oil and walnuts. The two omega-3 fatty acids which have particularly stirred the interest of researchers for their potential therapeutic value are eicosapentaenoic acid (EPA) and docosahexaenoic acid (DHA). It is important to recognize that our bodies cannot synthesize these acids. They must be consumed as part of our diet or by the use of supplements.

Omega-3 polyunsaturated fatty acids are one of the current hot items in a fad-prone culture attracting both researchers and the health-conscious public. Particularly exciting findings have been reported about coronary heart disease. Patients with coronary heart disease given omega-3 fatty acids were substantially less likely to suddenly die from sustained ventricular arrhythmias than patients not given these supplements.[32] Researchers have turned their attention to look for possible links of the omega-3 fatty acids to other diseases such as rheumatoid arthritis and quite interestingly, depression. Although large scale definitive studies proving beyond a reasonable doubt that increasing the amount of PUFAs in the body either by dietary supplements or by increasing the amount of fish in the diet will reduce the chances of becoming depressed or be a useful treatment for ongoing depression are still lacking, there are enough straws in the wind to make this a very attractive area for researchers to investigate.

Here are some of the straws in the wind. Studies have found statistical links between seafood consumption and prevalence rates for major depression. For example, in a note published in the British medical journal *Lancet*, Joseph Hibbeln looked at nine different countries and found that the countries in which seafood intake was highest had the lowest rates of depression.[33]

Researchers have reported that patients who are depressed had lower concentrations of PUFA's in their blood than controls. This finding has been replicated in several studies.[34]

In an interesting clinical report, physicians in Taiwan treating a pregnant woman who was suffering from recurrent major depressions but would not take antidepressant medicines for fear of hurting her unborn child was given omega-3 supplements. Within a month, her depression began to lift.[35]

In a study carried out in New York City 33 medication free depressed patients were assessed for levels of omega-3 fatty acid and then monitored over a two-year period for suicidal behavior. During the two years seven of the patients attempted suicide. These patients had lower levels of DHA in their initial assessments.[36]

Researchers in Israel carried out a study on 26 children with childhood depression. Half of the children were randomly selected to receive omega-3 fatty acids, half were given a placebo. Using a variety of measurements for depression, the children given the omega-3 fatty acids supplements were less depressed than the children given the placebo.[37]

In a study carried out in London, England, patients diagnosed with bipolar depression were randomly assigned to receive EPA or a placebo. After 12 weeks, the patients who had received EPA were less depressed than those receiving the placebo.[38]

Results such as these are certainly interesting!

A number of possible mechanisms have been proposed to explain why omega-3 fatty acids could have beneficial effects on depression. One of the more intriguing of these explanations is that omega-3 fatty acids affect the serotoninergic neurotransmitter system. Researchers have found evidence that levels of plasma DHA are related to levels of a serotonin metabolite, and we know that low levels of serotonin are a factor in depression.[39] It may be that adding omega-3 acids to the diet would affect serotonin activity in a somewhat similar way to taking SSRI antidepressant medications. This possibility needs further study.

Reports suggest that omega-3 fatty acids are generally well tolerated, although supplements may cause gastrointestinal distress and nausea in some people. It is an unsettled question of what might constitute an effective dose for treating depressive disorder. In some of the small clinical studies conducted to date, (e.g. the study carried out in London) a dose of 1 gram per day of EPA seemed to be effective. A helping of salmon or a tuna sandwich might well provide what is needed. Piling on supplements on the theory that if a small amount is helpful, more might be better could present problems, because high doses might pose a risk of bleeding and if one has a bleeding disorder, one should certainly exercise caution. But, substituting fish frequently for meat is not only good for your heart, it may be of value in ameliorating depression. Are we certain of this yet? By no means. The idea may yet fizzle when large scale randomized controlled studies are undertaken, but adding some fish to the diet is certainly about as low risk a strategy for possibly affecting depression that anyone has yet come up with.

Bright Light Therapy

Bright light therapy is an intuitive treatment for seasonal affective disorder. If the dark makes you depressed, turn on the lights! When the disorder was first elucidated in a 1984 paper in the *Archives of General Psychiatry* the authors also presented a study of the effectiveness of bright light therapy. They found that bright light therapy was an effective treatment for SAD and this finding has been replicated over the years.[40] Two of the questions that subsequently engaged researchers were (1) How could one use bright light therapy in the most effective way to treat SAD and, (2) Would this therapy have any value in treating depressive disorders besides SAD?

Among the issues relating to the first question was should the bright lights be used in the morning or evening? Or perhaps at both times? How long should the exposure to the bright light be? What kind of light and what intensity would work best? In a comprehensive review of bright light therapy Michael and Juian Su Terman examined the results of many studies and concluded that morning treatments were effective for more people than either evening or midday treatments. Adding a second session of exposure to the morning sessions was unlikely to improve the results. Brighter lights worked better than dimmer lights. Based on existing research the Termans recommended that SAD patients should initially try morning light shortly after awakening. They further recommended a light providing 10,000 lux be used for 30 minutes.[41]

As it is true that some people respond to bright light therapy better in the evening than they do in the morning, if morning light therapy doesn't work it makes sense for the individual to try it in the evening.

The answer to the second question, does bright light therapy work for depressive problems other than SAD appears to be a qualified "yes." The qualification is that the research basis is not yet that extensive to draw firm conclusions. However, some studies using patients diagnosed with major depressive disorders have reported significant beneficial effects. For example, a study published in *Psychological Medicine* reported a 50 percent remission rate in one measure of depression for patients treated with bright light therapy.[42] Given the relatively low risk in using bright lights, it seems worth a try for people suffering from major depressive disorder.

While bright light therapy appears to be a relatively benign treatment for depression, there are some potential side effects from its use. The principal side effects so far reported for bright light therapy are about what one might expect from being close to very bright lights for prolonged periods: headaches, nausea, and eye-irritation, and perhaps less predictable, jitteriness. Interestingly, there have been some cases of reported manic reactions to bright light therapy and several people using this therapy have committed suicide.[43] Whether the bright lights had anything to do with provoking these suicides is unknown.

To obtain the full benefits from bright light therapy, a special apparatus is required. Some people have constructed an apparatus, themselves, but the Termans do not recommend this, pointing out that some do-it-yourselfers have experienced corneal and eyelid burns. Commercial products come in different sizes and shapes. It is essential that the apparatus filter out ultraviolet light which is harmful. The apparatus should also be comfortable to sit near and be used for reading. The Termans describe a clinically tested model which uses high output white fluorescent lights which are elevated and tilted slightly downward. The device uses a polycarbonate diffusion screen for filtering out ultraviolet waves and yields an illumination of 10,000 lux.[44] In choosing an apparatus, it is clearly important to find manufacturers who are knowledgeable and experienced in designing and constructing these devices. Eye protection is of paramount importance in using bright light therapy.

15. The Problem of Recurrence

A patient diagnosed with major depressive disorder is being treated with an antidepressant. For awhile, the signs are encouraging. He is sleeping better, eating better, he has returned to work after a brief period of sick leave, and seems much more upbeat. Then, after a few weeks he seems to be going downhill again. This all too frequent situation is usually referred to as a *relapse*. While the depression had substantially improved, even appearing to be in remission, the patient has not yet reached the point where one could confidently assert that he was now experiencing a sustained recovery. And now, the attending physician has to once again make decisions about his medication.

If the patient has discontinued the antidepressant, should he be started on it again? If he is still using the medication, should the dose be increased or should another antidepressant be tried? Or should drug treatment be augmented by psychotherapy?

If the patient had discontinued the medicine when he felt better, chances are the prescribing physician will put him back on the medicine. There is a compelling logic in the argument that if the drug worked well before, why not try it again. Only this time, stay with it longer.

If the patient is still using the medicine, the usual thing to try is to raise the dose. There is empirical evidence that demonstrates that this strategy is often effective and a survey of over 400 clinicians indicated that increasing the dose is the most frequently reported "next step" in treatment.[1]

A relapse in depression and a recurrence of the disorder are very similar ideas. In both cases it appears that the depression has cleared up and seems to be in remission. The patient feels better and is doing better. However, in time the symptoms of depression flare-up again. The distinction between relapse and recovery has mostly to do with the length of the time the depression is in remission before symptoms of depression return. We call it a relapse when the remission of symptoms is a relatively short period and a recurrence when the period of remission is relatively long. One of the conventions proposed is that it is a relapse if the period of recovery is less than two months and a recurrence if the period is more than two months.[2] The distinction is, of course, arbitrary but the point is clear. After a decent interval of time the operative word is recurrence.

The recurrence of depression is one of the most nagging, troublesome problems facing mental health researchers and clinicians in their efforts to try to treat depression effectively. It must also be very discouraging to the patient and his or her family to have appeared to have shaken off the disorder only after a period of months or years to be faced with the problem all over again.

Now for many people who have experienced depression and have recovered, recurrence is not inevitable. A study carried out in California by Andrew Billings and Rudolph Moos demonstrated that many ex-patients do very well. In the study which followed up patients who had been treated in hospitals and community mental health centers, the researchers found that many patients were not only experiencing few depressive symptoms, but had improved self esteem and were coping better with stressful events. And although they still had relatively few friends and the interactions within their families were not as supportive as they could be, their social lives were getting better.[3]

In contrast to these ex-patients who were doing quite well, we know that many other patients experience a recurrence of depressive symptoms. The bad news is that neither treatment by medication nor psychotherapy is a guarantee that a person who has recovered substantially from an episode of depression will remain symptom free. And the same holds true for persons who have received electroconvulsive therapy. According to published reports, the chances are approximately one in two that people treated for unipolar depression will experience a recurrence of depression at some point during their lives and the odds rise precipitously that if there is a second episode, it will be followed by more.[4]

Some of the factors that promote the recurrence of depression are the same as the ones that promoted the risk of developing depression in the first place. Some are different. The patient's gender, for example, seems less predictive of recurrence than of experiencing the initial episode.[5]

Here, briefly are some of the factors that research has linked to increased risk for recurrence of depression.[6]

1. A family history of depression. Both genetic and experiential factors are probably involved here.
2. The initial episode of depression is severe.
3. The presence of comorbid disorders such as anxiety disorders and substance abuse.
4. Dysfunctional mind-sets and beliefs.
5. Continued high stress levels after recovery from the first episode.
6. Inadequate levels of social support.

If as research suggests, these are factors that promote the recurrence of depression, then we have an obvious starting place to offer suggestions about things to do to try to prevent such recurrences. The goal would be, wherever feasible, to mitigate the effects of these factors, to dampen them down.

A family history of depression is one of those roles of the dice that the new-born child has nothing to say about. A child comes into the world and has to take what he or she finds. We are beginning to make inroads into discovering the genes that contribute to depression and when the genetic influences are more fully understood, we may be able to find ways to counteract the effects of unhelpful genetic variations or perhaps even attempt to alter the genes themselves. This may well come, but we are not there yet.

At the present time, the environmental component of family influence may offer a more achievable target, particularly if we are dealing with a depressed child or adolescent. Family therapy offers a potential pathway to making changes in the child's environment to make it less depressogenic.

What about someone who has grown up in a dysfunctional family and is now a depressed adult? Would exploring these family dynamics in psychotherapy and hopefully coming to terms with what happened help prevent a recurrence of depression? I am not sure that there is research evidence which bears directly on this question, but it seems like a reasonable thing to try and I hope that in time research will address this issue move fully.

There is intuitive sense to the idea that a severe depression is more likely to persist in the face of treatment and more likely to recur than depression which is mild to moderate in severity. There is also empirical research which supports this view.[7] The severely depressed person may require a full range of antidepressant treatments — medication, psychotherapy, and possibly electroconvulsive therapy. At the present time the best hope for preventing recurrence of severe depression is through thorough treatment when it first occurs followed by some form of continuation or maintenance therapy which we shall discuss shortly.

In considering the impact of comorbid conditions on recurrence, I would like to use a metaphor. I would like to liken being depressed to being weighed down by a heavy load. For a moment, picture in your mind's eye a man or woman walking almost stooped shouldered by the weight they are carrying, perhaps a bundle of wood, or a sack of stones. The metaphor is not that far-fetched, for I have sat across from patients, their shoulders hunched, their eyes downcast looking very much as if they had been carrying a great load. Treatment for depression is something like taking this weight away.

But suppose that the individual has not only been carrying on one side of his shoulder that sack of stones but on the other side has been carrying and will continue to carry additional stones. With these additional burdens, it would not take a great deal of new stress on the other shoulder to weigh him or her down again.

The image of a man or woman caring a sack of stones or a pile of wood is, of course, only a metaphor but think for a moment of a person who is not only depressed, but is troubled by other problems such as anxiety disorders (e.g., phobias, panic attacks) or has a lingering problem of drug or alcohol abuse. Treating depression and not addressing these other problems leaves the individual with a perpetual drain on his or her psychological resources. With these ever-present vulnerabilities, it would not take a lot of stress to reactivate the depression.

As a preventive for the recurrence of depression, it makes sense to treat these comorbid conditions and get them under better control. For anxiety disorders there are anti-anxiety drugs (e.g., benzodiazepines) which can help at least in the short term for controlling anxiety disorders. Therapists trained in cognitive and behavioral techniques have effective procedures to deal with phobias and panic disorders. Twelve step programs are often the most effective ways of dealing with alcohol or drug abuse. The bottom-line is to treat, not ignore comorbid conditions as this may help prevent a recurrence of depression.

How does one change dysfunctional mind-sets such as a tendency towards overgeneralization or perfectionist thinking? Reading books like this which point out the links between such mind-sets and depression may help. Computerized programs of cognitive-behavior therapy such as Moodgym may be better. Working with a psychotherapist who is familiar with the techniques of cognitive therapy is probably the best bet. This approach to therapy has demonstrated effectiveness in treating depression, but like other forms of psychotherapy, it is no guarantor of recurrence of depression.[8]

Reducing stress in one's life is important for a great many people and particularly for people who are vulnerable to depression. While the most strategic time to do this is before there is an episode of depression — in the hope of preventing depression from ever occurring, the next best opportunity is during treatment for the initial episode and shortly thereafter, before depression becomes a recurrent problem. There are changes that one can make in one's life style that can reduce stress, such as increasing exercise and developing networks of supportive friends.

In addition to pursuing a range of self-help strategies, many people find that talking about their problems with a therapist is useful in controlling stress. Indeed, there is research evidence which supports the usefulness of psychotherapy in improving one's capability of dealing with stress. A recent study compared patients treated with either cognitive-behavioral or interpersonal therapy with patients treated with an antidepressant in terms of their post treatment resiliency to stressors. Compared to the patients receiving medication, the patients receiving therapy showed increased resiliency to stressors in the months following treatment.[9]

We have discussed the importance of social support in some detail earlier in the book. When things go bad, when problems arise, and stresses mount, there is nothing like having a sympathetic soul to talk to. A person with an understanding heart, an ability to listen, and empathize with what you're going through is a priceless commodity. Lucky the person who has such a friend! But lacking this, just to have somebody with whom you can sit down and talk over what is happening in your life can bring a sense of objectivity and perspective to your mounting concerns. Indeed, it may help prevent the escalation of negative thoughts and feelings into a depressive cycle.

Two practical suggestions. When you are depressed, utilize the help offered by the network of support groups for depression in this country. The Depression and Bipolar Support Alliance is a very good source for locating such support groups. When you are feeling well, try to increase your social contacts and when you can, make and nurture your friendships.

Continuation and Maintenance Therapies

The proponents of cognitive therapy are very good at carrying out research to demonstrate what they are doing. They report the good news that cognitive therapy or cognitive-behavioral therapy, as the case may be, is effective in treating depression. They present statistics on the percentage of cases that improve using standardized measures of depression and/or go into remission. To their credit, they also report the bad news—that significant numbers of patients who have successfully completed therapy began to develop depressive symptoms and not all that long after treatment is over. These flare-ups of depressive symptoms have been called discontinuation-risks or temporary spikes in symptoms. In other words the patient is showing signs of relapse to a greater or lesser extent. No one is sure what causes these flare-ups of symptoms. In a research paper, a research team led by T. M. Kashner suggested that these symptoms may have been temporarily suppressed by therapy only to emerge later when therapy had been completed. Or, alternatively that the discontinuation of therapy, itself, created sufficient stress to reignite the symptoms.[10] Critics of cognitive-behavioral therapy might argue that such therapy is too short-term and superficial to really dig down deep and root out the problem. For those who espouse this position, it seems to me that proponents of long term therapy should try to demonstrate in research that such therapy is followed by lower recurrence rates. I would be very interested in seeing such data.

How about medication and recurrence? When medication is stopped and the patient is on his or her own, recurrence statistics are likely to be no better than for cognitive-behavioral therapy. In fact, some data suggest that the recurrence rates may be worse.[11] All of which reinforces my own conclusion that whatever the initial treatment for depression — no matter what is done — it is a throw of the dice whether a single course of therapy will fix things up. Admittedly, a single course of therapy will work for many people. But for perhaps half of the people who are treated initially by psychotherapy or medication will sooner or later find that their improvement is only a temporary respite. In view of these hard facts, we need to rethink the model of treatment.

I have long held this view. In the first edition of *Understanding Depression*, I voiced the following opinion.

With regard to the use of psychotherapy as a preventive measure, it would take some rethinking of the traditional model of psychotherapy to utilize therapy as a preventive technique. In the traditional mode of therapy, a patient comes to the therapist with problems, has these problems thoroughly aired and hopefully resolved, and is then discharged. This traditional approach is based on an implicit assumption that bringing up and working through unresolved conflicts will result in a "cure" for the patient. While this may or may not be so for most emotional problems, we know that depression has a high rate of recurrence, so a different type of model may be more appropriate in treating depression. This model postulates that for many patients, there is a need for continuing contact on a much-reduced level between therapist and patient after initial discharge. It may be something like coming in for a visit once or twice a year-or, more importantly, when things begin to get rough.

My view is that for people who have suffered from recurrent depression, the time to see your psychotherapist is when stress is building up. Why wait until the stress level passes your tolerance level and the chances of a severe depressive reaction loom large? Wouldn't it be better to consult the therapist with whom you previously worked to help you over the difficulties *before* things get out of hand? This is the view that I left with my patients when they have finished the primary course of therapy.

Now, the view I expressed here — that for many patients it may be unrealistic to look at psychotherapy for depression as a single course of treatment with a fixed termination point — has been voiced by others as well. As far back as 1985, for example, researchers working at the University of Oregon expressed a similar position. Having completed a follow-up study of people with unipolar depression who were treated by cognitive-behavioral approaches, Linda Gonzales and her colleagues wrote, "The results suggest that although most patients are improved at the end of treatment, for some this improvement is relatively transient and by the LIFE criteria does not constitute recovery from the episode that led them to seek treatment. A potential implication of these results for cognitive behavioral treatments is that they are either too short to produce more enduring improvement in a greater proportion of patients and/or that they need to be supplemented with posttreatment maintenance and booster sessions to assist patients in maintaining the improvements they make in treatment."[12]

Procedures for continuation or maintenance therapy (e.g., seeing the patient on a reduced basis) have been developed by both practitioners of interpersonal therapy and cognitive-behavioral therapy. Researchers using interpersonal therapy have reported that seeing remitted patients as infrequently as once a month reduced the risk of recurrence.[13] Continuation-based cognitive therapy has also been found to lower the risk of recurrence.[14]

The need for continuation treatment with the use of antidepressant drugs has been widely recognized for some time. It has been recommended that following remission, patients should remain on antidepressant drugs for a period of up to nine months or perhaps a year, with people who have experienced recurrent episodes staying on the drug even longer.[15] The value of continuation therapy with antidepressant drugs has been demonstrated in a number of studies. Rates of recurrence diminish significantly with the continued use of the drugs. It has been suggested that the full dose of medicine used during treatment be maintained during the continuation period.[16]

With the high risk of recurrence of depression, I think it is altogether prudent for patients using antidepressant medicines which have proven effective for them to stay on the medicine for an extended period of time following remission of symptoms. For patients who have been through psychotherapy, it makes sense to maintain contact with the therapist and schedule occasional visitors to see the therapist, particularly when there are signs of trouble developing. There are no guarantees that these two steps or the self-help steps I outlined earlier will prevent the recurrence of depression, but it seems likely that a combination of such actions may have value as preventive measures.

16. Concluding Remarks

Depression, like other mental and emotional disorders, is a worldwide problem. One is likely to find the disorder in every corner of the globe. Joseph Westermeyer put it this way: "Psychiatric signs and symptoms are remarkably consistent from culture to culture. Patients everywhere complain of insomnia, worry, crying spells, weakness, suicidal ideation."[1]

Depression is not a new problem that has arisen in the wake of our modern technologically advanced society, although we may well be witnessing an increase in its prevalence. While depression has probably adversely affected people since the early days of recorded history, until recently we have not had much understanding of it or known how to treat it effectively. There were a few spots of light in this void. Freud, for example, offered some theoretical contributions highlighting the role of loss in depression and suggesting that self-directed anger plays a role in the disorder. Descriptive psychiatry produced some categories for classifying types of depression, but the distinctions were not all that clear and the terms were not universally accepted. In their early investigations, the biologically oriented researchers, lacking sophisticated techniques found little to write home about and the attention of research psychologists was turned elsewhere to problems that were more amenable to study. Over the past few decades the situation has changed dramatically.

Psychological and psychiatric journals have become inundated with research on depression. Researchers have been hard at work both improving the techniques needed to better study depression and producing substantive knowledge about the causes of depression and its treatment.

In listing the advances in knowledge brought about by this flurry of activity, one could begin by pointing to better methods of diagnosing depression. This has resulted in part from more clarity about the symptoms of depression. The *Diagnostic and Statistical Manual,* for example, lays out specific criteria to help the researcher and practitioner in making diagnoses of both depression and bipolar disorder. In addition, we now have both self-report and observationally-based psychological measures that can indicate with reasonable accuracy the presence of depression in adults. These measures are not only useful in clinical settings; they can also be used for large-scale studies in the community.

Community surveys have revealed that all groups in our society are susceptible to depression. Racial and ethnic backgrounds seem to make some difference in whether a person is at risk for depression. African Americans and Hispanic Americans tend to report symptoms of depression less frequently than non–Hispanic whites. Gender is probably a better indicator of risk. For reasons that we can only speculate about, women seem to be more vulnerable than men. While depression can occur at almost anytime during the life span, people in the prime time of life, those who have major responsibility for carrying out the workload of the society, seem to be particularly vulnerable. The latter finding points to stress as one of the factors that trigger depression. And, indeed, many psychological studies support this idea. Changes in life, particularly those involving personal loss, are related to depression. Cumulative stresses whether major or minor may also bring on depression.

Still, we know that not everyone subjected to stress becomes depressed. Studies have shown that the way we appraise stressful situations makes a difference. If we don't exaggerate the importance of what is happening, we are less likely to overact and less likely to experience an emotional downswing. The way we think about things makes a difference. Both theory and research indicate that thought patterns such as overgeneralization, perfectionistic and absolutist thinking and a predilection for fixing blame on oneself can interfere with making a rational appraisal of a stress provoking situation. Instead of reacting in a measured, problem-solving way, the tendency is to overreact, catastrophizing the situation, opening up the floodgates to depression.

While psychological researchers have been unraveling the thought processes that trigger and sustain depressed mood, researchers trained in the biological sciences have been exploiting new technologies to study the relation of depressed mood and the functioning of the body. Significant discoveries have been made linking depressed states to aberrations in the neurotransmitters in the brain. Genetic links to depression are being explored with interesting and provocative results. The day may not be far off when biological tests will be used in the diagnosis and treatment of depression.

I think it is fair to say that our understanding of depression is something that has gradually evolved over the past decades. While there have been occasional leaps forward in both our understanding of the disorder and how to treat it, such as the recognition of the role of the neurotransmitters in depression and the development of antidepressant drugs and forms of psychotherapy which are more targeted to deal with depression, with only a few exceptions (e.g., research on the serotonin transporter gene which may prove to be truly groundbreaking), a comparison between the first and second editions of *Understanding Depression* will show more of a tendency towards continuity and filling in the gaps in our knowledge than radical shifts in thinking about depression.

This suggests the study of depression is reaching a level of maturity in both the science base and in the treatment of depression. Obviously, there is a great deal more to learn and I feel confident that research over the next decades will add greatly to our understanding of the disorder.

Depression is a multilayered phenomenon. Even from fragmentary data we can see that there are social, cultural and environmental aspects of the disorder, as well as the more obvious psychological manifestations such as deep sadness which help define the disorder, and, of course, the underlying biological mechanisms. The lack of connectedness among many people in contemporary society and the high levels of stress generated in the society may be latent causes contributing to the increase in depression observed in our household surveys. While such social structures and institutions are difficult to change, one can envision potentially useful remedies such as support groups for people who experience stress and depression, as well as an expanded need to establish mechanisms in the workplace to reduce levels of stress. The treatment of depression, however, must almost inevitably focus on the psychological and biological levels. For here it is where the disorder is manifest, and here lie the treatments that are known to be efficacious.

Today the mental health profession can offer antidepressant medicines and psychotherapy. Both treatments are often effective. There is now a variety of antidepressant drugs which inhibit the reuptake of several important neurotransmitters, either singly or in combination, giving the prescribing physician more options in choosing medicines. These antidepressant medicines may improve mood and help get a person functioning. There is also a wider assortment of drugs with which to treat bipolar disorder. Psychotherapy can help change maladaptive thought patterns and destructive patterns of living which are contributing to the depressed state. While both types of treatment are helpful, neither is a panacea. Medicines have side effects that may not be tolerated by some patients. Therapy takes time and is expensive, and the patient has to be willing to put in the required time and effort. And there are a large number of people who are not helped by either medication or therapy.

Perhaps the biggest problem with current treatments for depression is that once the course of treatment is completed, there is a sizeable risk that in time — perhaps even in a matter of months— the symptoms may reappear. Not everyone experiences recurrence of symptoms, but enough people do to make it a worrisome possibility. At this point in time we are not certain of the best ways to prevent recurrence of depressive episodes. Continued use of antidepressant medicines well beyond the point of remission of symptoms can be helpful in preventing recurrence. I have recommended that when patients who have gone through psychotherapy begin to experience uncomfortable levels of stress in their lives, this is the time to consult their therapists, not wait until everything falls apart. A stitch in time may well save nine.

I believe that there is a good deal patients can do for themselves to help prevent further episodes of depression. A lifestyle that reduces the risk of depression is within the power of many people, just as a lifestyle that reduces the risk of a heart attack. In the latter case, if you stop smoking, keep your weight down, avoid dietary fats and unneeded salt and engage in a prudent program of exercise, the chances of developing coronary heart disease drop considerably. To reduce the risk of depression, you have to pay attention to the build-up of stress in order to take actions that keep it within acceptable limits. You should aim for a balanced lifestyle that includes activities that are personally gratifying.

It is also important to look at what is happening in life from a perspective that does not turn everyday problems into overwhelming ones. Give yourself a break when things go wrong. Don't get down on yourself to the point you can't make a comeback tomorrow. Remember that everyone has bad days. The trick is to learn to take them in stride. Research tells us that people who don't catastrophize events are less likely to become depressed.

In this book I have tried to present information and ideas that may be helpful to people who have experienced the symptoms of depression or have seen such symptoms in others who are close to them. I hope that this information will be useful in increasing your understanding of the nature of depressed mood and depression and the options that are available to treat depression.

I have tried to emphasize prevention and the importance of healthy attitudes and a balanced lifestyle. But when depressed feelings are severe or one has been in the throes of a protracted malaise that has eroded the joy of life, one would do well to consider consultation both with their physician and with a mental health professional. This book was not intended as a substitute for such consultation. I hope, however, that it will assist you in making an informed decision about what to do if such a time should come to pass.

Notes

Chapter 1

1. The technique was developed by E. Velten (1986).

2. See Forgas, et al. (1984).

3. Beck has written extensively about the cognitive approach to understanding and treating depression. See, for example, Beck, et al. (1979).

4. Four fluids (cardinal humors) were thought to influence one's health: blood, phlegm, choler, and melancholy (black bile).

5. See Goethe (1774), page 1.

6. See Folkenberg (1983), page 1.

7. See Jaminson (1993), pages 267–270.

8. See Kraepelin (1913).

9. This important reference has gone through several revisions. The current edition published in 1994 is known as DSM IV.

10. For studies of the facial muscle patterns of depressed people see Schwartz, et al. (1976) and Sirota & Schwartz (1982).

11. See, for example, Cornell, et al. (1984).

12. The study of driving skill was carried out by Bulmash, et al. (2006).

13. Freud (1959), page 155.

14. The empirical studies that have examined guilt in depressed patients seem to confirm the clinical picture. Robin Jarrett & Jan Weissenburger, for example, found that depressed patients reported higher levels of guilt than control subjects in a variety of situations: doing unintentional harm, failure of self-control, disregard for relationships, expression of anger, the failure to meet need and violation of principles. Jarrett & Weissenburger (1990).

15. See Dauber (1984) and the doctoral thesis of Schmidt (1981).

16. For examples of experimental demonstrations of the effects of depression on the processing of emotional materials, see Rinck & Becker (2005) and Weniger, et al. (2006).

17. Gallagher (1986), page 4.

18. Our sources for the risk factors for suicide in people with major depressive disorder studies are studies by Dumais et al. (2005), Oquendo, et al. (2004), McGirr, et al. (2006) and Solkero, et al. (2005).

19. Johnson & Magaro (1987), page 29.

20. The study in Norway was reported by Wang, et al. (2006)

21. See Robbins & Tanck (1982).

22. See Zimmerman, et al. (2006).

23. For a statistical study indicating that the dimensional model may be a better fit for depression than the category model, see Priscidiandaro & Roberts (2005).

24. See Hamilton (1960).

25. For the first version of the BDI, see Beck, et al. (1961). For the most recent, see Beck et al. (1996).

26. See Radloff (1977).

27. See Robbins & Tanck (1994).

28. See McMillan & Pihl (1987).

29. See Robbins & Tanck (1987).

30. Cook's narrative first appeared in 1909, was reprinted in 1998 (see Cook, 1998) and was excerpted in Palinkas (2003). The passage quoted here was taken from Palinkas, page 353.

31. See Palinkas, pages 353–354.

32. *Ibid.*, page 356.

33. Shakespeare, *The Tragedy of Richard the Third*, Act I, scene I. In Parrott, page 252.

34. See Rosenthal, et al. (1984).

35. The telephone survey of seasonal

mood changes was reported by Kasper, et al. (1989).

36. See Potkin, et al. (1986).

37. Wehr, et al. (1987), page 1603.

38. Falret's work is described in a paper by Sedler (1983).

39. See Spearing (2002).

40. Depue et al. (1981), pages 436–437.

41. These characteristics of rapid cyclers were reported by Kupka et al. (2005).

42. The study showing the stability of rapid cycling over time was carried out by Koukopoulos et al. (2003).

43. For reports of very rapid cycling, see Kramlinger and Post (1996).

44. The study comparing the personality patterns of type I bipolar patients, Type II bipolar patients and unipolar patients was reported by Akiskal, et al. (2006).

45. Studies with apparent conflicting findings were reported by Summers, et al. (2006) and Torrent, et al. (2006).

46. See Valtonen, et al. (2006) and Valtonen et al. (2005) for studies of suicide attempts in bipolar patients.

Chapter 2

1. Details on the development of the NIMH Interview Guide are given in Robins, et al. (1981).

2. Statistics for the lifetime prevalence of depressive disorder are presented in Robins, et al. (1984).

3. See Kessler, et al. (2005).

4. See Hasin, et al. (2005).

5. See Durkheim (1966).

6. This estimate was based on the research review by Goldbart (2006).

7. See McLearn, et al. (2006a).

8. See Goldbart (2006).

9. The meta analysis was reported by Carter, et al. (2006).

10. For a review of risk factors for postpartum depression see McCoy et al. (2006).

11. For an example of a study showing the relation of postpartum depressive levels and maternal-child behaviors see McLearn, et al. (2006b).

12. See Angold, et al. (1998).

13. See Brooks-Gunn and Warren (1989).

14. These data are reviewed in Hankin and Abramson (2001). See page 784.

15. Ibid., page 785.

16. Ibid., page 786.

17. Hammen and Peters (1977). See in particular pages 995–996.

18. The observations in New Guinea on the Kaluli tribe were made by Edward Schieffelin. The study of the Amish was carried out by Egeland and Hostetler (1983).

19. Blazer, et al. (1985). The statistically controlled analysis suggested that the rate of depression in urban areas was twice as high as in rural areas.

20. Rural-urban comparisons in other countries include studies by Weich, et al. (2006), St. John, et al. (2006), Kovess, et al. (1987), and Colla, et al. (2006).

21. The comparison of immigrants with native born Americans was reported by Grant, et al. (2004). See also the study by Ortega, et al. (2000).

22. See, for example, McGuire (1999).

23. See Breslau, et al. (2005).

24. Ibid.

25. See Grant, et al. (2004) and Ortega, et al. (2000).

26. Karno, et al. (1987). For a discussion of ethnic comparisons, see page 700.

27. The study of the use of health facilities by Asian Americans was reported by Bareto and Segal (2005).

28. The incident was described in Marcos, et al. (1979), page 173.

29. Sue and Sue (1987), page 480.

30. The Internet sample study was reported by Fogel and Ford (2005).

31. See Zhang and Snowden (1999).

32. See Takeuchi, et al. (1998).

33. The Oregon study was reported in an article by Lewinsohn, et al. (1986).

34. Kashani, et al. (1986), page 1141.

35. Lefkowitz and Tesiny (1980), page 43.

36. See Mcfarlane, et al. (1954).

37. See Hankin and Abramson (2001), page 774.

38. See Kovacs (1985) and Kovacs (1992).

39. The study of the Children's Depression Inventory carried out in Belgium was reported by Timbremont, et al. (2004).

40. Carey, et al. (1987), page 761.

41. See Doerfler, et al. (1988).

42. See Larson, et al. (1990).

43. See Kerr, et al. (1987).

44. For a discussion of adolescent suicide and suicidal ideation, see Robbins (1998).

45. See Reynolds and Coats (1982).

46. The study of French high school students was reported by Chabrol, et al. (2002).

47. A Graph showing the age distribution for the onset of bipolar illness was presented in Grant, et al. (2005), page 1210.

48. See, for example, the study by Sourander et al. (1999).

49. For data showing the risk of onset of depression during adolescence and young adulthood, see Burke, et al. (1990). See Hasin et al. (2005) for more recent data indicating a shift in maximum risk toward middle age.

50. The study in Canada of rural and urban elderly people was reported by J. L. Wang (2004).

51. See Kessler, et al. (2005).

52. The data showing the often prolonged nature of depression in the elderly was reported by Beekman, et al. (2002).

53. The study of physical decline in the depressed elderly was reported by Penninx, et al. (1998). Similar results were reported by Lenze, et al. (2005).

54. See Rapp, et al. (1988).

Chapter 3

1. Positron emission tomography (PET) and functional MRI (fMRI) are two of the more widely used techniques to measure activity levels in a given area of the brain. For a more extended description of PET see Robbins (2007).

2. For a review of family studies and depression, see Weissman (2006). The finding that people with a family history of depression often had early onset anxiety symptoms was reported by Weissman.

3. Data for second degree relatives of depressed people were cited in Sargent (1986).

4. See Kendler (1986).

5. The two twin studies were reported by Bierut, et al. (1999) and Kendler and Prescott (1999).

6. The studies reporting heritability estimates for bipolar disorder were reported by Kieseppa, et al. (2004) and McGuffin, et al. (2003).

7. The meta-analysis of studies comparing the size of the hippocampus in depressed

and non-depressed subjects was reported by Campbell, et al. (2004).

8. For a discussion of hippocampal nerve cell genesis see Dranovsky and Hen (2006).

9. Research on the amygdala in depressed patients is reviewed by Weniger, et al. (2006) and Campbell, et al. (2004).

10. See Weniger, et al. (2006).

11. For a review of MRI studies on early-onset bipolar patients, see Frazier, et al. (2005).

12. See Wurtman, et al. (1982).

13. See Neumeister, et al. (2004) and Neumeister et al. (2006).

14. See, for example, Owens and Nemeroff (1994) and Mann, et al. (1986). There are research findings indicating an increase in the number of serotonin binding sites in the frontal cortices of violent suicide victims. For a further discussion of this issue, see Pandy (1997).

15. See Gorman, et al. (2000).

16. See Siever and Davis (1985).

17. See Dickerson and Kemeny (2004).

18. For a discussion of the DST as a tool in the diagnosis of depression, see the report of the APA Task Force on Laboratory Tests in Psychiatry (1987).

19. *Ibid*. See, also Meller, et al. (1988).

20. The improvements using the DEX/CRH test in identifying depressed patients was reported by Heuser, et al. (1994). The findings for chronic depressed patients were reported by Watson, et al. (2002).

21. The study in Japan was reported by Kunugi, et al. (2006).

22. The study of bipolar patients was reported by Watson, et al. (2004).

23. For a discussions of REM studies in depressed patients see Kupfer (2006) and Shaffery, et al. (2003).

24. See Ehlers, et al. (1988). More recent estimates put the figures for 70 percent for outpatients and 80 percent for inpatients. See Lam (2006).

25. For a discussion of circadian rhythms and SAD, see Lewy, et al. (2006).

26. For a review of antidepressant medications and sleep, see Wilson and Argyrapoulos (2005) and Lam (2006).

27. See Kufper (2006).

28. The dreams of depressed people are discussed in Robbins (1988), Chapter 7. See also Robbins and Tanck (1988).

29. The study of the dreams of bipolar patients was reported by Beauchemin and Hays (1966).

30. See Blaise, et al. (1986).

31. See, for example, Denney, et al. (1988).

32. See Weisse (1992).

33. *Ibid.*, page 481.

34. For a non-technical discussion of the use of endophenotypes, see Dingfelder (2006). For an application of the concept to research on depression, see Hassler, et al. (2004).

35. Recently, the picture has become more complex, as functional variants have been identified in the long (L) form.

36. For a discussion of the serotonin transporter and the long and short variants, see Hariri and Holmes (2006).

37. See, for example, a meta-analysis reported by Sen, et al. (2004).

38. See Hariri (2002). See also Bertolino, et al. (2005).

39. See Caspi, et al. (2003).

40. See Zalsman, et al. (2006).

41. These data were presented as a follow-up report to the NIMH study of 2004. See Neumeister, et al. (2006).

Chapter 4

1. While Beck viewed, "the negative processing of information" as primary, in that it leads to the other symptoms of depression, he did not view negative thoughts as the cause of depression. In reviewing the status of cognitive therapy, he wrote, "It seems farfetched to assign a causal role to cognitions because the negative automatic thoughts constitute an integral part of depression, just like the motivational, affective, and behavioral symptoms. To conclude that cognitions cause depression is analogous to asserting that delusions cause schizophrenia." See Beck (1991), 373, 369.

2. See, for example, Incoviello, et al. (2006).

3. For research on the recognition of facial expressions, see Joorman and Gotlib (2006) and Surguiazde et al. (2004).

4. See Beck (1976), page 33.

5. See Buchwald (1977).

6. See, for example, Lewinsohn, et al. (1980).

7. The scale which has been widely used to measure the perceptions of the control of reinforcement was developed by Julian Rotter. See Rotter (1960).

8. See Benassi, et al. (1988), page 362.

9. For a review of research on learned helplessness, see the special February 1978 issue of the *Journal of Abnormal Psychology*, entitled "Learned Helplessness as a Model of Depression." See, in particular, the article by Seligman.

10. This experiment was carried out by Hiroto (1974).

11. See Altman and Winterborn (1980).

12. Anouilh (1959), Act 3, p. 64.

13. See Hawkins, et at. (1988).

14. See Wenzloff and Grozier (1988), page 93.

15. See Carver and Ganellen (1983), page 333.

16. The study identifying the aspects of perfectionism that had particular relevance to depression was carried out by Enns and Cox (1999). See also Packard (2006).

17. The study of people suffering from insomnia was reported by Vincent and Walker (2000).

18. See, for example, Blatt, et al. (1988), Zuroff, et al. (2000), and Hawley, et al. (2006).

19. See Ellis (1962).

20. See Beck (1976), page 255.

21. For a study of social comparisons and depression, see Bazner, et al. (2006). A meta-analysis of the results of many studies found that self-focusing was related to negative mood, anxiety and depression. See Mor and Winquest (2002).

22. See Freud (1959).

23. See Robbins and Tanck (1997).

24. The items for the automatic thoughts questionnaire are listed in Table I of the paper of Hollon and Kendall (1980). See page 389.

25. The Dysfunctional Attitudes Scale is described in Weissman and Beck (1978).

26. The study of dysfunctional attitudes and postpartum depression was reported by Church, et al. (2005).

27. See, for example, Seligman, et al. (1979).

28. For a discussion of the Attribution Style Questionnaire, see Peterson and Villanova (1988). The meta-analyses involved

thousands of subjects. A meta-analysis for adults was reported by Sweeney, et al. (1986). A meta-analysis for children was reported by Gladstone and Kaslow (1995).

29. See Meyersburg, et al. (1974), page 376.

30. See Lewinsohn, et al. (1980), page 205.

31. *Ibid.*, page 212.

32. *Ibid.*, page 211.

33. See Snyder (1984).

Chapter 5

1. See Bowlby (1982), page 668.

2. See, for example, Harlow (1958).

3. The study comparing attachment patterns of children from divorced families with those from intact families was reported by Nair and Murray (2005).

4. For a discussion of the early research relating to attachment, see articles by Goldsmith and Alansky (1987) and Cicchetti (1987).

5. See Ainsworth (1989), page 710.

6. The study of reactions to the play of toddlers was reported by Fagot (1997).

7. For reports of the longitudinal study of children evaluated in the strange situation, see Stroufe et al. (2005).

8. The study of attachment in nine- to eleven-year-old children was reported by Kearns et al. (2007).

9. The study of adult attachment and depression was carried out by Bifulco, et al. (2002a) and Bifulco, et al. (2000b).

10. The studies of fear of rejection and depression were conducted by Reis and Grenyer (2004).

11. See Blatt (1974).

12. This analysis was reported by Nelson (1982). See, also, Barnes and Prosen (1985).

13. See Agid, et al. (1999).

14. The study relating rejecting parents to self-hatred self-criticism was reported by Irons et al. (2006). See also Robbins and Tanck (1997).

15. See Parker (1979) and Parker, et al. (1979).

16. For a description of some of this research see Alloy, et al. (2006).

17. See Parker (1983).

18. See Alloy et al. (2006).

19. See McCraine and Bass (1984), page 7.

20. These statements were excerpted from Cofer and Winterborn (1980), page 313. See in particular Table 5.

21. These data were obtained in a study relating Beck Depression Inventory scores to reports of early memories. See Robbins and Tanck (1994).

22. The prospective studies varied in terms of the length of follow up. See Alloy et al. (2006). The follow-up period in one of the studies, Pilowsky et al. (2006) has now exceeded two decades.

23. These data were reported by Pilowsky et al. (2006).

24. See Kazdin et al. (1985), page 304.

25. Data linking childhood sexual abuse and psychiatric disturbances including depression was reported by Molnar et al. (2001).

26. See Alloy et al. (2006).

27. For a discussion of the psychological affects of divorce on children, see Hetherington (1989). For a recent report of a longitudinal study linking measures of parental discord to subsequent depression in the offspring, see Pilowsky et al. (2006).

28. See, for example, Coleg (1990).

29. See Lefkowitz and Tesiny (1980), page 44.

30. McGrath and Repetti (2002) found that children with more symptoms of depression underestimated their actual competence. See, also, related studies by Hoffman et al. (2000) and Kistner et al. (2006). For a more general look at the relation of childhood competence and depression, see Blechman et al. (1986).

31. This study was carried out by Rockhill et al. (2007).

32. See Leitenberg et al. (1986), pages 529–530.

33. See Seligman et al. (1984), page 238.

34. For illustrative studies pointing out these gender differences in adolescence, see Gjerde et al. (1988) and Oldenhinkel et al. (2007).

35. See Prinstein et al. (2005).

36. See, for example, Sund, et al. (2003).

Chapter 6

1. See Meyersburg et al. (1974), page 384.

2. The review was carried out by C. M. Mazure (1998). The statistics were cited in Hammen (2005).

3. There are a large number of studies which show the buffering effect of social support. For an example of a recent study, see Krohne and Slangen (2005). They found that social support reduced anxiety levels in patents undergoing surgery.

4. See Freud (1959) and Bowlby (1980).

5. While the evidence indicates that many people are able to cope with serious losses without experiencing depression, the chances of becoming depressed nonetheless are increased. A study by Patrick Shrout and his colleagues (1989) suggested that experiencing fateful losses such as the death of a spouse or child, the loss of a home or job or being unable to find treatment for a serious illness raises the odds of becoming depressed. A study by Stanley Murrell and Samuel Himmelfarb (1989) indicated that the depressive effects of bereavement in older adults began to dissipate within a year.

6. See Robbins and Tanck (1984).

7. See Kanner et al. (1981).

8. See Hammen (2005). The citation is on page 303.

9. The tendency for cortisol levels to be particularly elevated during stress arousing situations which are uncontrollable was reported in a review of research carried out by Dickerson and Kemeny (2004).

10. See Catrona et al. (2005).

11. *Ibid.*, page 12.

12. See Caspi et al. (2003).

13. See Hammen (2005), page 310.

14. See Hammen et al. (2000).

15. For an illustrative study of the relation of adult attachment style to childhood adverse events and current social relationships, see Bifulco et al. (2002).

16. For a review of the studies, see Hammen (2005). The importance of activating depressive cognitions was indicated in a study carried out by Abela et al. (2004).

17. See Hammen (2005), page 311.

18. See Folkman and Lazarus (1986), page 110, Table 2.

19. See Robbins and Tanck (1992), in particular Table 1, page 150. There have been a number of studies that related techniques people used to cope with stress to feelings of depression. An example would be the studies carried out by Charles Holahan and Rudolph Moos. They assessed their subjects on a number of measures including coping techniques, then followed the subject for several years. They reported, "We have found that personality characteristics that involve more self-confidence and more easy-going disposition, more family support, and fewer avoidant coping strategies predict lower levels of depression." See, Holahan and Moos (1991).

20. See Cole et al. (2006), page 40.

21. The concept of the sick role was elucidated by sociologist Talcott Parsons. See, for example, Parsons (1975).

22. See Cole et al. (2006).

23. The hypothesis of biological changes following repeated episodes of depression was developed in a seminal article by Post (1992).

24. See Monroe and Harkness (2005).

25. The study of assault victims was reported by Foa et al. (2006).

Chapter 7

1. See Crowe and George (1989), page 374.

2. A factor analytic study showing how items assessing these indicators form a factor of alcohol dependence was reported by Grant et al. (2006).

3. The 12 month prevalence for alcohol disorders was reported in a study by Stinson et al. (2005). See, in particular, page 109.

4. This assertion made by Benjamin Karpman was cited by Wall (1937).

5. See Clark et al. 1985, pages 483–485.

6. See Lutz's and Snow's (1985) review. These studies should be interpreted cautiously as the data are retrospective.

7. See Stinson et al. (2005). See, in particular, Table 2.

8. See Kuo et al. (2006).

9. For discussions of expectations from drinking see Brown et al. (1980) and Smith (1994).

10. See Crowe and George (1989), page 375.

11. See Nathan et al. (1970).

12. See Robbins and Nugent (1975).

13. The study carried out by Homish et al. was cited by Munsey in the *Monitor on Psychology* (2007).

14. These statistics on marijuana use were taken from Stinson et al. (2006).

15. See Robbins (1983), page 27.

16. See Keeler et al. (1971).

17. See Robbins and Tanck (1973).

18. These interesting findings relating to bipolar disorder were reported in Stinson, et al. (2006).

19. The study in Oakland was reported by Zweben et al. (2004).

20. The Internet study was reported by Looby and Earleywine (2007).

21. The study of arrestees was reported by Kalechstein et al. (2000).

22. The study on cocaine users was reported by Schmitz et al. (2000).

23. See, for example, Schmitz et al. (2001) and Galloway et al. (1994).

24. See Robbins and Nugent (1975). A recent study drawing from a very different population, heroin patients entering treatment centers in Australia reported major depressive disorder in about one-fourth of the subjects with higher rates among females than males. See Teesson et al. (2005).

25. For further discussion of these data, see Robbins (1974).

Chapter 8

1. Paul Hewitt and Gordon Flett developed a reliable scale to measure perfectionist tendencies. See Hewitt and Flett (1991).

2. See Heiby (1982).

3. The study linking a lack of self reinforcement to depression was reported by Wilkinson (1997).

4. The strategy of small wins was discussed in Weick (1984).

5. This line was attributed to J. L. Spaulding.

6. The randomized controlled trial studying the effects of exercise on depression was reported by Dunn et al. (2005).

7. For a discussion of community studies, see Harris et al. (2006).

8. *Ibid.*

9. See, for example, Noles et al. (1985)

and McCabe and Marwit (1993) for a study of this relation in children.

10. See the work of Betty Allgood-Merten et al. (1990). In discussing their research on adolescence, Allgood-Merten and her colleagues state, "The results also corroborate the finding that body image is an important correlate of depression in adolescence. (Body image) is a critically important aspect of self-esteem in this age group that functions as an antecedent as well as a strong correlate of depressive symptoms in adolescents." Allgood-Merten et al. (1990), page 61. See, also, Paxton et al. (2006).

11. A study reported by Douglas Needles and Lynn Abramson suggested that the introduction of pleasant activities into one's daily life would be most beneficial when accompanied by changes in the person's outlook and attitudes that enable him or her to more fully enjoy the activities. See Needles and Abramson (1990).

12. See Gladstone et al. (2007).

13. For examples of studies carried out abroad, see Stansfeld, et al. (1998), Ostberg and Lennartsson (2007), Aro, et al. (2001), and Koizumi, et al. (2005).

14. For illustrative studies, see Libet and Lewinsohn (1973) and Petty et al. (1994).

15. The comment was provided by DBSA.

16. This early review on self help manuals was written by Glasgow and Rosen (1978).

17. See Scogin et al. (1989) and Floyd et al. (2004).

18. See Griffiths and Christensen (2007) for a review of research using moodGYM.

19. For a study suggesting that while self-help information may increase knowledge about depression it may not translate into reduction of depressive symptoms. See Salkovskis, et al. (2006).

20. The study carried out in Germany was reported by Kronmuller (2007).

21. The review of evaluation studies for computerized cognitive-behavioral therapy was written by Kaltenthaler (2006). It should be stated that there are studies which report little effect from using these types of programs.

22. See Jewell and Mylander (1988).

23. See Nezu et al. (1989) and Nezu et al. (1990).

24. See Mahalik et al. (1988), page 241.

Chapter 9

1. See Neuringer (1982), page 185.
2. See Szasz (1986), page 809.
3. DBSA provides a number of helpful suggestions. See, for example, "Helping Someone with a Mood Disorder" posted on its website.
4. Papers by Veil and Kuhner (1990) and Veil (1993) describe these counterintuitive findings.
5. See, for example, Beach (1987).
6. For research of the social and psychological impact on the family, see Benazon and Coyne (2000), van Wijngaarden, et al. (2004), and Fadden, et al. (1987).
7. See Coyne, et al. (1987), page 350.
8. See, for example, Benazon and Coyne (2000).

Chapter 10

1. The often long delay between the onset of mental and emotional disorders and treatment for these disorders was reported by Wang at al. (2005).
2. See Wang et al. (2006).
3. These statistics for physician recognition of depression were reported by Simon and VonKorff (1995).
4. The study looking at difficulties in referral was reported by Trude and Stoddard (2003).
5. The decline in use of psychotherapy without medication was reported by Wang et al. (2006).
6. This conclusion was reached by Kessler et al. (2005).
7. Questions of the adequacy of treatment for depression by primary care physicians have been raised in a number of studies. See, for example, Young et al. (2001).
8. For a discussion of the changing relation between stress and depression, see Monroe and Harkness (2005).
9. For a look at the stigma associated with mental illness in past years, see Yarrow et al. (1955). The recent survey of attitudes about mental-health treatment was reported by Mojtabi (2007).
10. See Rost et al. (2007).
11. See Sue and Sue (1987).

12. For studies of underutilization of mental health services among minorities, see Alegria et al. (2002) and Neighbors et al. (2007).
13. See, for example, Kessler et al. (2005), and Olfson et al. (2002).

Chapter 11

1. These estimates for the effectiveness of antidepressant drugs are based on reviews and meta-analyses of many studies. See, for example Bollini, et al. (1999).
2. For an example of a study in which an antidepressant did not perform better than a placebo, see Moreno, et al. (2006).
3. The study showing the possible benefits of trying several antidepressants was reported by Quitkin, et al. (2005).
4. See *Medications for Mental Illness*, page 16.
5. See Kocsis et al. (1988).
6. The review of the efficacy of tricyclics and other antidepressants was reported by Einarson, et al. (1999).
7. The article in the *Emergency Medicine Journal* was written by Kerr, et al. (2001).
8. See FDA approves Emsam (selegiline) as first drug patch for depression (2006). See also Frampton and Plosker (2007) for studies of the use of this drug patch.
9. For a discussion of the treatment of atypical depression see Rapaport (2007).
10. The comparison between SSRIs and tricyclics was reported by Anderson (2000).
11. The study of the efficacy of the SSRI, citlapram was carried out by Trivedi et al. (2006).
12. See, for example, Anderson (2000).
13. The review of the efficacy of SSRIs in comparison with tricyclics when used in primary-care settings was reported by MacGillivray, et al. (2003). See, also, Arroll, et al. (2005).
14. The study carried out in United States primary-care clinics was reported by Clayton et al. (2002). The study in Spain was reported by Montejo et al. (2001).
15. For a discussion of the possible links between SSRIs and suicidal thinking, see Whittington (2005).

16. For studies evaluating the effects of using SSRIs during pregnancy on the newborn child, see Malm et al. (2005) and the article in the Health Section of the Washington Post, "Birth defects: Risks appear low when mother uses SSRI antidepressants."

17. See Serebruany (2006).

18. For a study comparing bupropion with SSRIs in terms of reported sexual dysfunction, see Clayton et al. (2002).

19. For a meta-analysis comparing the efficacy of the SNRI venlafaxine with that of SSRIs, see Einarson et al. (1999).

20. See, for example Sir, et al. (2005).

21. The comparison between duloxetine and escitalopram was reported by Nierenberg, et al. (2007).

22. See *Medicines for Mental Illness*, page 10.

23. *Ibid.*, page 11.

24. *Ibid.*, page 11.

25. *Ibid.*, page 11.

26. *Ibid.*, page 12.

27. *Ibid.*, page 13.

28. See, for example, Bridle, et al. (2004).

29. See Bridle et al. (2004) and Smith et al. (2007).

30. See *Medications for Mental Illness*, page 27.

Chapter 12

1. See Kazdin (1986), page 96.

2. See Freud's essay *Mourning and Melancholia,* republished (1959).

3. For a discussion of psychoanalytic thinking about depression see Bellak (1981).

4. Beck (1976), pages 213–14. Robert De-Rubeis and his colleagues (1990) suggest that the basis for the effectiveness of cognitive therapy lies not only in the changes in thinking that take place in therapy, but in the active application of their principles in the patient's everyday life. The same maxim would seem to hold for most forms of therapy; therapy does not stop in the therapist's office. One must practice what one has learned.

5. The case was excerpted from Safran et al. (1986). See pages 516–518.

6. A recent meta-analysis looking at the efficacy of the behavioral therapy technique, teaching activity scheduling to increase pos-

itive activities, as a treatment for depression revealed positive findings. The meta-analysis was carried out by Cuijpers et al. (2007).

7. See Klerman et al. (1984) for a discussion of interpersonal therapy including the case of Ellen F.

8. For a review of meta-analyses carried out for cognitive-behavioral therapy, see Butler et al. (2006).

9. The meta-analysis for interpersonal therapy was carried out by de Mello et al. (2005).

10. The review of studies which used interpersonal therapy with adolescents was reported by Brunstein-Klomek et al. (2007).

11. For recent papers looking at the efficacy of psychodynamic therapy for depression see Bond (2006) and Trowell et al. (2007).

12. This research is described by Weissman (2007).

13. See, for example, Nietzel et al. (1987).

14. See Wampold et al. (2002).

15. For examples of studies that show that people with more severe depression do less well in therapy, see Gonzales et al. (1985) and Hoberman et al. (1988). A recent meta-analysis showed that the severity of the disorder affects the outcome not only for depression but for anxiety disorders as well. See Haby et al. (2006).

16. See, for example, Hoberman et al. (1988).

17. See McBride et al. (2006).

18. See, for example, the review of research carried out by Steinbrueck et al. (1983) which concluded that, "Psychotherapy appears to be somewhat more effective than drug therapy."

19. The collaborative study is described in Elkin et al. (1989).

20. See Agency for Health Care Policy and Research (1993).

21. See DeRubeis et al. (1999).

22. See Conte et al. (1986).

23. For an illustrative study, see de Maat et al. (2007).

Chapter 13

1. See Way and Banks (2001).

2. The current telephone number for

the National Mental Health Information Center is 1-800-789-2647. Their web site is www.mentalhealth.samhsa.gov.

3. For a very readable account of the development of electroconvulsive therapy see Sabbatini (2007). For a general overview of electroconvulsive therapy, see Taylor (2007).

4. Personal communication

5. For a description of electroconvulsive therapy in modern dress, see S. Wang (2007).

6. See Consensus Development Conference Statement (1985).

7. See Taylor (2007). Taylor cites data which indicates that as many as 55 percent of depressed patients not helped by other treatments have responded well to electroconvulsive therapy.

8. The study of differential memory loss was reported by Lisandby et al. (2000).

9. See Taylor (2007).

10. *Ibid.*

11. The case study was reported by Goforth and Holsinger (2007).

Chapter 14

1. See Kessler et al. (2001) or Barnes et al. (2004).

2. See Ernst et al. (1999).

3. See *Meditation for Health Purposes* (2006), page 3.

4. *Ibid.*

5. See Cahn and Polich (2006), page 180.

6. *Ibid.*

7. See *Meditation for Health Purposes* (2006), page 2.

8. See Cahn and Polich, (2006), page 201.

9. *Ibid.*, page 182

10. *Ibid.*, page 181.

11. Most of these subjects in this study were retested in a three year follow-up. The improvements in depression and anxiety scores were maintained. See Kabat-Zinn et al. (1992).

12. See Lau and McMain (2005), page 864.

13. For Information on the development of MBCT, see Teasdale et al. (1995).

14. The study exploring the efficacy of MBCT was reported by Finucane and Mercer (2006).

15. The meta-analysis was reported by Toneatto and Nguyen (2007).

16. See Moyer et al. (2004), page 3.

17. The survey of massage therapists was reported by Sherman et al. (2005).

18. See Moyer et al. (2004), page 12.

19. The studies showing increased serotonin levels following massage therapy are described in Field et al. (2005).

20. See Moyer et al., page 14.

21. See Field et al. (2005), pages 1399–1400.

22. See Lee (2006). The article is in Korean. I have relied on the translated abstract.

23. The study comparing the effects of acupuncture and massage on depression measures was reported by Manber et al. (2004).

24. See *St. John's Wort and the Treatment of Depression* (2004), page 2.

25. The study in Brazil was carried out by Moreno et al. (2006).

26. The 1996 meta-analysis on the efficacy of St. John's wort was reported by Linde et al. (1996). The two subsequent meta-analyses were reported by Kim et al. (1999) and Whisky et al. (2001). The collaborative study carried out by the National Institutes of Health was cited in *St. John's Wort and the Treatment of Depression*, page 4. See the *Journal of the American Medical Association*, 2002, volume 287, page 1907 for more details.

27. See *St. John's Wort and the Treatment of Depression*, page 4.

28. *Ibid.*, page 1.

29. The study of St. John's wort carried out in Germany was reported by Szegedi, et al. (2005).

30. For a discussion of the incidence of adverse affects reported by users of St. John's wort, see Schultz (2006).

31. The two papers were authored by Caccia (2005) and by Wurglics and Schubert-Zsilavecz (2006).

32. These data were cited in Covington (2004).

33. See Hibbeln (1998).

34. See Sontrop and Campbell (2006) for a review of the studies.

35. The case was reported by Chiu et al.

(2003) in a letter to the *American Journal of Psychiatry*.

36. The study of suicide attempts was reported by Sublette et al. (2006).

37. The study of children in Israel was carried out by Nemets et al. (2006).

38. The study of bipolar patients was reported by Frangou et al. (2006).

39. See Hibbeln et al. (1998).

40. SAD and bright light therapy were described in Rosenthal, et al. (1984). For an example of a subsequent study, See, Lam et al. (2006).

41. The excellent review by the Termans covers many issues relating to the use of bright light therapy. See Terman and Terman (2005).

42. See Goel et al. (2005).

43. These reports were mentioned in the review of bright light therapy by Terman and Terman (2005).

44. *Ibid.*

Chapter 15

1. The survey of clinicians was reported by Friedman, et al. (2000). For a study showing the value of raising the dose of antidepressants to deal with relapse, see Fava et al. (2006).

2. For a discussion of the terms relapse and recurrence see the review of Burcusa and Iacono (2007).

3. See Billings and Moos (1984) and Billings and Moos (1985).

4. See Burcusa and Iacono (2007).

5. *Ibid.*

6. These factors, similar to ones listed in the 1993 edition of *Understanding Depression* were taken from Burcusa and Iacono (2007).

7. A study by Melartin et al. (2004) showed that the severity of depression was related to both the length of the episode and recurrence.

8. See Vittengl et al. (2007).

9. The study comparing psychotherapy and antidepressant medicine in terms of post treatment resiliency to stressors was carried out by Hawley et al. (2007).

10. See Kashner et al. (2007).

11. See Vittengl et al. (2007).

12. See Gonzales et al. (1985).

13. The study was reported by Frank et al. (2007).

14. See Vittengl et al. (2007), Kashner et al. (2007), and Bockting, et al. (2005).

15. See, for example, Thase (2006) and Fava et al. (2006).

16. See Thase (2006).

Chapter 16

1. See Westermeyer (1987), page 475.

Bibliography

Abela, J. R., Browa, K., & Seligman, M. E. (2004). A test of integration of the activation hypothesis and the diathesis-stress component of the hopelessness theory of depression. *British Journal of Clinical Psychology*, 43, 111–128.

Agency for Health Care Policy and Research (1993). *Clinical practice guidelines: Depression in primary care, Volume 2: Treatment of major depression.* Washington, D.C., U.S. Government Printing Office, AHCPR Publication 93-0551.

Agid, O., Shapira, B., Zislin, J., Ritsner, M., Hanin, B., Murad, H., Troudart, T., Bloch, M., Heresco-Levy, U., & Lerer, B. (1999). Environment and vulnerability to major psychiatric illness: A case control study of early parental loss in major depression, bipolar disorder, and schizophrenia. *Molecular Psychiatry*, 4, 163–172.

Ainsworth, M. D. S. (1989). Attachments beyond infancy. *American Psychologist*, 44, 709–716.

Akiskal, H. S., Kilzieh, N., Maser, J. D., Clayton, P. J., Schettler, P. J., Shea, M. T., Endicott, J., Scheftner, W., Hirschfeld, R. M. A., & Keller, M. B. (2006). The distinct temperament profiles of bipolar I, bipolar II and unipolar patients. *Journal of Affective Disorders*, 92, 19–33.

Alegria, M., Canino, G., Rios, R., Vera, M., Calderon, J., Rusch, D., & Ortega, A. N. (2002). Inequalities in use of specialty health services among Latinos, African-Americans, and non–Latino Whites *Psychiatric Services*, 53, 1547–1555.

Allgood-Merten, B., Lewinshon, P. M., & Hops, H. (1990). Sex differences and adolescent depression. *Journal of Abnormal Psychology*, 99, 55-63.

Alloy, L. B., Abramson, L. Y., Smith, J. M., Gibb, B. E., & Neeren, A. M. (2006). Role of parenting and maltreatment histories in unipolar and bipolar mood disorders: Mediation by cognitive vulnerability to depression. *Clinical Child and Family Psychology Review.*

Altman, J. H., & Winterborn, J. R. (1980). Depression-prone personality in women. *Journal of Abnormal Psychology*, 89, 303-308.

American Psychiatric Association (1994). *Diagnostic and statistical manual of mental disorders* (fourth edition). Washington, D.C.

Anderson, I. M. (2000). Selective serotonin reuptake inhibitors verses tricyclic antidepressants: A meta-analysis of efficacy and tolerability. *Journal of Affective Disorders*, 58, 19–36.

Angold, A., Costello, E. J., & Worthman, C. M. (1998). Puberty and depression: The roles of age, pubertal status and pubertal timing. *Psychological Medicine*, 28, 51–61.

Anouilh, J. (1959). Restless Heart. In Five Plays, Volume II. New York: Hill and Wang.

The APA Task Force on Laboratory Tests in Psychiatry (1987). The Dexamethasone Suppression Test: An overview of its current status in psychiatry. *American Journal of Psychiatry*, 144, 1253–1262.

Aro, A. R., Nyberg, N., Absetz, P., Henriksson, M., & Lonnqvist, J. (2001). Depressive symptoms in middle-aged women are more strongly associated with physical health and social support than with socioeconomic factors. *Nordic Journal of Psychiatry*, 55, 191–198.

Arroll, B. MacGillivray, S., Ogston, S., Reid, I., Sullivan, F., Williams, B., & Crombie, I. (2005).

Efficacy and tolerability of tricyclic antidepressants and SSRIs compared with placebo treatment for depression in primary care: A meta-analysis. *American Family Medicine,* 3, 449–456.

Barcusa, S. L., & Iacono, W. G. (2007). Risk for recurrence of depression. *Clinical Psychology Review* (in press).

Barnes, G. E., & Prosen, H. (1985). Parental death and depression. *Journal of Abnormal Psychology,* 94, 64–69.

Barnes, P., Powell-Griner, E., McFann, K., & Nahin, R. (2004). Complementary and alternative medicine use among adults: United States, 2002. *CDC Advance Data Report #343.* nccam.nih.gov/news/camsurvey.

Barreto R. M., & Segal, S. P. (2005). Use of mental health services by Asian Americans. *Psychiatric Services,* 56, 746–748.

Bazner, E., Bromer, P., Hamelstern, P., & Meyer, T. D. (2006). Current and former depression and their relationship to the effects of social comparison processes. Results of an internet study. *Journal of Affective Disorders,* 93, 97–103.

Beach, S. R. H., Sandeen, E. E., & O'Leary, K. D. (1987, November). Treatment for the depressed maritally discordant client: A comparison of behavioral marital therapy, individual cognitive therapy, and wait list. Paper presented at the annual meeting of the Association for the Advancement of Behavior Therapy, Boston, Massachusetts.

Beauchemin, K. M., & Hays, P. (1996). Dreaming away depression: The role of REM sleep and dreaming in affective disorders. *Journal of Affective Disorders,* 25, 125–133.

Beck, A. T. (1976). Cognitive therapy and the emotional disorders. New York: International University Press.

_____ (1991). Cognitive therapy: A 30-year retrospective. *American Psychologist,* 46, 368–375.

Beck, A. T., Rush, A. J., Shaw, B. F., & Emery, G. (1979). *Cognitive therapy for depression.* N.Y.: Gilford Press.

Beck, A. T., Steer, R. A., & Brown, G. K. (1996). Manual *for the Beck Depression Inventory-II.* San Antonio, Texas: Psychological Corporation.

Beck, A. T., Ward, C. H., Mendelson, M., Mock, J., & Erbaugh, J. (1961). An inventory for measuring depression. *Archives of General Psychiatry,* 4, 561–571.

Beekman A. T., Geerlings, S. W., Deeg, D. J., Smit, J. H., Schoevers, R. S., deBeurs, E., Braam, A. W., Penninx, B. W., & van Tilburg, W. (2002). The natural history of late-life depression: A 6-year prospective study in the community. *Archives of General Psychiatry,* 59, 605–611.

Bellak, L. (1981). Brief psychodynamic psychotherapy of nonpsychotic depression. *American Journal of Psychotherapy,* 35, 160–172.

Benassi, V. A., Sweeney, P. D., & Dufour, C. L. (1988). Is there a relation between locus of control orientation and depression? *Journal of Abnormal Psychology,* 97, 357–367.

Benazon, N. R., & Coyne, J. C. (2000). Living with a depressed spouse. *Journal of Family Psychology,* 14, 71–79.

Bertolino, A., Arciero, G. Rubino, V., Latorre, V., DeCandia, M., Mazzola, V., Blasi, G., Caforio, G., Hariri, A., Kalachana, B., Nardini, M., Weinberger, D. R., & Scarabino, T. (2005). Variation of human amygdala response during threatening stimuli as a function of 5- HTTLPR genotype and personality style. *Biological Psychiatry,* 57, 1517–1525.

Bierut, L. J., Heath, A. C., Bucholz, K. K., Dinwiddie, S. H., Madden, P. A., Statham, D. J., Dunne, M. P., & Martin, N. G. (1999). Major depressive disorder in a community-based twin sample: Are there different genetic and environmental contributions for men and women? *Archives of General Psychiatry,* 56, 557–563.

Bifulco, A., Moran, P. M., Ball, C., & Bernazzani, O. (2002). Adult attachment style: I. Its relationship to clinical depression. *Social Psychiatry and Psychiatric Epidemiology,* 37, 50–59.

Bifulco, A., Moran, P. M., Ball, C., & Lillie, A. (2002). Adult attachment style. II. Its relationship to psychosocial depressive-vulnerability. *Social Psychiatry and Psychiatric Epidemiology,* 37, 60–67.

Billings, A. G., & Moos, R. H. (1984). Treatment experiences of adults with unipolar depression: The influence of patient and life context factors. *Journal of Consulting and Clinical Psychology*, 52, 119–131.

_____ and _____ (1985). Psychosocial processes of remission in unipolar depression: Comparing depressed patients with matched community controls. *Journal of Consulting and Clinical Psychology*, 53, 314–25.

"Birth defects: Risk Appears Low when Mother Uses SSRI antidepressants." (2007). *Washington Post Health* Section, *Quick Study*. July 3, page F-2.

Blatt, S. J. (1974). Levels of object representation in anaclitic and introjective depression. *Psychoanalytic Study of the Child*, 29, 107–157.

_____, Zuroff, D. C., Bondi, C. M., Sanislow, C. A., III, & Pilkonis, P. A. (1998). When and how perfectionism impedes the brief treatment of depression: Further analysis of the National Institute of Mental Health treatment of depression collaborative research program." *Journal of Consulting and Clinical Psychology*, 66, 423–428.

Blazer, D., George, L. K., Landerman, R., Pennybacker, M., Melville, M. L., Woodbury, M., Manton, K. G., Jordan, K., & Locke, B. (1985). Psychiatric disorders: A rural/urban comparison.. *Archives of General Psychiatry*, 42, 651–656.

Blechman, E. A., McEnroe, M. J., Carella, E. T., & Audette, D. P. (1986). Childhood competence and depression. *Journal of Abnormal Psychology*, 95, 223–227.

Bliwise, D. L., Yesavage, J. A., Sink, J., Windrow, L., & Dement, W. C. (1986). Depressive symptoms and impaired respiration in sleep. *Journal of Consulting and Clinical Psychology*, 54, 734–35.

Bockting, C. L., Schene, A. H., Spinhoven, P., Koeter, M. W., Wooters, L. F., Huyser, J., & Kamphuis, J. H. (2005). Preventing relapse/reoccurrence in recurrent depression with cognitive therapy: A randomized controlled trial. *Journal of Consulting and Clinical Psychology*, 73, 647–657.

Bollini, P., Pampallona, S., Tibaldi, G., Kupelnick, B., & Munizza, C. (1999). Effectiveness of antidepressants: Meta-analysis of dose-effect relationships in randomized clinical trials. *British Journal of Psychiatry*, 174, 297–303.

Bond, M. (2006). Psychodynamic psychotherapy in the treatment of mood disorders. *Current Opinion in Psychiaty*, 19, 40–43.

Bowlby, J. (1980). *Loss: Sadness and depression* (Attachment and loss, Volume 3). New York: Basic Books.

_____ (1982). Attachment and loss: Retrospect and prospect. *American Journal of Orthopsychiatry*, 52, 664–678.

Breslau, J., Gaxiola, S. A., Kendler, K. S., Su, M., Williams, D., & Kessler, R. C. (2005). Specifying race-ethnic differences in risk for psychiatric disorder in a USA national sample. *Psychological Medicine*, 35, 1–12.

Bridle, C., Palmer, S., Bagnall. A. M, Darba, J., Duffy, S., Sculpher, M., & Riemsma, R. (2004). A rapid and systematic review and economic evaluation of the clinical and cost-effectiveness of newer drugs for treatment of mania associated with bipolar affective disorder. *Health Technology Assessment*, 8, 1–187.

Brooks-Gunn, J., & Warren, M. P. (1989). Biological and social contributions to negative affect expression in young adolescent girls. *Child Development*, 60, 40–55.

Brown, S. A., Goldman, M. S., Inn, A., & Anderson, L. R. (1980). Expectations of reinforcement from alcohol: Their domain and relation to drinking patterns. *Journal of Consulting and Clinical Psychology*, 48, 419–426.

Brunstein-Klomek, A., Zalsman, G., & Mufson, L. (2007). Interpersonal psychotherapy for depressed adolescents (IPT-A.). *Journal of Psychiatry and Related Sciences*, 44, 40–46.

Buchwald, A. M. (1977). Depressive mood and estimates of reinforcement frequency. *Journal of Abnormal Psychology*, 86, 443–446.

Bulmash, E. L., Moller, H. J., Kayumov, L., Shen, J., Wang, X., & Shapiro, C. M. (2006). Psychomotor disturbance in depression: Assessment using a driving simulator paradigm. *Journal of Affective Disorders*, 93, 213–218.

Burke, K. C., Burke, J. D., Jr., Regier, D. A., & Rae, D. S. (1990). Age at onset of selected mental disorders in five community populations. *Archives of General Psychiatry*, 47, 511–518.

Burns, D. D. (1980). *Feeling good: The new mood therapy*. N.Y: Morrow.

Butler, A. C., Chapman, J. E., Forman, E. M., & Beck, A. T. (2006). The empirical status of cognitive-behavioral therapy: A review of meta-analyses. *Clinical Psychology Review*, 26, 17–31.

Caccia, S. (2005). Antidepressant like components of hypericum perforatum extracts: An overview of their pharmacokinetics and metabolism. *Current Drug Metabolism*, 6, 531–543.

Cahn, B. R., & Polich, J. (2006). Meditation states and traits: EEG, ERP, and neuroimaging studies. *Psychological Bulletin*, 132, 180–211.

Campbell, S., Marriott, M., Nahmias, C., & MacQueen, G. M. (2004). Lower hippocampal volume in patients suffering from depression: A meta-analysis. *American Journal of Psychiatry*, 161, 598–607.

Carey, M. P., Faulstich, M. E., Gresham, F. M., Ruggiero, L., & Enyart, P. (1987). Children's Depression Inventory: Construct validity across clinical and nonreferred (control) populations. *Journal of Consulting and Clinical Psychology*, 55, 755–761.

Carter, F. A., Frampton, C. M., & Mulder, R. T. (2006). Caesarean section and postpartum depression: A review of the evidence examining the link. *Psychosomatic Medicine*, 68, 321–330.

Carver, C. S., & Ganellen, R. J. (1983). Depression and components of selfpunitiveness: High standards, self criticism, and overgeneralization. *Journal of Abnormal Psychology*, 92, 330–337.

Caspi A., Sugden, K., Moffitt, T. E., Taylor, A., Craig, I. W., Harrington, H., McCloy, J., Nill, J., Martin, J., Braithwaite, A., & Poulton, R. (2003). Influence of life stress on depression: Moderation by a polymorphism on the 5-HTT gene. *Science*, 301, 386–389.

Chabrol, H., Montovany, A., Chouicha, K., & Duconge, E. (2002). Study of the CES-D on a sample of 1953 adolescent students. *Encephale*, 28, 429–432.

Chiu, C-C., Huang, S-Y., Shen, W. W., & Su, K-P. (2003). Omega-3 fatty acids for depression in pregnancy. *American Journal of Psychiatry*, 160, 385.

Church, N. F., Brechman-Toussaint, M. L., & Hine, D. W. (2005). Do dysfunctional cognitions mediate the relationship between risk factors and postnatal depression symptomatology? *Journal of Affective Disorders*, 87, 65–72.

Cicchetti, D. (1987). Developmental psychopathology in infancy: Illustration from the study of maltreated youngsters. *Journal of Consulting and Clinical Psychology*, 55, 837–845.

Clark, D. C., Gibbons, R. D., Fawcet, J., Aagesen, C. A., & Sellers, D. (1985). Unbiased criteria for severity of depression in alcoholic inpatients. *Journal of Nervous and Mental Disease*, 173, 482–487.

Clayton, A. H., Pradko, J. F., Croft, H. A., Montano, C. B., Leadbetter, R. A., Bolden-Watson, C., Bass, K. I., Donahue, R. M., Jamerson, B. D., & Metz, A. (2002). Prevalence of sexual dysfunction among newer antidepressants. *Journal of Clinical Psychiatry*, 63, 357–366.

Cofer, D., & Winterborn, J. R. (1980). Personality characteristics of formally depressed women. *Journal of Abnormal Psychology*, 89, 309–314.

Cole, D. A., Nolen-Hoeksema, S., Girgus, J., & Gilda, P. (2006). Stress exposure and stress generation in child and adolescent depression: A latent trait-state-error approach to longitudinal analyses. *Journal of Abnormal Psychology* 115, 40–51.

Coleg, E. A. (1990). Relation of social and academic competence to depressive symptoms in childhood. *Journal of Abnormal Psychology*, 99, 422–429.

Colla, J., Buka, S., Harrington, D., & Murphy, J. M. (2006). Repression and modernization: A cross-cultural study of women. *Social Psychiatry and Psychiatric Epidemiology*, 41, 271–279.

Consensus Development Conference Statement (1985). *Electroconvulsive Therapy*. 5, no. 11, National Institutes of Health.

Conte, H. R., Plutchik, R., Wild, K. V., & Karasu, T. B. (1986). Combined psychotherapy and pharmacotherapy for depression. *Archives of General Psychiatry*, 43, 471–479.

Cook, F. A. (1998). *Through the first anarctic night 1898–1899*. Pittsburgh, PA.: Polar. First published 1909.

Cornell, D. G., Suarez, R., & Berent, S. (1984). Psychomotor retardation in melancholic and nonmelancholic depression: Cognitive and motor components. *Journal of Abnormal Psychology*, 93, 150–157.

Covington, M. B. (2004). Omega-3 fatty acids. *American Family Physician*, 70.

Coyne, J. C., Kessler, R. C., Tal, M., Turnbull, J., Wortman, C. B., & Greden, J. F. (1987). Living with a depressed person. *Journal of Consulting and Clinical Psychology*, 55, 347–352.

Crowe, L. C., & George, W. H. (1989). Alcohol and human sexuality: Review and integration. *Psychological Bulletin*, 105, 374–386.

Cuijpers, P., Van Stratten, A., & Warmerdam, L. (2007). Behavioral activation treatments of depression: A meta-analysis. *Clinical Psychology Review*, 27, 318–326.

Cutrona, C. E., Russell, D. W., Brown, P. A., Clark, L. A., Hessling, R. M., & Gardner, K. A. (2005). Neighborhood context, personality, and stressful life events as predictors of depression among African American women. *Journal of Abnormal Psychology*, 2005, 114, 3–15.

Dauber, R. B. (1984). Subliminal psychodynamic activation in depression: On the role of autonomy issues in depressed college women. *Journal of Abnormal Psychology*, 93, 9–18.

De Maat, S. M., Dekker, J., Schoevers, R. A., & de Jonghe, F. (2007). Relative efficacy of psychotherapy and combined therapy in the treatment of depression: A meta-analysis. *European Psychiatry*, 22, 1–8.

de Mello, M. F., de Jesus, Mari, J., Bacaltchuk, J., Verdeli, H., & Neugebauer, R. (2005). A systematic review of research findings on the efficacy of interpersonal therapy for depressive disorders. *European Archives of Psychiatry and Clinical Neuroscience*, 255, 75–82.

Denney, D. R., Stephenson, L. A., Penick, E. C., & Weller, R. A. (1988). Lymphocyte subclass and depression. *Journal of Abnormal Psychology*, 97, 499–502.

Depue, R. A., Slater, J. F, Wolfsetter-Kausch, H., Klein, D., Goplerud, E., & Farr, D. (1981). A behavioral paradigm for identifying persons at risk for bipolar depressive disorder: A conceptual framework and five validation studies. *Journal of Abnormal Psychology*, 90, 381–438.

DeRubeis, R. J., Evans, M. D., Hollon, S. D., Garvey, M. J., Grove, W. M., & Tuason, V. B. (1990). How does cognitive therapy work? Cognitive change and symptom change in cognitive therapy and pharmacotherapy for depression. *Journal of Consulting and Clinical Psychology*, 58, 862–869.

DeRubeis, R. J., Gelfand, C. A., Tang, T. Z., Simons, A. D. (1999). Medications versus cognitive behavior therapy for severely depressed outpatients: Mega-analysis of four randomized comparisons. *American Journal of Psychiatry*, 156, 1007–1013.

Deutsch, A. (1948). The shame of the states. New York: Harcourt, Brace. Development conference statement (1985). Electroconvulsive therapy. 5, No.11. National Institutes of Health.

Dickens, C. (1981). *David Copperfield*. Oxford: Oxford University Press.

Dickerson, S. S., & Kemeny, M. E. (2004). Acute stressors and cortisol responses: A theoretical integration and synthesis of laboratory research. *Psychological Bulletin*, 130, 355–391.

Dingfelder, S. F. (2006). The hunt for endophenotypes: Psychologists are leading the charge to uncover the steps from genes to mental illness. *Monitor on Psychology*, 37, 20–21.

Doerfler, L. A., Felner, R. D., Rowlison,, R. T., Raley, P. A., & Evans, E. (1988). Depression in children and adolescence: A comparative analysis of the utility and the construct validity of two assessment measures. *Journal of Consulting and Clinical Psychology*, 56, 769–772.

Dranovsky, A., & Hen, R. (2006) Hippocampus neurogenesis: Regulation by stress and antidepressants. *Biological Psychiatry*, 59, 1136–1143.

Dumais, A., Lesage, A. D., Alda, M., Rouleau, G., Dumont, M., Chawky, N., Roy, M., Mann, J. J., Benkelfat, C., & Turecki, G. (2005). Risk factors for suicide completion in major depression: A case-controlled study of impulsive and aggressive behaviors in men. *American Journal of Psychiatry*, 162, 2114–2116.

Dunn, A. L., Trivedi, M. H., Kampert, J. B., Clark, C. G., & Chambliss, H. O. (2005). Exercise treatment for depression: Efficacy and dose response. *American Journal of Preventive Medicine, 28,* 1–8.

Durkheim, E. (1966). *Suicide.* New York: Free Press.

Egeland, J. A & Hostetter, A. M. (1983). Amish study: I. Affective disorders among the Amish, 1976–1980. *American Journal of Psychiatry, 140,* 56–61.

Ehlers, C. L., Frank, E., & Kupfer, D. J. (1988). Social zeitgebers and biological rhythms. *Archives of General Psychiatry, 45,* 948–952.

Einarson, T. R., Arikian, S. R., Casciano, J., & Doyle, J. J. (1999). Comparison of extended-release venlafaxine, selective serotonin reuptake inhibitors, and tricyclic antidepressants in the treatment of depression: A meta-analysis of randomized controlled trials. *Clinical therapy, 21,* 296–308.

Elkin, L., Shea, T., Watkins, J. T., Imber, S. D., Sotsky, S. M., Collins, J. F., Glass, D. R., Pilkonia, P. A., Leber, W. R., Docherty, J. P., Fiester, S. J., & Parloff, M. B. (1989). National Institute of Mental Health Treatment of Depression Collaborative Research program: General effectiveness of treatments. *Archives of General Psychiatry, 46,* 971–982.

Ellis, A. (1962). *Reason and emotion in psychotherapy.* New York: Lyle Stuart.

Enns, H. W., & Cox, B. J. (1999). Perfectionism and depressive symptom severity in major depressive disorder. *Behavior Research and Therapy, 37,* 783–794.

Ernst, E., Rand, J. I., & Stevinson, C. (1998). Complementary therapies for depression: An overview. *Archives of General Psychiatry, 55,* 1026–1032.

Fadden, G., Bebbington, P., Kuipers, L. (1987). Caring and its burdens. A study of the spouses of depressed patients. *British Journal of Psychiatry, 151,* 660–667.

Fagot, B. I. (1997) Attachment, parenting, and peer interactions of toddler children. *Developmental Psychology, 33,* 489–499.

Fava, M., Detke, M. J., Balestrieri, M., Wang, F., Raskin, J., & Perahia, D. (2006). Management of depression relapse: Re-initiation of duloxetine treatment or dose increase. *Journal of Psychiatric Research, 40,* 328–336.

FDA approves Emsam (selegiline) as first drug patch for depression. (2006). *FDA News* (February 28th, 2006). Http://www.fda.gov/bbs/topics/news/2006New01326.html.

Field, T., Hernandez-Reif, M., Diego, M., Schanberg, S., & Kuhn, C. (2005). Cortisol decreases and serotonin and dopamine increase following massage therapy. *International Journal of Neuroscience, 115,* 1397–1413.

Finucane, A., & Mercer, S. W. (2006). An exploratory mixed methods study of the acceptability and effectiveness of mindfulness-based cognitive therapy for patients with active depression and anxiety in primary care. *BMC Psychiatry, 6,* 14.

Floyd, M., Rohen, N., Shakelford, J. A., Huibbard, K. L., Parnell, M. B., Scogin, F., & Coates, A. (2006). Two-year follow-up of bibliotherapy and individual cognitive therapy for depressed older adults. *Behavior Modification, 30,* 281–294.

Foa, E. B., Zoellner, L. A., & Feeny, N. C. (2006). An evaluation of three brief programs for facilitating recovery after assault. *Journal of Traumatic Stress, 19,* 29–43.

Fogel, J., & Ford, D. E. (2005). Stigma beliefs of Asian Americans with depression in an internet sample. *Canadian Journal of Psychiatry, 50,* 470–478.

Folkenberg, J. (1983, October). Using drugs to lift that dark veil of depression. *FDA Consumer,* 16–19.

Folkman, S., & Lazarus, R. S. (1986). Stress processes and depressive symptomatology. *Journal of Abnormal Psychology, 95,* 107–113.

Forgas, J. P., Bower, G. H., & Krantz, S. E. (1984). The influence of mood on perceptions of social interactions. *Journal of Experimental Social Psychology, 20,* 497–513.

Frampton, J. E. & Plosker, G. L. (2007). Selegiline transdermal system in the treatment of major depressive disorder. *Drugs, 67,* 257–265.

Frangou, S., Lewis, M., & McCrone, P. (2006). Efficacy of ethyl-eicosapentaenoic acid in bipolar depression: Randomized double-blind placebo-controlled study. *British Journal of Psychiatry, 188,* 46–50.

Frank, E., Kupfer, D. J., Buysse, D. J., Swartz, H. A., Pilkonis, P. A., Houck, P. R., Rucci, P., Novick, D. M., Grochocinski, V. J., & Stapf, D. M. (2007). Randomized trial of weekly, twice-monthly, and monthly interpersonal psychotherapy as maintenance treatment for women with recurrent depression. *American Journal of Psychiatry*, 164, 7, 761–767.

Frazier, J. A., Ahn, M. S., Dejong, S., Bent, K. E.. (2005). Magnetic resonance imaging studies in early-onset bipolar disorder: A Critical Review. *Harvard Review of Psychiatry*, 13, 125–140.

Freedman, S. J., Fava, M., Kienke, A. S., White, C. H., Nierenberg, A. A., & Rosenbaum, J. F. (2000). Partial response, nonresponse, and relapse with selective serotonin reuptake inhibitors in major depression: A survey of current "next-step" practices. *Journal of Clinical Psychiatry*, 61, 403–418.

Freud, S. (1959). *Mourning and melancholia*. In Collected Papers, Volume 4, 152–170. New York: Basic Books.

Friedman, R. A., Mitchel, J., & Kocsis, J. H. (1995). Retreatment for relapse following desipramine discontinuation in dysthymia. *American Journal of Psychiatry*, 152, 921.

Gallagher, W. (1986, May). The dark affliction of mind and body. *Discover*, 7, no. 5, 6.

Galloway, G. P., Newmeyer, J., Knapp, T., Stalcup, S. A., & Smith D. (1994). Imipramine for the treatment of cocaine and methamphetamine dependence. *Journal of Addictive Disorders*, 13, 201–216.

Gjerde, P. F., Block, J., & Block, J. (1988) Depressive symptoms and personality during late adolescence: Gender differences in externalization of symptom expression. *Journal of Abnormal Psychology*, 97, 475–486.

Gladstone, T. R., & Kaslow, N. J. (1995). Depression and attributions in children and adolescents: A meta-analytic review. *Journal of Abnormal Child Psychology*, 23, 597–606.

Glascoe, R. E., & Rosen, G. M. (1978). Behavioral bibliotherapy: A review of self-help behavior therapy manuals. *Psychological Bulletin*, 85, 1–23.

Goel, N., Terman, M., Terman, J. S., Macchi, M. M., & Stewart, J. W. (2005). Controlled trial of bright light and negative air ions for chronic depression. *Psychological Medicine*, 35, 945–955.

Goethe, J. W. von (1774). *The Sorrows of Young Werther*. New York: Random House. (1971).

Goforth, H. W., & Holsinger, T. (2007). Rapid relief of severe major depressive disorder by use of preoperative ketamine and electroconvulsive therapy. *Journal: ECT*, 23, 23–25.

Goldbort, J. (2006). Transcultural analysis of postpartum depression. *MCN American Journal of Maternal Child Nursing*, 31, 121–126.

Goldsmith, H. H., & Alansky, J. A. (1987). Attachment: A meta-analytic review. *Journal of Consulting and Clinical Psychology*, 55, 805–816.

Gonzales, L. R., Lewinsohn, P. M., & Clarke, G. N. (1985). Longitudinal follow-up of unipolar depressives: An investigation of predictors of relapse. *Journal of Consulting and Clinical Psychology*, 53, 461–469.

Gorman, J., & Sullivan, G. (2000). Noradrenergic approaches to antidepressant therapy. *Journal of Clinical Psychiatry*, 61, Supplement 1: 13–6.

Grant, B. F., Harford, T. C., Muthen, B. O., Yi, H. Y., Hasin, D. S., & Stinson, F. S. (2006). DSM-IV alcohol dependence and abuse: Further evidence of validity in the general population. *Drug and Alcohol Dependence*.

Grant, B. F., Stinson, F. S., Hasin, D. S., Dawson, D. A., Chou, S. P., Anderson, K. (2004). Immigration and lifetime prevalence of DSM-IV psychiatric disorders among Mexican Americans and non–Hispanic Whites in the United States: Results from the National Epidemiological Survey on Alcohol and Related Conditions. *Archives of General Psychiatry*, 61, 1226–1233.

Grant, B. F., Stinson, F. S., Hasin, D. S., Dawson, D. A., Chou, S. P., Ruan, W. J., & Huang, B..(2005). Prevalence, correlates, and comorbidity of bipolar I disorder and axis I and axis II disorders: Results from the National Epidemiologic Survey on Alcohol and Related Conditions. *Journal of Clinical Psychiatry*, 66, 1205–1215.

Griffiths, K. M., & Christensen, H. (2007). Internet-based mental health programs: A powerful tool in the rural health kit. *Australian Journal of Rural Health*, 15, 81–88.

Haby, M. M., Donnelly, M., Corry, J., & Vos, T. (2006). Cognitive behavioural therapy for depression, panic disorder and generalized anxiety disorder: A mega regression of factors that may predict outcome. *Australian and New Zealand Journal of Psychiatry*, 40, 9–19.

Hamilton, M. A. (1960). A rating scale for depression. *Journal of Neurology, Neurosurgery, and Psychiatry*, 23, 56–62.

Hammen, C. (2005). Stress and depression. *Annual Review of Clinical Psychology*, 1, 293–319.

_____, Henry, R., & Daley, S. E. (2000). Depression and sensitization to stressors among young women as a function of childhood adversity. *Journal of Consulting and Clinical Psychology*, 68, 782–787.

Hammen, C. L., & Peters, S. D. (1977). Differential responses to male and female depressive reactions. *Journal of Consulting and Clinical Psychology*, 45, 994–1001.

Hankin, B. L., & Abramson, L. Y. (2001). Development of gender differences in depression: An elaborated cognitive vulnerability-transactional stress theory. *Psychological Bulletin*, 127, 773–796.

Hariri, A. R., & Holmes, A. (2006). Genetics of emotional regulation: The role of the serotonin transporter in neural function. *Trends in Cognitive Science*, 10, 182–191.

Hariri, A. R., Murray, V. S., Tessitore, A., Kolachana, B., Fera, F., & Goldman, D. (2002). Serotonin transporter genetic variation and the response of the human amygdala. *Science*, 297, 400–403.

Harlow, H. F. (1958). The nature of love. *American Psychologist*, 13, 673–685.

Harris, A. H. S., Cronkite, R., & Moos, R. (2006). Physical activity, exercise coping, and depression in a 10-year cohort study of depressed patients. *Journal of Affective Disorders*, 93, 79–85.

Hasin, D. S., Goodwin, R. D., Stinson, F. S., & Grant, B. F. (2005). Epidemiology of major depressive disorder: Results from the National Epidemiological Survey on Alcoholism and Related Conditions. *Archives of General Psychiatry*, 62, 1097–1106.

Hasler, G., Drevets, W. C., Manji, H. K., & Charney, D. S. (2004). Discovering endophenotypes for major depression. *Neuropsychopharmacology*, 10, 1765–1781.

Hawkins, W. L., French, L. C., Crawford, B. D., & Enzle, M. E. (1988). Depressed affect and time perspective. *Journal of Abnormal Psychology*, 97, 275–280.

Hawley, L. L, Zuroff, D. C., Ho, M-HR, & Blatt, S. J. (2007). Stress reactivity following brief treatment for depression: Differential effects of psychotherapy and medication. *Journal of Consulting and Clinical Psychology*, 75, 244–256.

Healy, D. (1997). *The Antidepressant Era*. Cambridge, MA: Harvard University Press.

Heiby, E. M. (1982). A self-reinforcement questionnaire. *Behavior Research and Therapy*, 20, 391–401.

Hetherington, E. M., Hagan, M. S., Anderson, E. T. (1989). Marital transitions: A child's perspective. *American Psychologist*, 44, 303–312.

Heuser, I., Yassouridis, A., & Holsboer, F. (1994). The combined dexamethasone/CRH test: A refined laboratory test for psychiatric disorders. *Journal of Psychiatric Research*, 28, 341–356.

Hewitt, P. L., & Flett, G. L. (1991). Dimensions of perfectionism in unipolar depression. *Journal of Abnormal Psychology*, 100, 98–101.

Hibbeln, J. R. (1998). Fish consumption and major depression. *Lancet*, 351, 1213.

_____, Umhau, J. C., Linnoila, M., George, D. T., Ragan, P. W., Shoaf, S. E., Vaughan, M. R., Rawlings, R., & Salem, Jr., N. (1998 b). A replication study of violent and non-violent subjects: Cerebrospinal fluid metabolites of serotonin and dopamine are predicted by plasma essential fatty acids. *Biological Psychiatry*, 44, 235–249.

Hiroto, D. S. (1974). Locus of control and learned helplessness. *Journal of Experimental Psychology*, 102, 187–193.

Hoberman, H. M., Lewinshon, P. M., & Tilson, M. (1988). Group treatment of depression: Individual predictors of outcome. *Journal of Consulting and Clinical Psychology*, 56, 393–398.

Hoffman, K. B., Cole, D. A., Martin, J. M., Tram, J., & Seroczynski, A. D. (2000). Are the discrepancies between self and others' appraisals of confidence predictive or reflective of depressive symptoms in children and adolescents: A longitudinal study, Part II. *Journal of Abnormal Psychology*, 106, 651–652.

Holahan, C. J., & Moos, R. H. (1991). Life stressors, personal and social resources, and depression: A four-year structural model. *Journal of Abnormal Psychology*, 100, 31–38.

Hollon, S. D., & Kendall, P. C. (1980). Cognitive self-statements in depression: Development of an automatic thoughts questionnaire. *Cognitive Therapy and Research*, 4, 383–395.

Incoviello, B. M., Alloy, B., Abramson, L. Y., Whitehouse, W. G., & Hogan, E. (2006). The course of depression in individuals with high and low cognitive risk for depression: A prospective study. *Journal of Affective Disorders*, 93, 61–69.

Irons, C., Gilbert, P., Baldwin, M. W., Baccus, J. R., & Palmer, M.. (2006). Parental recall, attachment relating and self-attacking/self-reassurance: Their relationship with depression. *British Journal of Clinical Psychology*, 45, 297–308.

Jamison, K. R. (1993). *Touched with fire: Manic-depressive illness and the artistic temperament*. New York: Free Press.

Jarrett, R. B., & Weissenburger, D. E. (1990). Guilt in depressed outpatients. *Journal of Consulting and Clinical Psychology*, 58, 495–498.

Jewell, D. S., & Mylander, M. (1988). The psychology of stress: Run silent, run deep. In G. P. Chorousos, D. L. Loriaux, & P. W. Gold (Eds.), *Mechanisms of physical and emotional stress*. New York: Plenum.

Johnson, M. H., & Magaro, P. A. (1987). Effects of mood and severity on memory processes in depression and mania. *Psychological Bulletin*, 101, 28–40.

Joormann, J., & Gotlib, I. H. (2006). Is this happiness I see? Biases in the identification of emotional facial expression in depression and social phobia. *Journal of Abnormal Psychology*, 115, 705–714.

Kabat-Zinn, J., Massion, A. O., Kristeller, J., Peterson, L. G., Fletcher, K. E., Pbert, L., Lenderking, W. R., & Santorelli, S. F. (1992). Effectiveness of a meditation-based stress reduction program in the treatment of anxiety disorders. *American Journal of Psychiatry*, 149, 936–943.

Kalechstein, A. D., Newton, T. F., Longshore, D., Anglin, M. D., van Gorp, W. G., & Gawin, F. H. (2000). Psychiatric comorbidity of methamphetamine dependence in a forensic sample. *Journal of Neuropsychiatry and Clinical Neuroscience*, 12, 480–484.

Kaltenthaler, E., Brazier, J., Denigris, E., Tumur, I., Ferriter, M., Beverley, C., Parry, G., Rooney, G., & Sutcliffe, P. (2006). Computerized cognitive behaviour therapy for depression and anxiety update: A systematic review and economic evaluation. *Health Technology Assessment*, 10, 1–168.

Kanner, A. D., Coyne, J. C., Schaefer, C., & Lazarus, R. S. (1981). Two modes of stress measurement: Daily hassles and uplifts verses major life events. *Journal of Behavioral Medicine*, 4, 1–39.

Karno, M., Hough, R. L., Burnam, A., Escobar, J. L., Timbers, D. M. (1987). Lifetime prevalence of specific psychiatric disorders among Mexican Americans and non–Hispanic whites in Los Angeles. *Archives of General Psychiatry*, 44, 695–701. Archives of General Psychiatry, 44, 695–701.

Kashani, J. H., Holcomb, W. R., & Orvaschel, H. (1986). Depression and depressive symptoms in preschool children from the general population. *American Journal of Psychiatry*, 143, 1138–1143.

Kashner, T. M., Henley, S. S., Golden, R. M., Rush, A. J., & Jarrett, R. B. (2007). Assessing the preventive effects of cognitive therapy following relief of depression: A methodological innovation. *Journal of Affective Disorders* (in press).

Kasper, S., Anghelescu, I. G., Szegedi, A., Dienel, A., & Kieser, M. (2006). Superior efficacy of St. John's wort extract WS5570 compared to placebo in patients with major depression: A randomized double-blind, placebo-controlled, multi-center trial. *BMC Medicine*, 4, 14.

Kasper, S., Wehr, T. A., Bartko, J. J., Gaist, P. A., & Rosenthal, N. E. (1989). Epidemiological findings of seasonal changes in mood and behavior. A telephone survey of Montgomery County, Maryland. *Archives of General Psychiatry, 46*, 823–833.

Kazdin, A. E. (1986). Comparative outcome studies of psychotherapy: Methodological issues and strategies. *Journal of Consulting and Clinical Psychology, 54*, 95–105.

Keats, J. (1958). The *poetical works of John Keats*. Oxford: Oxford University Press.

Keeler, M. H., Ewing, J. A., & Rouse, B. A. (1971). Hallucinogenic effects of marijuana as currently used. *American Journal of Psychiatry, 128*, 213–216.

Kendler, K. S., Heath, A., Martin, N. G., & Eaves, L. J. (1986). Symptoms of anxiety and depression in a volunteer twin population. *Archives of General Psychiatry, 43*, 213–221.

Kendler, K. S., Prescott, C. A. (1999). A population-based twin study of lifetime major depression in men and women. *Archives of General Psychiatry, 56*, 39–44.

Kerns, K. A., Abrambham, M. M., Schlegelmilch, A., & Morgan, T. A. (2007). Mother-child attachment in later middle childhood: Assessment approaches and associations with mood and emotion regulation. *Attachment and Human Development, 9*, 33–53.

Kerr, G. W., McGuffie, A. C., & Wilkie, S. (2001). Tricyclic antidepressant overdose: A review. *Emergency Medicine Journal, 18*, 236–241.

Kerr, M. M., Hoier, T. S., & Versi, M. (1987). Methodological issues in childhood depression: A review of the literature. *American Journal of Orthopsychiatry, 57*, 193–198.

Kessler, R. C., Bergland, P., Demier, O., Jin, R., & Walters, E. E. (2005). Lifetime prevalence and age-of-onset distribution of DSM-IV disorders in the National Comorbidity Survey Replication. *Archives of General Psychiatry, 62*, 593–602.

Kessler. R. C., Demier, O., Frank, R. G., Olfson, M., Pincus, H. A., Walters, E. E., Wang, P., Wells, K. B., & Zaslavsky, A. M. (2005). Prevalence and treatment of mental disorders, 1990 to 2003. *New England Journal of Medicine, 352*, 2515–2523.

Kessler, R. C., Soukup, J., Davis, R. B., Foster, D. F., Wilkey, S. A., van Rompay, M. I., & Eisenberg, D. M. (2001). The use of complementary and alternative therapies to treat anxiety and depression in the United States. *American Journal of Psychiatry, 158*, 289–294.

Kieseppa, T., Partonen, T., Haiskka, J., Kaprio, J., & Lonnqvist, J. (2004). High concordance of bipolar I disorder in a nationwide sample of twins. American Journal of Psychiatry, 161, 1814–1821.

Kim, H. L., Streltzer, J,, & Goebert, D. (1999). St. John's wort for depression: A meta-analysis of well-defined clinical trials. *Journal of Nervous and Mental Disease, 187*, 532–538.

Kistner, J. A., David-Ferdan, C. F., Repper, K. K., & Joiner, T. E., Jr. (2006). Bias and accuracy of children's perceptions of peer acceptance: Prospective associations with depressive symptoms. *Journal of Abnormal Child Psychology, 34*, 349–361.

Klerman, G. L., Weissman, M. M., Rounsvaile, B. J., & Chevron, E. (1984). *Interpersonal psychotherapy of depression*. New York: Basic Books.

Kocsis, J. H., Frances, A. J., Voss, C., Mann, J. J., Mason, B. J., & Sweeney, J. (1988). Imipramine treatment for chronic depression. *Archives of General Psychiatry, 45*, 253–257.

Koizumi, Y., Awata, S., Kuriyama, S., Ohmori, K., Hozawa, A., Seki, T., Matsuoka, H., & Tsuji, I. (2005). Association between social support and depression status in the elderly: Results of a 1-year community-based prospective cohort study in Japan. *Psychiatric Clinical Neuroscience, 2005, 5*, 563–569.

Koukopoulos, A., Sani, G., Koukopoulos, A. E., Minnai, G. P., Giardi, P., Pani, L., Albert, M. J., & Reginaldi, D. (2003). Duration and stability of the rapid-cycling course: A long-term personal follow-up of 109 patients. *Journal of Affective Disorders, 73*, 75–85.

Kovacs, M. (1985). The Childrens Depression Inventory (CDI). *Psychopharmacology Bulletin, 21*, 995–998.

_____ (1992). *Children Depression Inventory Manual*. Los Angeles: Western Psychological Services.

Kovess, V., Murphy, H. B., & Tousignant, M. (1987). Urban-rural comparisons of depressive disorders in French Canada. *Journal of Mental and Nervous Disease, 175*, 457–466.

Kraeplin, E. (1913). *Textbook of Psychiatry*. (R. M. Barclay, trans.). Edinburgh: Livingston.

Kramlinger, K. G., & Post, R. M. (1996). Ultra-rapid and ultradian cycling in bipolar affective illness. *British Journal of Psychiatry*, 168, 314–323.

Krohne, H. W., & Slangen, K. E. (2005). Influence of social support on adaptation to surgery. *Health Psychology*, 24, 101–105.

Kronmueller, K. T., Victor, D., Schenkenbach, C., Postelnicu, I., Bachenstrass, M., Schroder, J., & Mundt, C. (2007). Knowledge about affective disorders and outcome of depression. *Journal of Affective Disorders* (in press).

Kunugi, H., Ida, I., Owashi, T., Kimura, M., Inoue, Y., Nakagawa, S., Yabana, T., Urushibara, T., Kanal, R., Alhara, M., Yuuki, N., Otsubo, T., Oshima, A., Kuda, A., Inoue, T., Kitaichi, Y., Shirakawa, O., Isogawa, K., Nagayama, H., Kamijima, K., Nanko, S., Kanba, S., Higuchi, T., & Mikuni, M. (2006). Assessment of the dexamethasone/CRH as a state-dependent marker for hypothalamic-pituitary-adrenal (HPA) axis abnormalities in major depressive disorders: A multicenter study. *Neuropsychopharmacology*, 31, 212–220.

Kuo, P. H., Gardner, C. O., Kendler, K. S., & Prescott, C. A. (2006). The temporal relationship of the onsets of alcohol dependence and major depression: Using a genetically informative study design. *Psychological Medicine*, 36, 1153–1162.

Kupfer, D. J. (2006). Depression and associated sleep disturbances: Patient benefits with agomelatine. *European Neuropsychopharmacology*, 16, supplement 5, S639–643.

Kupka, R. W., Luckenbaugh, D. A., Post, R. M., Suppes, T., Altshuler, L. L., Keck, P. E., Jr., Frye, M. A., Denicoff, K. D., Grunze, H., Leverich, G. S., McElroy, S. L., Walden, J., & Nolen, W. A. (2005). Comparison of rapid-cycling and non–rapid-cycling bipolar disorder based on prospective mood ratings in 539 outpatients. *American Journal of Psychiatry*, 162, 1273–1280.

Lam, R. W. (2006). Sleep disturbances and depression: A challenge for antidepressants. *International Clinical Psychopharmacology*, 21, Supplement 1, S25–29.

_____, Levitt, A. J., Levitan, R. D., Enns, M. W., Morehouse, R., Michalak, E. E., & Tam, E. M. (2006). The Can-SAD study: A randomized controlled trial of the effectiveness of light therapy and fluoxetine in patients with winter seasonal affective disorder. *American Journal of Psychiatry*, 163, 805–812.

Larson, R. W., Rafaelli, M., Richards, M. H., Ham, M., & Jewell, L (1990). Ecology of depression in late childhood and early adolescence: A profile of daily states and activities. *Journal of Abnormal Psychology*, 99, 92–102.

Lau, M. A., & McMain, S. F. (2005). Integrating mindfulness meditation with cognitive and behavioral therapies: The challenge of combining acceptance and change-based strategies. *Canadian Journal of Psychiatry*, 50, 863–869.

Lee, Y. M. (2006). Effect of self-foot reflexology massage on depression, stress responses and immune functions of middle aged women. *Taehan Kanho Hakhoe Chi.*, 36, 179–188 (translation of abstract).

Lefkowitz, M. M., & Tesiny, E. (1980). Assessment of childhood depression. *Journal of Consulting and Clinical Psychology*, 48, 43–50.

Leitenberg, H., Yost, L. W., & Carroll-Wilson, M. (1986). Negative cognitive errors in children: Questionnaire development, normative data, and comparisons between children with and without self-reported symptoms of depression, low self-esteem, and evaluation anxiety. *Journal of Consulting and Clinical Psychology*, 54, 528–536.

Lenze, E. J., Schulz, R., Martire, L. M., Zdaniuk, B., Glass, T., Kop, W. J., Jackson, S. A., & Reynolds, C. F., III. (2005). The course of functional decline in older people with persistently elevated depressive symptoms: Longitudinal findings from the Cardiovascular Health Study. *Journal of the American Geriatrics Society*, 53, 569–575.

Lewinsohn, P. M., Duncan E. M., Stanton, A. K., & Hautzinger, M. (1986). Age at first onset for nonbipolar depression. *Journal of Abnormal Psychology*, 95, 378–383.

Lewinsohn, P. M., Mischel, W., Chaplin, W., & Barton, R. (1980). Social competency and depression: The role of illusory self-perceptions. *Journal of Abnormal Psychology*, 89, 203–212.

Lewinsohn, P. M., Munoz, R. F., Youngren, M. A., & Zeiss, A. M. 1986. *Control your depression.* Englewood Cliffs, N. J.: Prentice-Hall.

Lewy, A. J., Lefler, B. J., Emens, J. S., & Bauer, V. K. (2006). The circadian basis of winter depression. *Proceedings of the National Academy of Sciences,* 103, 7414–7419.

Libet, J. M., & Lewinsohn, P. M. (1973). The concept of social skills with special reference to the behavior of depressed persons. *Journal of Consulting and Clinical Psychology,* 40, 304–312.

Lindy, K., Ramirez, G., Mulrow, C. D., Pauls, A., Weidenhammer, W., & Melchart, D. (1996). St. John's wort for depression-an overview and meta-analysis of randomized clinical trials. *British Medical Journal,* 313, 253–258.

Lisanby, S. H., Maddox, J. H., Prudic, J., Devanand, D. P., & Sackeim, H. A. (2000). The effects of electroconvulsive therapy on memory of autobiographical and public events. *Archives of General Psychiatry,* 57, 581–590.

Looby, A., & Earleywine, M. (2007). The impact of methamphetamine use on subjective well-being in an internet survey: Preliminary finding. *Human Psychopharmacology,* 22, 167–172.

Lutz, D. L., & Snow, P. A. (1985). Understanding the role of depression in the alcoholic. *Clinical Psychology Review,* 5, 535–551.

Macfarlane, J. W., Allen, L., & Honzik, M. P. (1954). *Developmental study of the behavior problems of normal children between twenty-one months and fourteen years.* Berkeley: University of California Press.

MacGillivray, S., Arroll, B., Hatcher, S., Ogston, S., Reid, I., Sullivan, F., Williams, B., & Crombie, I. (2003). Efficacy and tolerability of selective serotonin reuptake inhibitors compared with tricyclic antidepressants in depression treated in primary care. Systematic review and meta-analysis. *British Medical Journal,* 326, 1014.

Mahalik, J. R., & Kivlighan, D. M., Jr. (1988). Self-help treatment for depression: Who succeeds? *Journal of Counseling Psychology,* 35, 237–242.

Malm, H., Klavkka, T., & Neuvonen, P. J. (2005). Risks associated with selective serotonin reuptake inhibitors in pregnancy. *Obstetrics and Gynecology,* 106, 1289–1296.

Manber, R, Schnyer, R. N., Allen, J. J., Rush, A. J., & Blasey, C. M. (2004). Accupuncture: A promising treatment for depression during pregnancy. *Journal of Affective Disorders,* 15, 89–95.

Mann, J. J., Stanley, M., McBride, P. A., & McEwen, B. S. (1986). Increase serotonin and B-adrenergic receptor binding and the frontal cortices of suicide victims. *Archives of General Psychiatry,* 43, 954–959.

Marcos, L. R. (1979). Effects of interpreters on the evaluation of psychopathology in non–English speaking patients. *American Journal of Psychiatry,* 136, 171–174.

Mazure, C. M. (1998). Life stressors as risk factors in depression. *Clinical Psychology Science and Practice,* 5, 291–313.

McBride, C., Atkinson, L., Quilty, L. C., & Bagby, R. M. (2006). Attachment as moderator of treatment outcome in major depression: A randomized controlled trial of interpersonal psychotherapy verses cognitive behavior therapy. *Journal of Consulting and Clinical Psychology,* 74, 1041–1054.

McCabe, M., & Marwit, S. J. (1993). Depressive symptomatology, perceptions of attractiveness, and body image in children. *Journal of Child Psychology and Psychiatry,* 34, 1117–1124.

McCoy, S. J., Beal, J. M., Shipman, S. B., Payton, M. E., & Watson, G. H. (2006). Risk factors for postpartum depression: A retrospective investigation at four-weeks postnatal and a review of the literature. *Journal of the American Osteopathic Association,* 106, 181–182.

McCranie, E. W., & Bass, J. D. (1984). Childhood family antecedents of dependency and self-criticism: Implications for depression. *Journal of Abnormal Psychology,* 93, 3–8.

McGirr, A., Renaud, J., Segin, M., Alda, M., Benkelfat, C., Lesage, A., & Turecki, G. (2006). An examination of DSM-IV depressive symptoms and risk for suicide completion: A psychological autopsy study. *Journal of Affective Disorders* (in press).

McGrath, E. P., & Repetti, R. L. (2002). A longitudinal study of children's depressive symptoms, self-perceptions, and cognitive distortions about the self. *Journal of Abnormal Psychology*, 111, 77–87.

McGuffin, P., Rijsdijk, F., Andrew, M., Sham, P., Katz, R., & Cardino, A. (2003). The heritability of bipolar affective disorder and the genetic relationship to unipolar depression. *Archives of General Psychiatry*, 60, 497–502.

McGuire, P. A. (1999). Worker stress reaching critical point. *APA Monitor*, 30, 1.

McLearn, K. T., Minkovitz, C. S., Strobino, D. M., Marks, E., & Hou, W. (2006a). Maternal depressive symptoms at 2 to 4 months post partum and early parenting practices. *Archives of Pediatric and Adolescent Medicine*, 160, 279–284.

_____ (2006b). The timing of maternal depressive symptoms and mother's parenting practices with young children: Implication for pediatric practice. *Pediatrics*, 118, 174–182.

McMillan, M. J., & Pihl, R. O. (1987). Premenstrual depression: A distinct entity. *Journal of Abnormal Psychology*, 96, 149–154.

Medications for mental illness. Fifth edition. (2005). Bethesda, MD: National Institute of Mental Health, NIH publication number 05–3929.

Meditation for health purposes. (2006). Backgrounder. National Center for Complementary and Alternative Medicine. Bethesda, MD: National Institutes of Health.

Melartin, T. K., Rytsala, H. J., Leskela, U. S., Lesstella-Mielonen, P. S., Sokero, T. P., & Isometsa, E. T. (2004). Severity and comorbidity predict duration and recurrence of DSM-IV major depressive disorder. *Journal of Clinical Psychiatry*, 65, 810–819.

Meller, W., Kathol, R. G., Jaeckle, R. S., Grambsch, P., & Lopez, J. F. (1988). HPA axis abnormalities in depressed patients with normal response to the DST. *American Journal of Psychiatry*, 145, 318–324.

Meyersburg, H. A., Ablon, S. L., & Kotin, J. (1974). A reverberating psychic mechanism in the depressive processes. *Psychiatry*, 37, 372–386.

Mezulis, A. H., Abramson, L. Y., Hyde, J. S., & Hankin, B. L. (2004). Is there a universal positivity bias in attribution? A meta-analytic review of individual, developmental, and cultural differences in the self-serving attribution bias. *Psychological Bulletin*, 130, 711–747.

Miller, T. Q., Smith, T. W., Turner, C. W., Guijario, M. L., & Hullet, A. J. (1996). A meta-analytic review of research on hostility and physical health. *Psychological Bulletin*, 119, 322–348.

Mojtabai, R. (2007). Americans' attitudes towards mental-health treatment seeking: 1990–2003. *Psychiatric Services*, 58, 642–651.

Molnar, B. E., Buka, S. L., & Kessler, R. C. (2001). Child sexual abuse and subsequent psychopathology: Results from the National Comorbidity Survey. *American Journal of Public Health*, 91, 753–760.

Monroe, S. M., & Harkness, K. L. (2005). Life stress, the "kindling" hypothesis, and the recurrence of depression: Considerations from a life stress perspective. *Psychological Review*, 112, 417–445.

Monroe, S. M., Torres, L. D., Guillaumot, J., Harkness, K. L., Roberts, J. E., Frank, E., & Kupfer, D. (2006). Life stress and the long-term treatment course of recurrent depression: III. Nonsevere life events predict recurrence for medicated patients over 3 years. *Journal of Consulting and Clinical Psychology*, 74, 112–120.

Montejo, A L., Llorca, G., Izquierdo, J. A., & Rico-Villademoros, F. (2001). Incidence of sexual dysfunction associated with antidepressant agents: A prospective study of 1022 outpatients. Spanish Working Group for the Study of Psychotropic-Related Sexual Dysfunction. *Journal of Clinical Psychiatry*, 62, Supplement 3, 10–21.

Mor, N., & Winquist, J. (2002). Self-focused attention and negative affect: A meta-analysis. *Psychological Bulletin*, 128, 638–662.

Moreno, R. A., Teng, C. T., Almeida, K. M., & Tarares, H., Jr. (2006). Hypericum perforatum versus fluoxetine in the treatment of mild to moderate depression: A randomized double-blind trial in a Brazilian sample. *Revista Brasileira Psiquiatria de*, 28, 29–32.

Moyer, C. A., Rounds, J., & Hannum, J. W. (2004). A meta-analysis of massage therapy research. *Psychological Bulletin*, 130, 3–18.

Munsey, C. (2007, April). Differences in heavy alcohol use can jeopardize marriages. *Monitor on Psychology*, 38, 11.

Murrell, S. A., & Himmelfarb, S. (1989). Effects of attachment bereavement and pre-event conditions on subsequent depressive symptoms in older adults. *Psychology and Aging*, 4, 166–172.

Nair, H., & Murray, A. D. (2005). Predictors of attachment security in preschool children from intact and divorced families. *Journal of Genetic Psychology* 166, 245–263.

Nathan, P. E., Titler, N. A., Lowenstein, L. M., Solomon, P., & Rossie, A. M. (1970). Behavioral analysis of chronic alcoholism. *Archives of General Psychiatry*, 22, 419–430.

Needles, D. J., & Abramson, L. Y. (1990). Positive life events, attributional style, and hopefulness: Testing a model of recovery from depression. *Journal of Abnormal Psychology*, 99, 156–165.

Neighbors. H. W., Caldwell, C., Williams, D. R., Nesse, R., Taylor, R. J., Bullard, K. M., Torres, M., & Jackson, J. S. (2007). Race, ethnicity, and the use of services for mental disorders: Results from the national survey of American life. *Archives of General Psychiatry*, 64, 485–494.

Nelson, G. (1982). Parental death during childhood and adult depression: Some additional data. *Social Psychiatry*, 17, 37–42.

Nemets, H. Nemets, B., Apter, A., Bracha, Z., Belmaker, R. H. (2006). Omega-3 treatment of childhood depression: A controlled double-blind pilot study. *American Journal of Psychiatry*, 163, 1098–1100.

Neumeister, A., Nugent, A. C., Waldeck, T., Geraci, M., Schwartz, M., Bonne, O., Bain, E. E., Luckenbaugh, D. A., Herscovitch, P., Charney, D. S., & Drevets, W. C. (2004). Neural and behavioral responses to tryptophan depletion in unmedicated patients with remitted by major depressive disorder and controls. *Archives of General Psychiatry*, 61, 765–773.

Neumeister, A., Xian-Zhang, H., Luckenbaugh, D. A., Schwartz, M., Nugent, A. C., Bonne, O., Herscovitch, P., Goldman, D., Drevets, W. C., & Charney, D. S. (2006). Differential effects of 5-HTTLPR genotypes in the behavioral and neural responses to tryptophan depletion in patients with major depressive disorder and controls. *Archives of General Psychiatry*, 63, 978–986.

Neuringer, C. (1982). Affect configurations and changes in women who threaten suicide following a crisis. *Journal of Consulting and Clinical Psychology*, 50, 182–186.

Nezu, A. M., & Nezu, C. M. (1990). Psychotherapy for adults within a problem-solving framework: Focus on depression. *Journal of Cognitive Psychotherapy*, 4, 247–256.

Nezu, A. M., Nezu, C. M., & Perri, M. G. (1989). *Problem-solving therapy for depression: Theory, research and clinical guidelines*. New York: Wiley.

Nierenberg, A. A., Greist, J. H., Mallinckrodt, C. H., Prakash, A., Sambunaris, A., Tollefson, G. D., & Wohlreich, M. M. (2007). Duloxetine versus escitalopram and placebo in the treatment of patients with major depressive disorder: Onset of antidepressant action, a non-inferiority study. *Current Medical Research and Opinion*, 23, 401–416.

Nierenberg, A. A., Trivedi, M. H., Fava, M., Biggs, M. M., Shores-Wilson, K., Wisniewski, S. R., Blasubramani, G. K., & Rush, A. J. (2006). Family history of mood disorder and characteristics of major depressive disorder: A Star* D (sequenced treatment alternatives to relieve depression) study. *Journal of Psychiatric Research* (in press).

Nietzel, M. T., Russell, R. L., Hemmings, K. A., & Gretter, M. L. (1987). Clinical significance of psychotherapy for unipolar depression: A meta-analytic approach to social comparison. *Journal of Consulting and Clinical Psychology*, 55, 156–161.

Noles, S. W., Cash, T. F., & Winstead, B. A. (1985). Body image, physical attractiveness, and depression. *Journal of Consulting and Clinical Psychology*, 53, 88–94.

Oldenhinkel, A. J., Rosmalen, J. G., Veenstra, R., Dijkstra, J. K., & Ormel, J. (2007). Being admired or being liked: Classroom social status and depressive problems in early adolescent girls and boys. *Journal of Abnormal Child Psychology* (in press).

Olfson, M., Marcus, S. C., Druss, B., Elinson, L., Tanielian, T., & Pincus, H. A. (2002). National trends in the outpatient treatment of depression. *Journal of the American Medical Association, 287,* 203–209.

O'Malley, S. S., Foley, S. H., Rounsaville, B. J., Watkins, J. T., Sotsky, S., Imber, S. D., & Elkin, I. (1988). Therapist competence and patient outcome in interpersonal psychotherapy of depression. *Journal of Consulting and Clinical Psychology, 56,* 496–501.

Oquendo, M. A., Galfalvy, H., Russo, S., Ellis, S. P., Grunebaum, M. F., Burke, A., & Mann, J. J. (2004). Prospective study of clinical predictors of suicidal acts after a major depressive disorder or bipolar disorder. *American Journal of Psychiatry, 161,* 1433–1441.

Ortega, A. N., Rosenheck, R., Alegria, M., & Desai, R. A. (2000). Acculturation and the lifetime risk of psychiatric and substance abuse disorders among Hispanics. *Journal of Nervous and Mental Disease, 188,* 728–735.

Ostberg, V., & Lennartsson, C. (2007). Getting by with a little help: The importance of various types of social support for health problems. *Scandinavian Journal of Public Health, 35,* 197–204.

Owens, M. J & Nemeroff, C. B. (1994). Role of serotonin in the psychophysiology of depression: Focus on the serotonin transporter. *Clinical Chemistry, 40,* 288–295.

Packard, E. (2006). Perfectionists more vulnerable to depression, study finds. *Monitor on Psychology, 37,* 14.

Palinkas, L. A. (2003). The psychology of isolated and confined environments: Understanding human behavior in Antarctica. *American Psychologist, 58,* 353–363.

Pandey, G. A. (1997). Altered serotonin function in suicide: Evidence from platelet and neuroendrocine studies. *Annals of the New York Academy of Science, 836,* 182–200.

Parker, G. (1979). Parental characteristics in relation to depressive disorders. *British Journal of Psychiatry, 134,* 138–147.

_____ (1983). Parental "affectionless control" as an antecedent to adult depression: A risk factor delineated. *Archives of General Psychiatry, 40,* 956–960.

_____, Tupling, H., & Brown, L. B. (1979). A parental bonding instrument. *British Journal of Psychiatry, 52,* 1–11.

Parsons, T. (1975). The sick role and the role of the physician reconsidered. *Milbank Memorial Fund Quarterly, 53,* 257–278.

Paxton, S. J., Neumark-Sztainer, D., Hannan, P. J., & Eisenberg, M. E. (2006). Body dissatisfaction prospectively predicts depressive mood and low self-esteem in adolescent girls and boys. *Journal of Clinical Child and Adolescent Psychology, 35,* 539–549.

Penninx, B. W., Guralinik, J. M., Ferrucci, L., Simonsick, E. M., Deeg, D. J., & Wallace, R. B. (1998). Depressive symptoms and physical decline in community-dwelling-older persons. *Journal of the American Medical Association, 279,* 1720–1726.

Peterson, C., & Villanova, P. (1988). An expanded attributional style questionnaire. *Journal of Abnormal Psychology, 97,* 87–89.

Petty, S. C., Sachs-Ericsson, N., & Joiner, T. E., Jr. (2004). Interpersonal functioning deficits: Temporary or stable characteristics of depressed individuals? *Journal of Affective Disorders 81,* 115–122.

Pilowsky, D. J., Wickramaratne, P., Nomura, Y., & Weissman, M. M. (2006). Family discord, parental depression, and psychopathology in offspring: 20-year follow-up. *Journal of the American Academy of Child and Adolescent Psychiatry, 45,* 452–460.

Post, R. M. (1992). Transduction of psychosocial stress into the neurobiology of recurrent affective disorder. *American Journal of Psychiatry, 149,* 999–1010.

Potkin, S. G., Zetin, M., Stamnekovic, V., Kripke, D., & Bunney, W. E., Jr. (1986). Seasonal affective disorder: Prevalence varies with latitude and climate. *Clinical Neuropharmacology, 9,* 181–183.

Prinstein, M. J., Borelli, J. L., Cheah, C. S., Simon, V. A., & Aikins, J. W. (2005). Adolescent girls' interpersonal vulnerability to depressive emotions: A longitudinal examination of reassurance-seeking and peer relationships. *Journal of Abnormal Psychology, 114,* 676–688.

Prisciandaro, J. J., & Roberts, J. E. (2005). A taxometric investigation of unipolar depression in the National Comorbidity Survey. *Journal of Abnormal Psychology*, 114, 718–728.

Quitkin, F. M., McGrath, P. J., Stewart, J. W., Deliyannides, D., Taylor, B. P., Davies, C. A., & Klein, D. F. (2005). Remission rates with 3 consecutive antidepressant trials: Effectiveness for depressed outpatients. *Journal of Clinical Psychiatry*, 66, 670–676.

Radloff, L. S. (1977). The CES-D Scale: A self-report depression scale for research in the general population. *Applied Psychological Measurement*. 1, 385–401.

Rapaport, M. H. (2007). Translating the evidence on atypical depression into clinical practice. *Journal of Clinical Psychiatry*, 68, Supplement 3, 31–36.

Rapp, S. R., Parisi, S. A., Walsh, D. A., & Wallace, C. E. (1988). Detecting depression in elderly medical inpatients. *Journal of Consulting and Clinical Psychology*, 56, 509–513.

Reis, S., & Grenyer, B. F. (2004). Fear of intimacy in women: Relationship between attachment styles and depressive symptoms. *Psychopathology*, 37, 299–303.

Reynolds, W. M., & Coats, K. I. (1982). Depression in adolescents: Incidents, depth, and correlates. Paper presented at the 10th International Congress, International Association of Child and Adolescent Psychiatry and Allied Professions, Dublin, Ireland.

Rinck, M., & Becker, E. S. (2005). A comparison of attentional biases and memory biases in women with social phobia and major depression. *Journal of Abnormal Psychology*, 114, 62–74.

Robbins, P. R. (1974). Depression and drug addiction. *Psychiatric Quarterly*, 48, 374–386.

_____ (1983). *Marijuana: A short course. Update for the eighties.* Brookline Village, MA: Branden.

_____ (1988). *The psychology of dreams.* Jefferson, NC: McFarland.

_____ (1998). *Adolescent Suicide.* Jefferson, NC: McFarland.

_____ (2007). *Coping with stress: Commonsense strategies.* Jefferson, NC: McFarland.

Robbins, P. R., & Nugent, J. F., III (1975). Perceived consequences of addiction: A comparison between alcoholics and heroin-addicted patients. *Journal of Clinical Psychology*, 31, 367–369.

Robbins, P. R., & Tanck, R. H. (1973). Psychological correlates of marijuana use: An exploratory study. *Psychological Reports*, 33, 703–706.

_____ and _____ (1982). Further research using a psychological diary technique to investigate psychosomatic relationships. *Journal of Clinical Psychology*, 38, 356–359.

_____ and _____ (1984). Sex differences in problems related to depression. *Sex Roles*, 11, 703–707.

_____ and _____ (1985, October 23). There are ways to fight college anxiety and stress. *Washington Post*, Health Section.

_____ and _____ (1987). A study of diurnal patterns of depressed mood. *Motivation and Emotion*, 11, 37–49.

_____ and _____ (1988). Depressed mood, dream recall and contentless dreams. *Imagination, Cognition and Personality*, 8, 165–174.

_____ and _____ (1992). Stress, coping techniques, and depressed affect: Explorations within a normal sample. *Psychological Reports*, 70, 147–152.

_____ and _____ (1994). Depressed mood and early memories: Some negative findings. *Psychological Reports*, 75, 465–466.

_____ and _____ (1997). Anger and depressed affect: Interindividual and intraindividual perspectives. *Journal of Psychology*, 131, 489–500.

Robins, L. N., Helzer, J. E., Croughan, J., & Ratcliff, K. S. (1981). National Institute of Mental Health Diagnostic Interview Schedule: Its history, characteristics and validity. *Archives of General Psychiatry*, 38, 381–389.

Robins, L. N., Helzer, J. E., Wiessman, M. M., Orvaschel, H., Gruenberg, E., Burke, J. D., Regier, D. A. (1984). Lifetime prevalence of specific psychiatric disorders in three sites. *Archives of General Psychiatry*, 41, 949–958.

Rockhill, C. M., Fan, M. Y., Katon, W. J., McCauley, E., Crick, N. R., & Pleck, J. H. (2007). Friendship interactions in children with and without depressive symptoms: Observation of emotion during game-playing interactions and post-game evaluations. *Journal of Abnormal Child Psychology* (in press).

Rosenthal, N. E., Sack, D. A., Gillin, J. C., Lewy, A. J., Goodwin, F. K., Davenport, Y., Mueller, P. S., Newsome, D. A., & Wehr, T. A. (1984). Seasonal affective disorder: A description of the syndrome and preliminary findings with light therapy. *Archives of General Psychiatry*, 41, 72–80.

Rost, K., Adams, S., Xu, S., & Dong, F. (2007). Rural-urban differences in hospitalization rates of primary care patients with depression. *Psychiatric Services*, 58, 503–508.

Rotter, J. B. (1960). Generalized expectancies for internal verses external control of reinforcement. *Psychological Monographs*, 80, 609.

Sabbatini, R. (2007). The history of shock therapy in psychiatry. http://www.cerebromente. org.br/n04/historia/shock:i.htm.

Safran, J. D., Vallis, T. M., Segal, Z. V., & Shaw, B. F. (1986). Assessment of core cognitive processes in cognitive therapy. *Cognitive Therapy and Research*, 10, 509–526.

St. John, P. D., Blanford, A. A., & Strain, L. A. (2006). Depressive symptoms among older adults in urban and rural areas. *International Journal of Geriatric Psychiatry* (in press).

St. John's wort and the treatment of depression. (2004). Bethesda, MD.: National Center for Complementary and Alternative Medicine.

Salkovskis, P., Rimes, K., Stephenson, D., Sacks, G., & Scott, J. (2006). A randomized controlled trial of the use of self-help materials in addition to standard general practice treatment of depression compared to standard treatment alone. *Psychological Medicine*, 36, 325–333.

Sargent, M. (1986). *Depressive disorders: Treatments brings new hope.* Publication no. ADM 86-1491.

Schmidt, J. M. (1981). The effects of subliminally presented anaclitic and introjective stimuli on normal young adults. Unpublished doctoral dissertation, University of Southern Mississippi.

Schmitz, J. M., Averill, P., Stotts, A. L., Moeller, F. G., Rhoades, H. M., & Grabowski, J. (2001). Fluoxetine treatment of cocaine-dependent patients with major depressive disorder. *Drug and Alcohol Dependence*, 63, 207–214.

Schmitz, J. M., Stotts, A. L., Averill, P. M., Rothfleisch, J. M., Bailley, S. E., Sayre, S. L., & Grabowski, J. (2000). Cocaine dependence with and without comorbid depression: A comparison of patient characteristics. *Drug and Alcohol Dependence*, 60, 189–198.

Schulz, V. (2006). Safety of St. John's wort extract compared to synthetic antidepressants. *Phytomedicine*, 3, 199–204.

Schwartz, G. E., Fair, P. L., Salt, P., Mandel, M. R., &, Klerman, G. L. (1976). Facial muscles patterning to affective imagery in depressed and nondepressed subjects. *Science*, 192, 489–491.

Scogin, F., Jamison, C., & Gochneaur, K. (1989). Comparative efficacy of cognitive and behavioral bibliotherapy for mildly and moderately depressed older adults. *Journal of Consulting and Clinical Psychology*, 57, 403–407.

Sedler, M. J. (1983). Falret's Discovery: The origin of the concept of bipolar affective illness. *American Journal of Psychiatry*, 140, 1127–1133.

Seligman, M. E. P., Abramson, L. Y., Semmel, A., & von Baeyer, C. (1979). Depressive attributional style. *Journal of Abnormal Psychology*, 88, 242–248.

Seligman, M. E. P., Peterson, C., Kaslow, N. J., Tasnenbaum, R. L., Alloy, L. B., & Abramson, L. Y. (1984). Attributional styles and depressive symptoms among children. *Journal of Abnormal Psychology*, 93, 235–238.

Sen, S., Burmeister, M., & Ghosh, D. (2004). Meta-analysis of the association between a serotonin transporter promoter polymorphism (5HTTLPR) and anxiety-related personality traits. *American Journal of Medical Genetics. B. Neuropsychiatric Genetics*, 127, 85–89.

Serebruany, V. L. (2006). Selective serotonin reuptake inhibitors and increased bleeding risk: Are we missing something? *American Journal of Medicine*, 119, 113–116.

Shaffery, J., Hoffmann, R., & Armitage, R. (2003). The neurobiology of depression: Perspectives from animal and human sleep studies. *Neuroscientist*, 9, 82–98.

Shakespeare, W. (1938). *The tragedy of Richard the Third*. In Shakespeare: Twenty-three plays and the sonnets. New York: Scribners.

Sherman, K. J., Cherkin, D. C., Kahn, J., Erro, J., Herbec, A., Deyo, R. A., & Eisenberg, D. M. (2005). A survey of training and practice patterns of massage therapists in two U.S. States. *BMC Complimentary and Alternative Medicine*, 14, 13.

Shrout, P. E., Link, B. G., Dohrenwend, B. P., Skodol, A. E., Stueve, A., & Mirotznik, J. (1989). Characterizing life events as risk factors for depression: The role of fateful loss events. *Journal of Abnormal Psychology*, 98, 460–467.

Siever, L. J., & Davis, K. L. (1985). Overview: Toward a dysregulation hypothesis of depression. *American Journal of Psychiatry*, 142, 1017–1031.

Simon, G. E., & Von Korff, M. (1995). Recognition, management, and outcome of depression in primary care. *Archives of Family Medicine*, 4, 99–105.

Sir, A., D'Souza, R. F., Uguz, S., George, T., Vahip, S., Hopwood, M., Martin, A. J., Lam, W., & Burt, T. (2005). Randomized trial of sertraline versus venlafaxine XR in major depression: Efficacy and discontinuation symptoms. *Journal of Clinical Psychiatry*, 66, 1312–1320.

Sirota, A. D., & Schwartz, G. E. (1982). Facial muscle patterning and lateralization during elation and depression imagery. *Journal of Abnormal Psychology*, 91, 25–34.

Smith, G. T. (1994). Psychological expectancy as mediator of vulnerability to alcoholism. *Annals of the New York Academy of Sciences*, 708, 165–171.

Smith, J. A., Cornelius, V., Warnock, A., Bell, A., & Young, A. H. (2007). Effectiveness of mood stabilizers and antipsychotics in the maintenance phase of bipolar disorder: A systematic review of randomized controlled trials. *Bipolar Disorder*, 9, 394–412.

Snyder, C. R. (1984, September). Excuses, excuses. *Psychology Today*, 18, 50–55.

Solkero, T. P., Melartin, T. K., Rytsala, H. J., Leskela, U. S., Lestela-Mielonen, P. S., & Isometsa, E. T. (2005). Prospective study of risk factors for attempted suicide among patients with DSM-IV major depressive disorder. *British Journal of Psychiatry*, 186, 314–318.

Sontrop, J., & Campbell, M. K. (2006). W-3 polysaturated fatty acids and depression: A review of the evidence and a methodological critique. *Preventive Medicine*, 42, 4–13.

Sourander, A., Koskelainen, M., & Helenius, H. (1999). Mood, latitude, and seasonality among adolescents. *Journal of the American Academy of Child and Adolescent Psychiatry*, 38, 1271–1276.

Spearing, M. (2002). A story of bipolar disorder (manic depressive illness). Bethesda, Md.: NIH Publication No. 06–5085.

Spitz, R. A. (1946). Anaclitic Depression. *Psychoanalytic Study of the Child*, 2, 313–342.

Stansfeld, S. A., Fuhrer, R., & Shipley, M. J. (1998). Types of social support as predictors of psychiatric morbidity in a cohort of British civil servants (Whitehall II study). *Psychological Medicine*, 28, 881–892.

Steinbrueck, S. M., Maxwell, S. E. and Howard, G. S. (1983). A meta-analysis of psychotherapy and drug therapy in the treatment of unipolar depression with adults. *Journal of Consulting and Clinical Psychology*, 51, 856–863.

Stinson, F. S., Grant, B. F., Dawson, D. A., Huang, B., & Saha, T. (2005). Comorbidity between DSM-IV alcohol and specific drug use disorders in the United States: Results from the National Epidemiologic Survey on Alcohol and Related Conditions. *Drug and Alcohol Dependence*, 80, 105–116.

Stinson, F. S., Ruan, W. J., Pickering, R., & Grant, B. F. (2006). Cannabis use disorders in the U.S.A.: Prevalence, correlates and co-morbidity. *Psychological Medicine* (in press).

Stroufe, L. A. (2005). Attachment and development: A prospective, longitudinal study from birth to adulthood. *Attachment and Human Development*, 7, 349–367.

Sublette, M. E., Hibbeln, J. R., Galfalvy, H., Oquendo, M. A., & Mann, J. J. (2006). Omega-3 polyunsaturated essential fatty acid status as a predictor of future suicide risk. *American Journal of Psychiatry*, 163, 1100–1102.

Sue, D., & Sue, S. (1987). Cultural factors and the clinical assessment of Asian Americans. *Journal of Consulting and Clinical Psychology*, 55, 479–487.

Summers, M., Papadopoulou, K., Bruno, S., Cipolotti, L., & Rou, M. A. (2006). Bipolar I and bipolar II disorder: Cognition and emotion processing. *Psychological Medicine* (in press).

Sund, A. M., Larsson, B., & Wichstrom, L. (2003). Psychosocial correlates of depressive symptoms among 12 to 14-year-old Norwegian adolescents. *Journal of Child Psychology and Psychiatry*, 44, 588–597.

Surguiadze, S. A., Young, A. W., Senior, C., Brebion, G., Travis, M. J., & Phillips, M. L. (2004). Recognition accuracy and response bias to happy and sad facial expressions in patients with major depression. *Neuropsychology*, 18, 212–218.

Sweeney, P. D., Anderson, K., & Bailey, S. (1986). Attributional style in depression: A meta-analytic review. *Journal of Personality and Social Psychology*, 50, 974–991.

Szasz, T. (1986). The case against suicide prevention. *American Psychologist*, 41, 806–812.

Szegedi, A., Kohnen, R., Dienel, A., & Kieser, M. (2005). Acute treatment of moderate to severe depression with hypericum extract WS5570 (St. John's wort): Randomized controlled double blind non-inferiority trial versus paroxetine. http://bmjournals.com/cgi

Takeuchi, D. T., Chung, R. C. Lin, K. M., Shen, H., Kurasaki, K., Chun, C. A., & Sue, S. (1998). Lifetime and twelve-month prevalence rates of major depressive episodes and dysthymia among Chinese Americans in Los Angeles. *American Journal of Psychiatry*, 155, 1407–1414.

Taylor, S. (2007). Electroconvulsive therapy: A review of history, patient selection, technique, and medication management. *Southern Medical Journal*, 100, 494–498.

Teasdale, J. D., Segal, Z. V., & Williams, J. M. G. (1995). How does cognitive therapy prevent depressive relapse and why should attentional control (mindfulness) training help? *Behavior Research and Therapy*, 33, 25–39.

Teesson, M., Harvard, A., Fairbairn, S., Ross, J., Lynskey, M., & Darke, S. (2005). Depression among entrants to treatment for heroin dependence in the Australian Treatment Outcomes Study (ATOS): Prevalence, correlates and treatment seeking. *Drug and Alcohol Dependence*, 78, 309–315.

Terman, M., & Terman, J. S. (2005). Light therapy for seasonal and nonseasonal depression: Efficacy, protocol, safety, and side effects. *CNS Spectrum*, 10, 647–663.

Thase, M. E. (2006). Preventing relapse and recurrence of depression: A brief review of therapeutic options. *CNS Spectrum*, 11, 12–21, Supplement 15.

Timbremont, B., Braet, C., & Dreessen, L. (2004). Assessing depression in youth: Relation between the Children's Depression Inventory and a structured interview. *Journal of Clinical Child and Adolescent Psychiatry*, 33, 149–157.

Toneatto, T., & Nguyen, L. (2007). Does mindfulness meditation improve anxiety and mood symptoms? A review of the controlled research. *Canadian Journal of Psychiatry*, 52, 260–266.

Torrent, C., Martinez-Aran, A., Daban, C., Sanchez-Moreno, J., Comes, M., Goikolea, J. U., Salamero, M., & Vieta, E. (2006). Cognitive impairment in bipolar II disorder. *British Journal of Psychiatry*, 189, 254–259.

Trivedi, M. H., Rush, A. J., Wisniewski, S. R., Nierenberg, A. A., Warden, D., Ritz, L., Norquist, G., Lebowitz, B., McGrath, P. J., Shores-Wilson, K., Biggs, M. M., Balasubramani, G. K., & Fava, M. (2006). Evaluation of outcomes with citalopram for depression using measurement-based care in STAR*-D: Implications for clinical practice. *American Journal of Psychiatry*, 163, 28–40.

Trowell, J., Joffe, I., Campbell, J., Clemente, C., Almqvist, F., Soininen, M., Koskenranta-Aalto, U., Weintraub, S., Kolaitis, G., Tomaras, V., Anastasopoulos, D., Grayson, K., Barnes, J., & Tsiantis, J. (2007). Childhood depression: A place for psychotherapy. An outcome study comparing individual psychodynamic psychotherapy and family therapy. *European Child and Adolescent Psychiatry*, 16, 157–167.

Trude, S., & Stoddard, J. J. (2003). Referral gridlock: Primary care physicians and mental health services. *Journal of General Internal Medicine*, 18, 442–449.

Valtonen, H., Suominen, K., Mantere, O., Leppamaki, S., Arvilommi, P., & Isometsa, E. T.

(2005). Suicidal ideation and attempts in bipolar I and II disorders. *Journal of Clinical Psychiatry*, 66, 1456–1462.

Valtonen, H. M., Suominen, K., Mantere, O., Leppamaki, S., Arvilommi, P., & Isometsa, E. (2006). Suicidal behavior during different phases of bipolar disorder. *Journal of Affective Disorders* (in press).

Van Wijngaarden, B., Schene, A. H., & Koeter, M. W. (2004). Family caregiving in depression: Impact on caregivers' daily life, distress, and help seeking. *Journal of Affective Disorders*, 81, 211–222.

Veiel, H. O. (1993). Detrimental effects of kin support networks on the course of depression. *Journal of Abnormal Psychology*, 102, 419–429.

_____, & Kuhner, C. (1990) Relatives and depressive relapse: The critical period after discharge from in-patient treatment. *Psychological Medicine*, 20, 977–984.

Velten, E. (1986). A laboratory test for induction of mood states. *Behaviour Research and Therapy*, 6, 473–482.

Vincent, N. K., & Walker, J. R. (2000). Perfectionism and chronic insomnia. *Journal of Psychosomatic Research*, 49, 349–354.

Vittengl, J. R., Clark, L. A., Dunn, T. W., & Jarrett, R. B. (2007). Reducing relapse and recurrence in unipolar depression: A comparative meta-analysis of cognitive-behavioral therapy's effects. *Journal of Consulting and Clinical Psychology*, 75, 475–488.

Wall, J. H. (1937). A study of alcoholism in women. *American Journal of Psychiatry*, 93, 942–955.

Wampold, B. E., Minami, T., Baskin, T. W., & Callen, T. S. (2002). A meta-(re)analysis of the effects of cognitive therapy versus other therapies for depression. *Journal of Affective Disorders*, 68, 159–165.

Wang, C. E., Halvorsen, M., Sundet, K., Steffensen, A. L., Holte, A., & Waterloo, K. (2006). Verbal memory performance of mildly to moderately depressed outpatient younger adults. *Journal of Affective Disorders*, 92, 283–286.

Wang, J. L. (2004). Rural-urban differences in the prevalence of major depression and associated impairment. *Social Psychiatry Psychiatric Epidemiology*, 39, 19–25.

Wang, P. S., Berglund, P., Olfson, M., Pincus, H. A., Wells, K. B., & Kessler, R. C. (2005). Failure and delay in initial treatment contact after first onset of mental disorders in the National Comorbidity Survey Replication. *Archives of General Psychiatry*, 62, 590–592.

Wang, P. S., Demier, O., Olfson, M., Pincus, H. A., Wells, K. B., & Kessler, R. C. (2006). Changing profiles of service sectors used for mental health care in the United States. *American Journal of Psychiatry*, 163, 1187–1198.

Wang, S. (2007). Shock value: Electroconvulsive therapy saves lives. But 70 years after it first gained currency as a treatment for major depression, ECT continues to court controversy. *Washington Post. Health Section*, July 24. Page F-1.

Watson, S., Gallagher, P., Del-Estal, D., Hearn, A., Ferrier, I. N., & Young, A. H. (2002). Hypothalamic-pituitary-adrenal axis function in patients with chronic depression. *Psychosomatic Medicine*, 32, 1021–1028.

Watson, S., Gallagher, P., Ritchie, J. C., Ferrier, I. N., & Young, A. H. (2004). Hypothalamic-pituitary-adrenal axis function in patients with bipolar disorder. *British Journal of Psychiatry*, 184, 496–502.

Way, B. B., & Banks, S. (2001). Clinical factors related to admission and release decisions in psychiatric emergency services. *Psychiatric Services*, 52, 214–218.

Wehr, T. A., Sack, D. A., & Rosenthal, N. E. (1987). Seasonal affective disorder with summer depression and winter hypomania. *American Journal of Psychiatry*, 144, 1602–1603.

Weich, S., Twigg, L., & Lewis, G. (2006). Rural/non-rural differences in rates of common mental disorders in Britain: Prospective multicultural cohort study. *British Journal of Psychiatry*, 188, 51–57.

Weick, K. E. (1984). Small wins: Redefining the scale of social problems. *American Psychologist*, 39, 40–49.

Weisman, R. (1984, March). Nutrition and neurotransmitters: The research of Richard Wurtman. *NIMH Science Reporter*, 1–8.

Weisse, C. S. (1992). Depression and immunocompetence: A review of the literature. *Psychological Bulletin*, 111, 475–489.

Weissman, A. N., & Beck, A. T. (1978). Development and validation of the Dysfunctional Attitudes Scale: A preliminary investigation. Paper presented at the 12th Annual American Educational Research Association meeting. Toronto, Ontario, Canada.

Weissman, M. M. (2006). Recent advances in depression across the generations. *Epidemiologia e Psichiatria Sociale*, 15, 16–19.

Weissman, M. M. (2007). Cognitive therapy and interpersonal psychotherapy summit: 30 years later. *American Journal of Psychiatry*, 164, 693–696.

Weniger, G., Lange, C., & Irle, E. (2006). Abnormal size of the amygdala predicts impaired emotional memory in major depressive disorder. *Journal of Affective Disorders*, 94, 219–229.

Wenzlaff, R. M., & Grozier, S. A. (1988). Depression and the magnification of failure. *Journal of Abnormal Psychology*, 97, 90–93.

Westermeyer, J. (1987). Cultural factors and clinical assessment. *Journal of Consulting and Clinical Psychology*, 55, 471–478.

Whiskey, E., Werneke, U., & Taylor, D. (2001). A systematic review and meta-analysis of Hypericum perforatum in depression: A comprehensive clinical review. *International Clinical Psychopharmacology*, 16, 239–252.

Whittington, C. J., Kendall, T., & Pilling, S. (2005). Are the SSRIs and atypical antidepressants safe and effective for children and adolescents? *Current Opinion in Psychiatry*, 18, 21–25.

Wilkinson, R. B. (1997). Interactions between self and external reinforcement in predicting depressive symptoms. *Behavior Research and Therapy*, 35, 281–289.

Wilson, S., & Argyropoulos, S. (2005). Antidepressants and sleep: A qualitative review of the literature. *Drugs*, 65, 927–947.

Wurglics, M., & Schubert-Zsilavecz, M. (2006). Hypericum perforatum: A 'Modern' herbal antidepressant: Pharmacokinetics of acute ingrediieints. *Clinical Pharmacokinetics*, 45, 449–468.

Wurtman, R. J. (1982). Nutrients that modify brain function. *Scientific American*, 246, 50–59.

Yarrow, M. R., Clausen, J. A., & Robbins, P. R. (1955). The social meaning of mental illness. *Journal of Social Issues*, 11, 33–48.

Young, A. S., Klap, R., Sherbourne, C. D., & Wells, K. B. (2001). The quality of care for depressive and anxiety disorders in the United States. *Archives of General Psychiatry*, 58, 55–61.

Zalsman, G., Huang, Y. Y., Oquendo, M. A., Burke, A. K., Hu, X. Z., Brent, D. A., Ellis, S. P., Goldman, D., & Mann, J. J. (2006). Association of a triallelic serotonin transporter gene promoter region (5-HITTLPR) polymorphism with stressful life events and severity of depression. *American Journal of Psychiatry*, 163, 1588–1593.

Zhang, A. Y., & Snowden, L. R. (1999). Ethnic characteristics of mental disorders in five U.S. communities. *Cultural Diversity and Ethnic and Minority Psychology*, 5, 134–146.

Zimmerman, M., McGlinchey, J. B., Young, D., Chelminski, I. (2006). Diagnosing major depressive disorder. III. Can some symptoms be eliminated from the diagnostic criteria? *Journal of Nervous and Mental Disease*, 194, 313–317.

Zuroff, D. C., Blatt, S. J., Sotsky, S. M., Krupnick, J. L., Martin, D. J., Sanislow, C. A., III, & Simmens, S. (2000). Relation of therapeutic alliance and perfectionism to outcome in brief outpatient treatment of depression. *Journal of Consulting and Clinical Psychology*, 68, 114–124.

Zweben, J. E., Cohen, J. B., Christian, D., Galloway, G. P., Salinardy, M., Parent, D., & Iguchi, M. (2004). Psychiatric symptoms in methamphetamine users. *American Journal of Addiction*, 13, 181–190.

Index